Pigments

Pigments

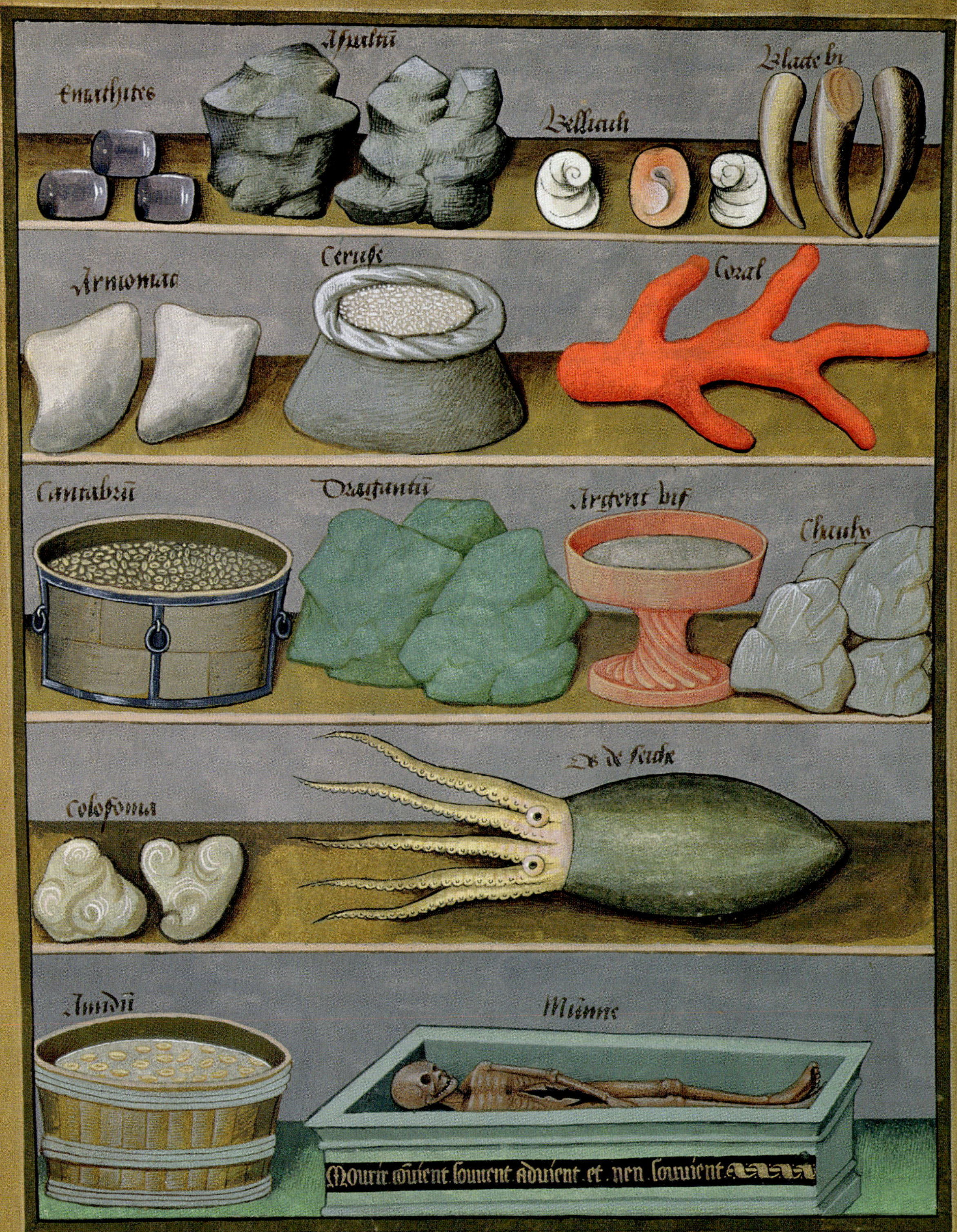

Enarthites
Asfaltū
Belliach
Blacte bū
Arnomac
Cerusī
Coral
Cantabrū
Dragantū
Argent vif
Chaulx
Colofonia
Os de seiche
Amidū
Mienne
Mourir couvient. souvent. aduient. et. nen. couuient.

ART/WORK   Edited by Caroline Fowler and Ittai Weinryb

Pigments

Barbara H. Berrie
Caroline Fowler
Karin Leonhard
Ittai Weinryb

Princeton University Press
Princeton and Oxford

Copyright © 2024 by Princeton University Press

Princeton University Press is committed to the protection of copyright and the intellectual property our authors entrust to us. Copyright promotes the progress and integrity of knowledge. Thank you for supporting free speech and the global exchange of ideas by purchasing an authorized edition of this book. If you wish to reproduce or distribute any part of it in any form, please obtain permission.

Requests for permission to reproduce material from this work should be sent to permissions@press.princeton.edu

Published by
Princeton University Press
41 William Street
Princeton, New Jersey 08540

In the United Kingdom:
Princeton University Press
99 Banbury Road
Oxford OX2 6JX

press.princeton.edu

All Rights Reserved

Printed on acid-free paper. ∞

ISBN (pbk.) 978-0-691-22371-1
ISBN (ebook) 978-0-691-25662-7

Library of Congress Control Number: 2023946906

British Library Cataloging-in-Publication Data is available

Design and composition:
Binocular, New York

This book has been composed in Sole Serif and Sole Sans.

Cover images: (Front, left to right) Image of a piece of Lapis Lazuli from Badakhshan province, Afghanistan; Vincent van Gogh, *Self Portrait*, 1889; Cueva de las Manos, UNESCO World Heritage Site. (Back, left to right) White Shaman Mural, photograph courtesy of Shumla Archaeological Research and Education Center; Wassily Kandinsky, *Palette*, ca. 1939, Wood, © droits réservés.

Frontispiece: Examples of *pharmakeia*, in Matthaeus Platearius, *Liber de simplici medicina*, ca. 1470. Ink and tempera on parchment. National Library, St. Petersburg, Russia.

Printed in China

10 9 8 7 6 5 4 3 2 1

Contents

Pigments

Pigment Worlds: An Introduction

Caroline Fowler and Ittai Weinryb

In the Santa Cruz region of Argentina, a cave wall is covered with an orchestra of red ocher handprints. Variations of earth tones, from deep blood red to rose pink, echo as the ocher commingles with a white chalky pigment [FIG. 1]. The mural evokes geology and earth, as the pigments were created from mineral deposits. The harmonic concatenation of hands across the wall presents a visual echo and rhythm that mirror the acoustics of the interior space, so that the voices that echoed ephemerally within the cave become visually transcribed onto the walls. Archaeologists suggest that these works were created by blowing the pigment from the mouth, creating a "halo effect." Some scholars conjecture that this mingling of pigment, breath, and saliva embodied "breathing life" onto the wall, infusing breath's brevity with the endurance of stone mediated through ocher pigment. Instead of carving lines—sculpting and incising—these artists archived their relationship to space and time with pigment and breath. We use this iconic image to begin the volume to demonstrate that pigment is inseparable from the desire of the human species to archive, impress, and create. As Carolyn Boyd argues in her case study, pigment begets life.

But first, **what are pigments?** On a technical level, they are insoluble materials that contain color. Most pigments must be processed to release their color. For example, ultramarine is made from lapis lazuli, a hard stone. The mineral is ground into a powder to create the colorant, then the powder is mixed with a material like pine resin or beeswax to produce a doughlike substance. This material is massaged and worked in a solution of warm ash to separate out the blue pigments, which would be mixed with a binder, perhaps egg yolk, if the artist wanted a tempera paint. This recipe is only one of thousands for extracting a pigment from a naturally occurring substance. Although this book is not intended as a compendium of pigment recipes, we share this process to demonstrate

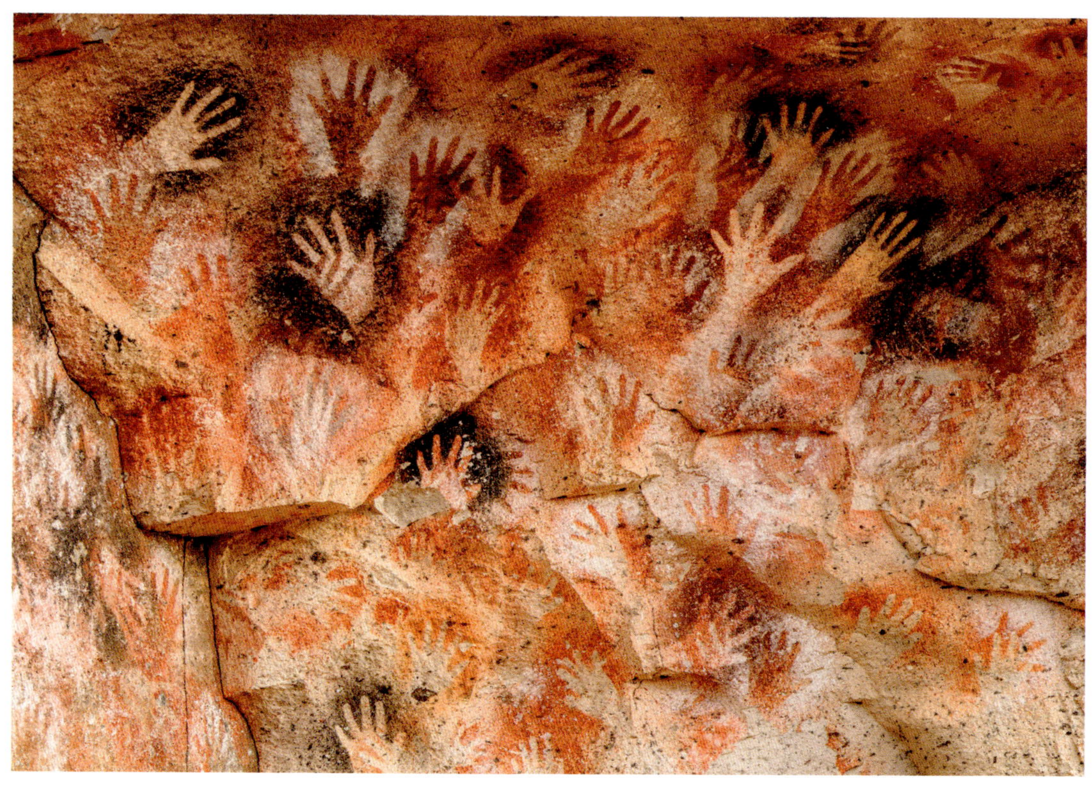

[FIG. 1]
Cueva de las Manos,
UNESCO World Heritage
Site, Rio Pinturas Canyon,
Santa Cruz Province,
Patagonia, Argentina.

that the production of pigments demands labor, time, and knowledge about the natural world.

Today, many pigments are born in a chemist's laboratory. Vantablack, for example, is an engineered super-black pigment consisting of carbon nanotubes that absorb more than 99 percent of all light. This technology is far-removed from the ocher pigments employed in the Argentinian caves that were made by oxidizing clay. Moreover, Vantablack was not originally intended for artistic production. Nevertheless, Anish Kapoor bought the exclusive rights to it and instigated a heated debate about intellectual property and artistic production [FIG. 2]. Yet, Kapoor's purchase of Vantablack belongs in a tradition of artists engaged with technology and trade secrets. Whereas illuminators in medieval guilds might have guarded their recipes in their workshop, Kapoor gained his technical expertise through financial and legal means.

While pigments are one central colorant in our world, dyes are another. Both pigments and dyes are powders extracted from natural and synthetic materials that may be combined with binders to create substances of varying liquidity. Typical binders for paints include animal fat, eggs, linseed oil, and, more recently, acrylic and vinyl polymers, to name only a few. For the most part, pigments are insoluble, and dyes are soluble. In this volume, we focus on pigments and how their insolubility and structure are fundamental to the history of art. When a pigment is combined with animal fat, a common binder for cave painting, it will not dissolve. It retains its structure. In contrast, dye dissolves when mixed with a binder. Typically, dyes are used for textiles whereas pigments are the painter's medium (there are, of course, important exceptions). Dyes absorb into their material support while pigments rest on the surface of their ground—for instance, wood panel or canvas. Moreover, pigments are suspended in their binder, which means that they are constantly in relationship to the material world instead of being absorbed into it.

Pigments and dyes can be made from the same original material, though dyes are often made of organic compounds and pigments are made of inorganic compounds—that is, they do not have carbon-hydrogen bonds. Pigments frequently come from the earth: charcoal and ocher, minerals and rocks. The color known as sienna, for example, is an earth pigment containing iron and sometimes manganese. It will change from yellow to red when heat is applied. Although its chemical composition is found in cave paintings, it was produced in Siena during the Renaissance and bears this geographic history in its name. Stones and semiprecious stones are also sources of pigments. Azurite and malachite, ground into a powder, produce blue and green, respectively. Pigments are also mined or are a by-product of mining. The ore cinnabar (mercury sulfide) and its synthetic form, vermilion, were used interchangeably

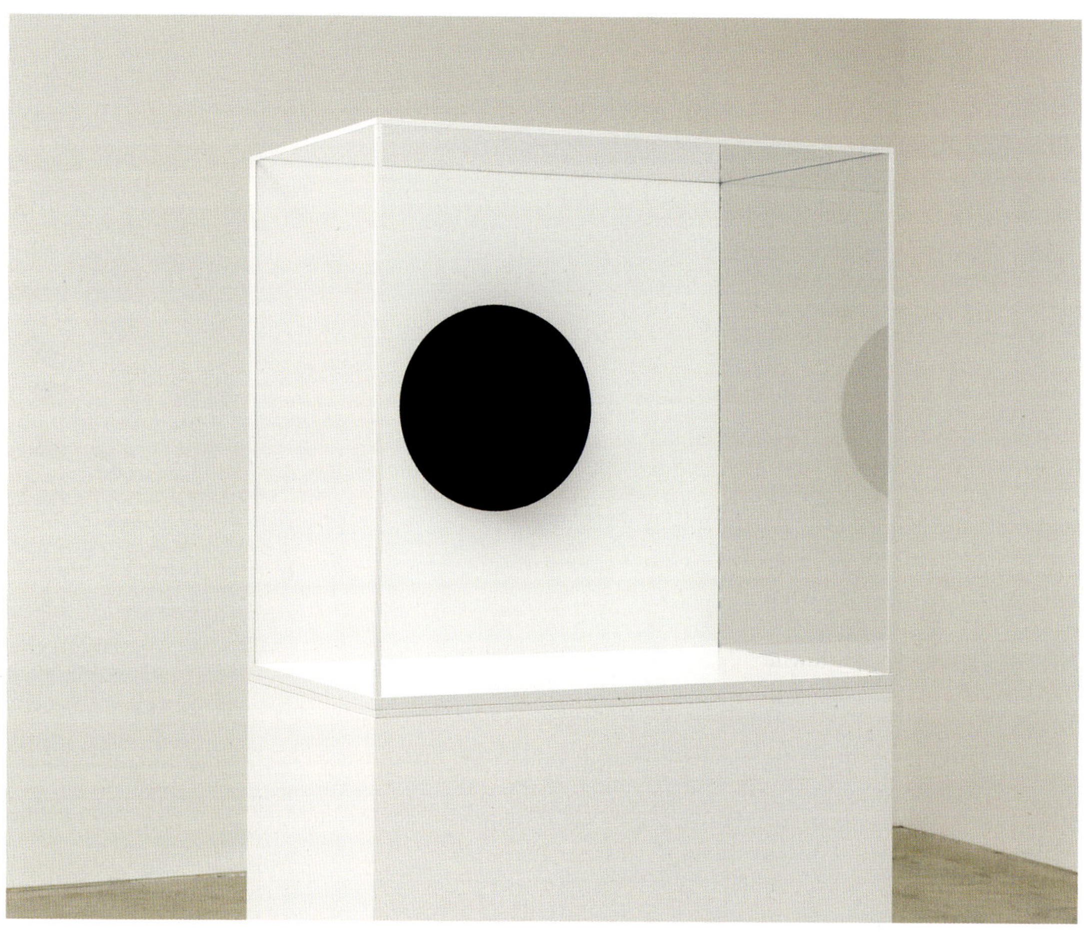

[FIG. 2]
Anish Kapoor, *Non-Object
Black*, 2019.

until the seventeenth century. Both were valuable detritus created from the mining of mercury.

Pigments are also derived from plant sources: red from madder root, or gamboge, a yellow or orange resin from the Garcinia tree in Southeast Asia. One well-known pigment—indigo—is extracted from the indigo plant. Indigo arrived in Europe from India in the seventeenth century and transformed the blue-pigment market, offering a less expensive alternative to the ultramarines harvested from lapis lazuli. Indigo was also one of the major cash crops driving the trans-Atlantic slave trade in North America. Therefore, beginning with the first contact between Europeans and Americans and the expansion of global trade in the sixteenth and seventeenth centuries, pigments began to be part of an economic system that was responsible for the rise of exploitative labor.

Cochineal, made from insects, was another red pigment that played a central role in early modern artistic practice. The insects were dried to extract carminic acid, which was then processed into either dyes or pigments. Cochineal was an established part of many cultures in the Americas, and Europeans immediately took an interest in transferring the technology to their own workshops [FIG. 3]. Although cochineal was predominantly important for the textile industry, it was also used by artists as a lake pigment, which is one of several organic pigments. Lake pigments are created when the liquid dye is transformed into a solid substance and combined with a binder—for example, chalk or crushed bones. These pigments produced from organic dyes are often not lightfast. Some paintings by Rembrandt van Rijn (1606–1669) have traces of cochineal, testifying to the impact of the technology on the European market and to the predilection of seventeenth-century European painters for these fugitive materials.

For the most part, synthetic pigments—that is, not derived from nature—developed with the rise of chemistry, though there are earlier examples. The earliest known example is Egyptian blue, made by heating quartz sand, alkali, lime, and copper. It was used extensively in ancient Egyptian tomb paintings until the technology was lost during the Roman period. Ancient Egyptians not only made the first synthetic pigment, but they also introduced a form of painting called *encaustic*, which was used for portraits on mummies such as the one in the Art Institute of Chicago [FIG. 4]. Kept in cool, dry, dark spaces, mummy portraits maintained their original brilliance, which embodied a lifelike rendition of the deceased's face. The artists achieved this effect by binding the pigment with clarified beeswax, so that the image would "shine." The process of encaustic (from the Greek meaning "to burn in") includes mixing pigment with clarified beeswax and also sometimes with resin or tallow and applying the hot material to the surface. This form of painting requires the use of special

6

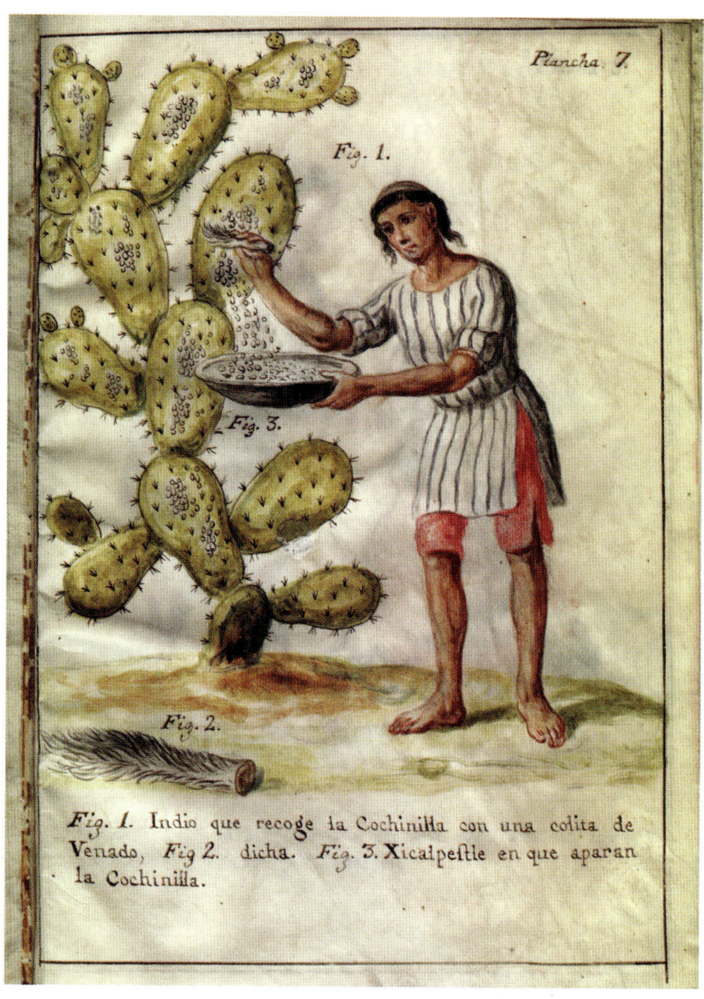

[FIG. 3]
Illustration of cochineal collection, in José Antonio de Alzate y Ramírez, *Memoria sobre la naturaleza, cultivo, y beneficio de la grana . . .* (Essay on the nature, cultivation, and benefits of the cochineal insect), 1777. Colored pigment on vellum.

metal tools, and the result comes from the unique properties of wax. Wax is not, however, a stable binder, and when exposed to light or heat, it shifts the properties of paint. Mummy portraits survive mainly because they were locked in dark tombs. Once they were discovered and brought into the light, their brilliance began to fade.

A central fact about pigments is that they are often unstable. Paintings are inherently stable or unstable depending on the use of pigments, binders, and supports. Even stable colorants such as umbers and ochers are constantly mutating, particularly in response to shifting atmospheric conditions. Knowledge about pigments allows for an understanding that nothing in artistic production is fixed. All works of art are on a trajectory of metamorphosis and perhaps even degradation. The study of pigments, therefore, becomes a theorization of time and temporality. As Karin Leonhard articulates in this volume, pigments and their ability to degrade demand that we see objects less like fixed objects and instead like faces and physiognomies that will age. Experience with pigments allows a viewer to perceive the multiple temporalities that are often present in a single work of art as its various materials age at different rates.

This process of degradation becomes even more rapid with the transport of artworks from their original locations as well as climate change and pollution. Pigments, therefore, always exist in relationship to their external environment. Conservators, curators, and scientists determine to what degree to intervene in the life of work. To examine the shifting nature of pigments and their relative stability or instability, conservation scientists have developed a range of techniques that Barbara Berrie outlines in her essay. Intervention with fading pigments presents philosophical challenges to conservators. While there is a desire to preserve the structural integrity of the original work as it was intended by the artist, that presumes a seamless relationship between the work and the maker, even though works of art often express their own integrity beyond the intentions of the artist. The process of time on a work of art, and its multiple subsequent receptions, becomes a part of its history. Painters were often aware that their pigments might be fugitive—that they might lighten, darken, or even disappear—and they often took that into consideration. Works of art, therefore, hold multiple stages in their lives, and we should not expect a painting to look as it did when the artist first put down the brush. Approaching a painting with a material understanding of pigment allows a better understanding of what has been lost and what remains, as David Bomford illustrates in his contribution to this volume.

One of the most well-known projects in recent decades to bridge the world of original appearance with historical degradation took place at the Harvard Art Museums with murals painted by Mark Rothko (1903–1970) in the 1960s [FIG. 5]. The murals consist of five canvases created with

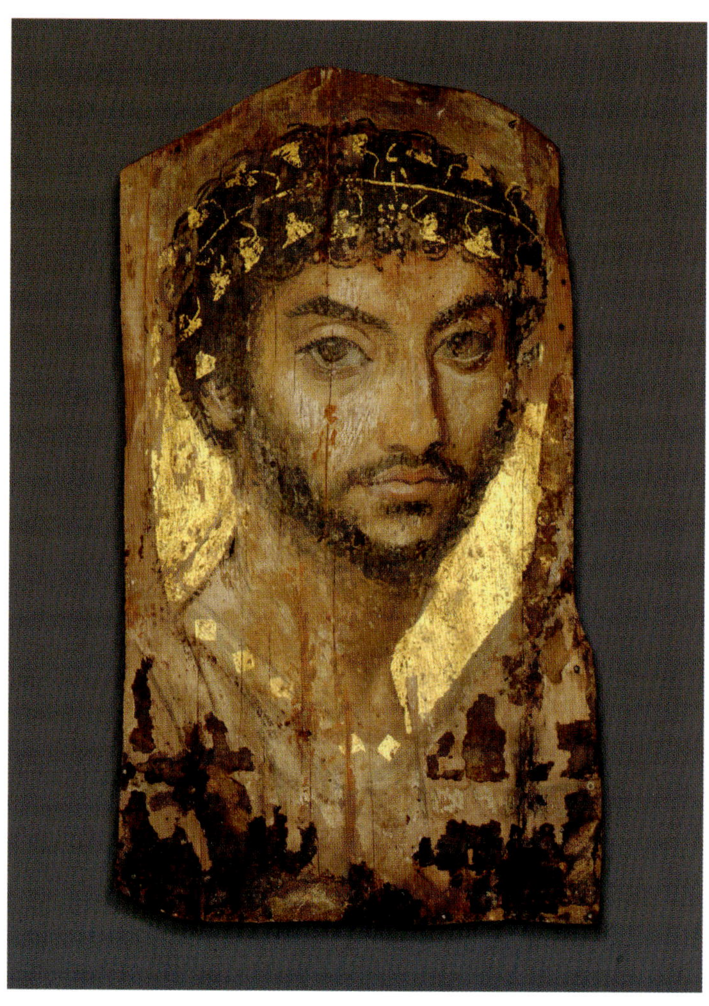

Portrait of a Man Wearing a Laurel Wreath. Egypt, early to mid-2nd century. Lime (linden) wood, beeswax, pigments, gold, textile, natural resin. Art Institute of Chicago, Gift of Emily Crane Chadbourne (1922.4798).

shifting variations of red and rectangular shapes. Rothko painted on an unprepared canvas and eschewed commercial paints, preferring to experiment with pigments and binders. His paintings are, therefore, not only an exploration of color and form on a monumental scale but also the representation of his knowledge about the materials of his craft. Almost immediately after their installation, the murals changed dramatically, becoming darker and losing the brightness of the original red. To give viewers a sense of the original works, the conservation team at Harvard Art Museums installed a light projector. When beams of light reflect off the canvas, the conservators achieve the glow of the original works. When the projectors are turned off, the viewers see the dramatic shift in hue and pigment. This technique was noninvasive, yet it allowed viewers to appreciate the metamorphosis of the works over nearly a half-century. The installation created conditions for the works to exist both as historical artifacts marked by degradation and time and as paintings that could be returned to their brilliant red created by Rothko.

The Harvard Art Museums have a legacy of conservation, science, and the study of pigments. In the early twentieth century, Edward Forbes—a leader in museums and conservation—amassed a collection of thousands of pigments to be kept at the Fogg Museum. For Forbes, the collection was a means to better understand the material history of painting in order to know the past, to conserve it for the future. As he wrote, "We are born to die; these frescoes are born to live." Collecting and mining pigments ensured that works of art would exist for generations, as conservators could utilize the historical collection to create pigments like those used centuries earlier. Forbes also realized that works of art are breathing objects that react to their environments. He pointed out that furnaces and heating systems often destroy paintings and their sensitive surface structures formed by pigments and binders. For example, the dryness in the air from heat might cause pigments suspended on the surface of their ground to swell, shrink, and ultimately detach from the support.

The Forbes Pigment Collection at the Harvard Art Museums demonstrates the ways in which trade networks, colonial expansion, and exploitation of labor and natural resources were central to the history of painting and its materials, a history that remains within the labels and names of many pigments on display [FIG. 6]. It tells a geographic history of art and reminds us how color is often derived from specific geographic areas; labels describe the fossil resin of amber "found on the shores of the Baltic sea" and the gum Arabic from acacia "growing in Africa, India, and Australia." Like the encyclopedic collections of the Harvard Art Museums, the Forbes Pigment Collection embodies the geographic and temporal ambitions of a universal collection. Nevertheless, the names of the pigments and their extraction mirror the same histories

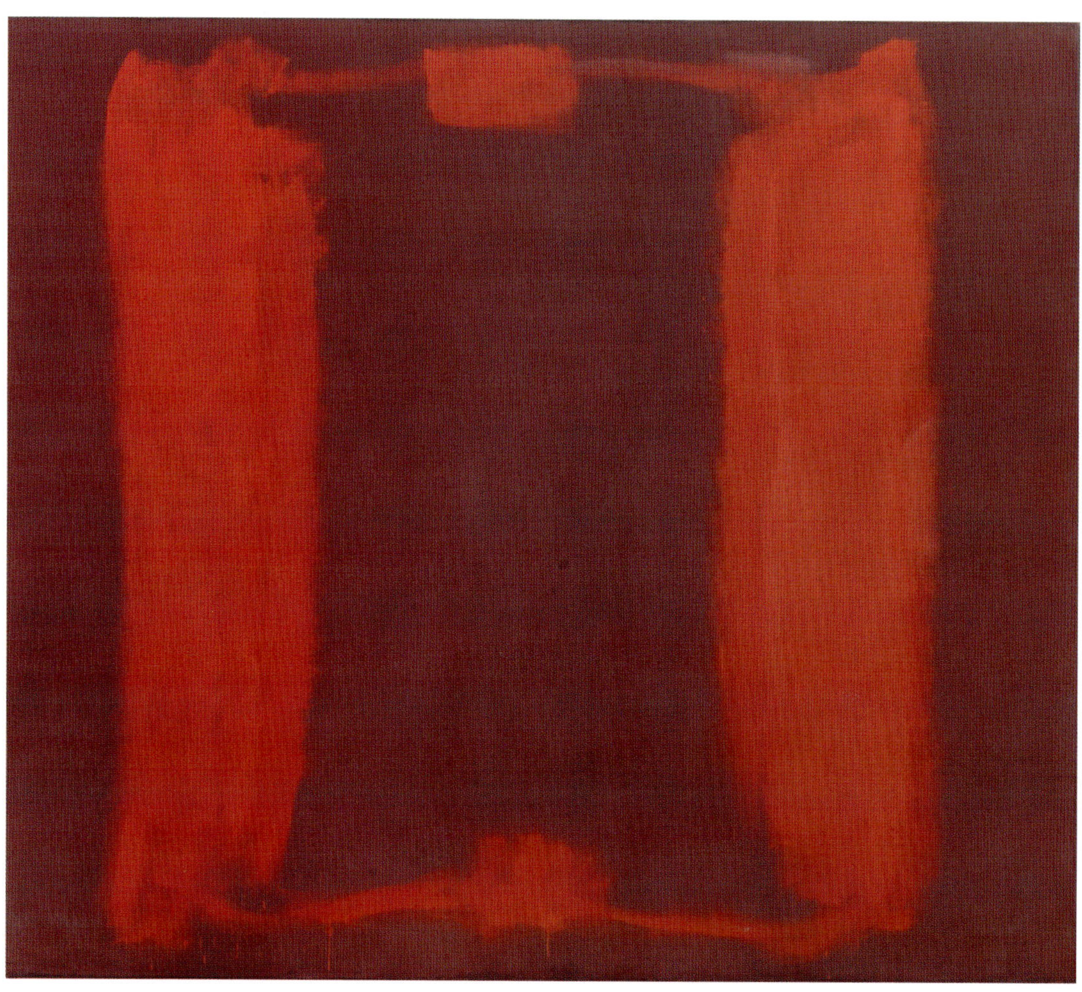

[FIG. 5]
Mark Rothko, *Panel One*
(*Harvard Mural Triptych*),
1962. Egg tempera and
distemper on canvas,
267.3 × 297.8 cm. Harvard
Art Museums/Fogg
Museum, Transfer from
Harvard University, Gift
of the Artist (2011.638.1).

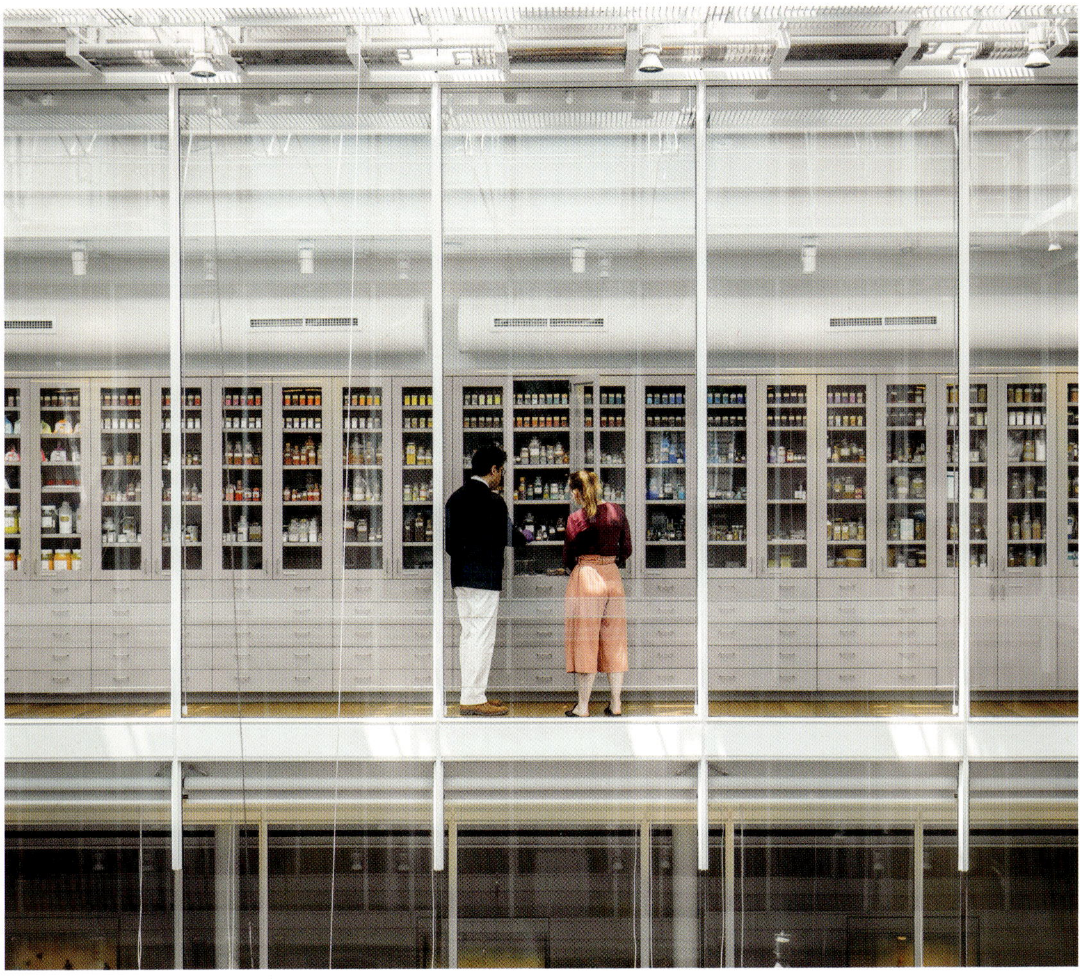

[FIG. 6]
Forbes Pigment Collection
and Gettens Collection
of Binding Media and
Varnishes at Harvard Art
Museums' Straus Center
for Conservation and
Technical Studies.

of exploitation and colonialism that have been central to the concept and formation of collections since the sixteenth century. As a resource for study, it is invaluable. Yet, like the plants and parasites of indigo and cochineal, many specimens in the Forbes collection contain their own microhistories of agricultural development under industrial capitalism and violent extraction.

Forbes was not the only scientist, conservator, and artist who took an interest in building a collection of pigments at the turn of the twentieth century. George Washington Carver (ca. 1864–1943), born enslaved at the end of the Civil War, was one of the foremost agricultural scientists of the twentieth century and an innovator in the science of pigments. His writings about sustainable practices in farming, particularly aimed at farmers struggling to make a living from land that was destroyed by the monoculture of the plantation economy, were formative for twentieth-century agriculture. At Tuskegee University, where he was the head of the Department of Agriculture, Carver wrote on a variety of topics, from the importance of crop rotation to introducing new cash crops that would add nutrients to the soil. He was also a painter and created pigments from the Alabama soil that local farmers could use to paint their houses. For him, these pigments allowed the development of an aesthetic language for buildings that were often overlooked: "No place can be called a school in the truest sense that has no pictures on the wall, no paint or whitewash on the buildings, either inside or outside, no trees, shrubs, vines, grasses or properly laid out walks and paths, which appeal to the child's aesthetic nature and sets before him the most important of all secular lessons—order and system." For Carver, making pigments to beautify the vernacular architecture with the local Alabama clays and soil was a means to create a visual vocabulary. Carver saw the local landscape as a resource for agricultural innovation and artistic materials. "Of the many attractive features of our beautiful country," he wrote, "I think there is possibly none that elicit such universal admiration and praise as the vast deposits of multi-colored clays, ranging from snow-white, through many gradations, to the richest Sienna and Indian reds on the one hand, and from the deepest yellow ochre to the palest cream tintings on the other." Carver also created pigments from tomato vines, Osage oranges, radishes, wood ashes, the bark of maple trees, dandelions, and sweet potato peels and vines.

His work demonstrates that pigments and their extraction from the earth can tell local histories and stories, demonstrating the intersections among the sciences of food, medicine, and art. For Carver, who always reminded farmers to "be kind to the soil," making pigments from Alabama clay was a means to build a new society from the ruins of plantations and the slave trade [FIG. 7]. His work in local pigments and ecologies allowed agricultural society in the South to recuperate, following the

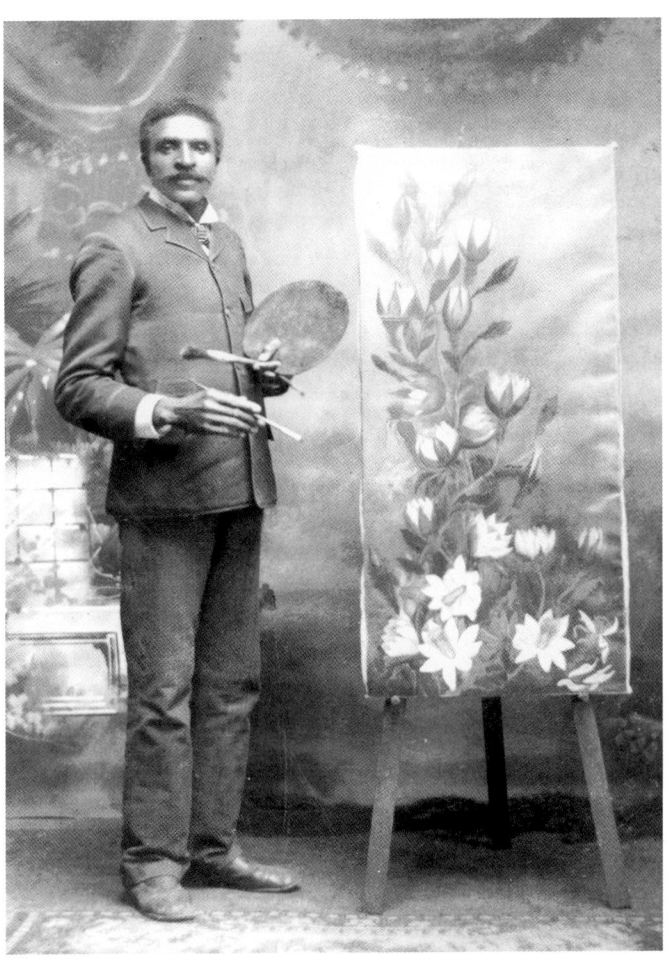

[FIG. 7]
George Washington Carver (1864–1943) and His Art.
Photograph.

devastation of the global trade in cotton. Carver's work was also an early form of conservation of the earth itself. Carver's legacy testifies that the history of art conservation has always intimately been connected to the earth. Pigments tell stories about survival, as they are not only made from earth, but they also track our relationship to the earth as a site of worship, extraction, development, plenitude, and exhaustion.

How might knowing more about pigments change how we look at painting? This book is not intended as a complete history of pigments across time. We focus primarily on organic rather than inorganic pigments. This book is an introduction to what constitutes a pigment and a study in method, engaging with a variety of specialists who are knowledgeable about pigments from different perspectives and demonstrate how that understanding impacts their writing about art. All the essays in this book articulate the vital work happening across disciplines as art historians, scientists, anthropologists, and conservators enter into conversation with one another.

In the longer essays, art historian Karin Leonhard and conservation scientist Barbara Berrie introduce the language needed to think about pigment. Leonhard discusses the critical vocabulary and theoretical structure around color and pigment in early modern European painting, outlining the theorization in relationship to discourses on light and perception. Berrie offers key terms in the conservation science of pigment that will be a resource for readers looking to understand the tools at play in the scientist's laboratory. The case study by conservator David Bomford examines the impact of pigment and discoloration on European painting. The other four case studies explore pigment beyond the context of European painting, recognizing the limitations of thinking about pigment from that perspective. Carolyn Boyd demonstrates how technical study of pigment contextualizes the White Shaman Mural from nearly five thousand years ago in the American Southwest and Coahuila, Mexico. Technical analysis reveals that the artists did not use the readily available red ocher pigment but instead produced a red pigment from yellow siltstones using a labor-intensive process. As she argues, the difficulty of making the red pigment imbues the mural cycles with fire and life, so that they not only represent creation but also embody it within their material construction. Boyd's case demonstrates how to interweave technical analysis into an essay to make an argument about cosmological meaning.

Quincy Ngan considers copper-based pigments in relationship to ancient Chinese bronzes from the Shang and Zhou dynasties (ca. 1600–256 BCE) and their enduring impact on Chinese painting into the nineteenth century. Drawing on technical analysis, Ngan traces the transmediality of copper-based pigments in Chinese art from ancient bronzes to nineteenth-century painting. Gabriela Siracusano illustrates the importance of technical analysis of pigment to historicize the Amerindian artists working between Indigenous and colonial painting practices. Siracusano calls her method an "archaeology of making," bringing together chemical analysis and art history to study the ongoing legacy of ancestral material memory realized in the choice of pigment for Amerindian artists working in the Viceroyalty of Peru.

For the most part, these essays focus on pigment and its role in temporality, sacred geographies, and infusing objects with human presence and ancestral histories. Yet, the final essay, by Anne Lafont, demonstrates how the perception of pigment—particularly skin pigment—dehumanized and refused presence to those whose skin color was not white, a history of science and race that is necessary to contextualizing the ongoing legacy of racism today and its impact on certain technologies such as color printing. Lafont demonstrates how the concept of pigment in regard to skin color enters the history of art at the same time as innovations in pastel and color printing, so that artists "prepared the scholar's eye" to recognize variations in skin color. Lafont's essay makes clear that the study and recognition of pigments in European art cannot be dissociated from the formation of the discipline of art history itself in the eighteenth century.

Despite radically different time periods and geographic areas, all the cases offer modes by which to engage technical analysis with art-historical methods to narrate complex histories in which color and pigment are not merely mimetic or symbolic but reorient art history. This short book is intended only as an introduction to thinking about pigment as a method in art history, introducing the work of scholars who use a technical understanding of pigment in relationship to other models of art-historical analysis. While the book can be read in any order, the essays collectively demonstrate how pigment illuminates the interaction between nature and culture. Studying the history of art through the lens of pigment reveals that artists often depicted the natural world and depended on the physical world for their materials—from rock to parasitic insect. Pigments themselves are creative works, held within each coarsely ground molecule of powder. They are laborious, time-consuming, and imaginative endeavors, and most great painters have studied not only line and form but also the qualities of the material world through pigments and binders. Pigment demonstrates the insoluble nature of color and how we have left our mark on the surface of this earth through the extraction of reds, blues and violets, greens and yellows across the visible and the invisible spectrum, a history that is as much about art as our relationship to nature and to one another.

Pigment Histories in European Painting

Karin Leonhard

A few years ago, over a cup of coffee in Berlin, the following conversation took place between a conservation scientist and an art historian: "When looking at a painting, you say, 'The Madonna is wearing a blue cloak,' while we say, 'The Madonna's cloak is painted with lapis lazuli'" [FIG. 8]. They were referring to a divergent focus inasmuch as art historians refer to the perception of a viewer ("we see a blue color"), while art technologists or conservators emphasize the material substance inducing this perception ("we see pigments such as lapis lazuli").

It was a friendly exchange, but the sting remained: What do we, as art historians, really know about the material nature of the artworks we study so closely? During my studies, this issue was hardly raised, and the differences between artistic techniques, pigments, coloring agents, and binders barely seemed worth mentioning. Much has changed since then, and the material turn in the humanities has drawn new attention to the colorants used and their artistic or artisanal application as a meaningful part of a work of art. Another realization has also changed the discipline of art history. Once we understand that paintings are *physical* objects that travel across space and time and may sustain damage or age in the process, our own perception is called into question. Do we know what a painting or artwork looked like when it was created? What are we seeing in a museum? To what extent has time already been at work, in the form of a chemical aging process or a history of restoration?

Transforming Nature into Art

For the Russian avant-garde painter Wassily Kandinsky (1866–1944), the sight of paint coming out of a tube amounted to a lavish feast for the senses. In 1879 he bought himself a box of oil paints: "When I was thirteen or fourteen, I bought a paintbox with oil paints from money slowly saved up. The feeling I had at the time—or better: the experience of the color coming out of the tube—is with me to this day. A pressure of the fingers—and jubilant, joyous, thoughtful, dreamy, self-absorbed, with deep seriousness, with bubbling roguishness, with the sigh of liberation, with sensitive unstableness of balance came one after another these unique beings we call colors—each alive in and for itself, independent, endowed with all necessary qualities for further independent life and ready and willing at every moment to submit to new combinations, to mix among themselves and create endless series of new worlds." His fascination with being able to press lightly on the tube from a paintbox to create an entire work, gushing out from the tube as if by itself, led to works with a cosmological quality. In his paintings, wars are waged between colors and forms, and harmonies are created that are indebted to the sensation of gushing paint from a tube that he explained in his autobiography [FIG. 9].

Kandinsky used industrially produced paints that he bought in tubes or a paintbox—a recent invention that we should not take for granted. The history of the paintbox, developed in the nineteenth century in the wake of plein air painting, is worth a study of its own. In earlier centuries, artists made their own paints. Painters or their apprentices painstakingly ground the pigments then added binding agents to make them spreadable. These agents were water-soluble for book illumination, oil-soluble for panel and canvas painting and polychrome decoration, and lime-binding for wall painting. Depending on the colorant and the painting technique, the pigments were mixed in shells or arranged on palettes, or small linen cloths were soaked in the paint so it could be stored and reused for a prolonged period.

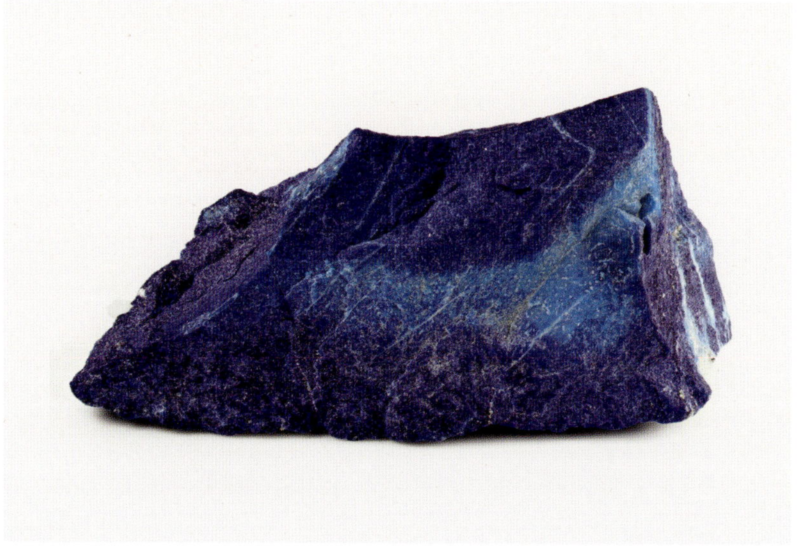

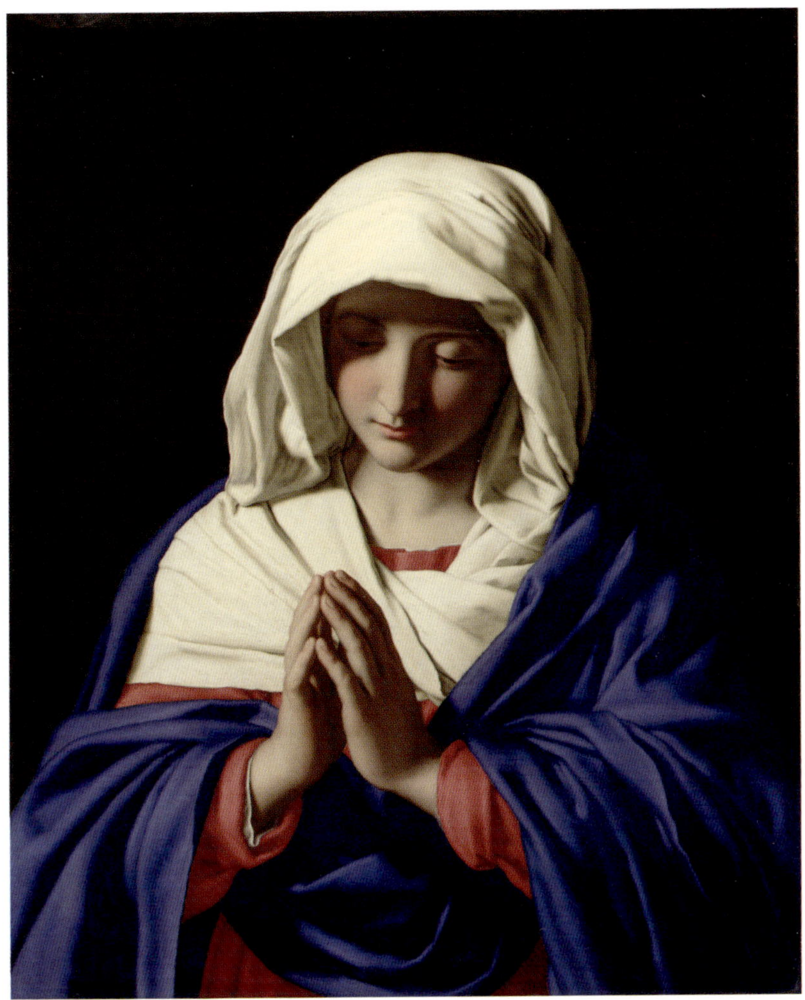

[FIG. 8]
(above) Sassoferrato, *The Virgin in Prayer*, 1640–50. Oil on canvas, 73 × 57.7 cm. National Gallery, London, Bequeathed by Richard Simmons, 1846 (NG200). (opposite) Lapis lazuli from Badakhshan Province, Afghanistan.

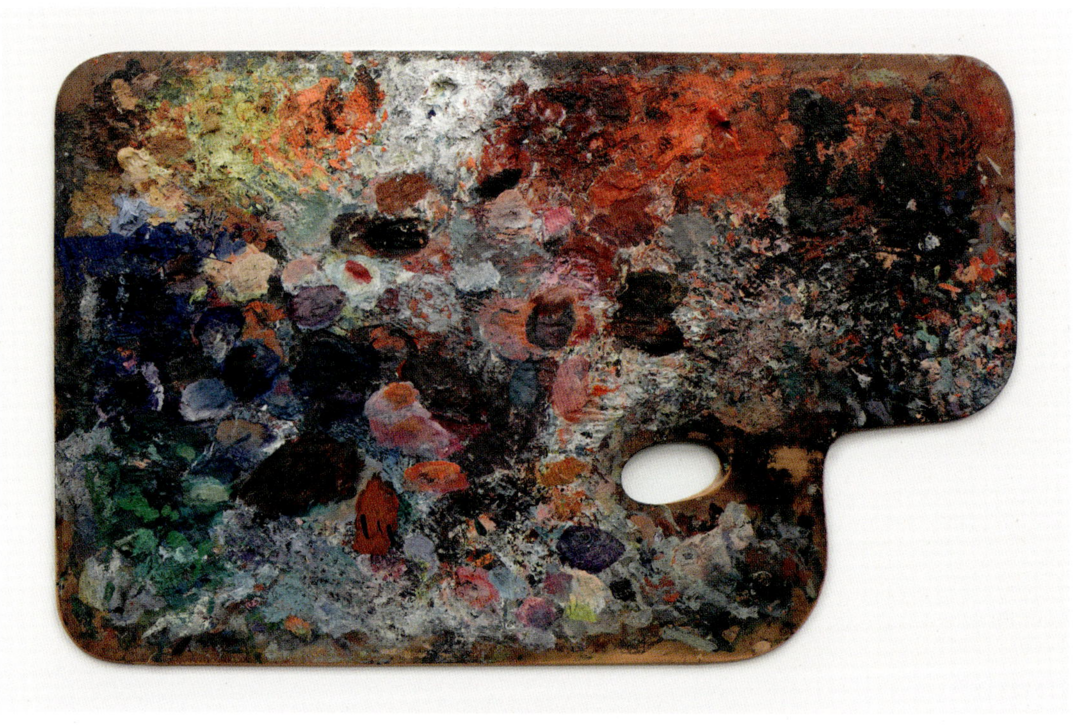

[FIG. 9]
Wassily Kandinsky,
Palette, ca. 1939. Wood.
© Musée National d'Art
Moderne / Centre Georges
Pompidou, Bequest of
Nina Kandinsky, 1981.

The ways in which colors were extracted varied as well. While some pigments had to be dug from the earth then ground into powder, washed, and slurried for use, colorants of animal origin were often boiled or subjected to chemical processes. The production process was at times harmful to health. Just think of the manufacture of toxic lead white paint, made from strips of lead that were rolled into spirals and placed in stoneware vessels over sharp vinegar. The vessels, in turn, were loosely covered and buried in horse manure or used tanner's bark in an oxidation room. Heat and carbon dioxide produced from decomposition caused the metallic lead to change into lead white. Verdigris was similarly obtained by attaching strips of copper to the inside of a hollowed-out block or wooden barrel with vinegar at the bottom and burying the container in manure. The verdigris that formed on the copper surfaces could be scraped off and used as paint. The instructions for making pigment from natural materials such as minerals, plants, and other organic substances circulated in workshops and were passed on orally from one generation to the next. Occasionally, they were also compiled in written workshop records and collections of recipes that also addressed the addition of binding agents and mixing with other colors. Such source texts are crucial for an understanding of historical processes. The scientific identification of a pigment may tell us its chemical composition, but to understand how certain paints were produced in the past we need contemporary recipes and thus are forced to adopt a cultural-historical perspective on artistic techniques and materials.

After the invention of the printing press, the practical knowledge of color moved from medieval manuscripts into printed works such as treatises, artists' manuals, and large-scale volumes on medicine and botany. Early modern printers and publishers also produced a slew of pharmaceutical literature, ranging from costly hand-colored herbaria to inexpensive "daily companions." Such manuals were popular because, as their introductions announced, they tended to "summarize the magical and physical properties of trees and herbs as well as their healing powers against nearly every disease." In addition, there was a veritable boom in the publication of "Books of Wonder" or "Books of Secrets" that provided recipes for color extraction and instructions about engraving, making ink, gilding, and varnishing as well as cosmetics. They were often bound together with books on the arts of dyeing and distilling, and all the texts drew connections between man-made paints and natural resources. In 1677 the German physician, botanist, and naturalist Johann Sigismund Elsholtz (1623–1688) refers to "the so great variety of Colour in the Herbs, Roots, Leaves and Flowers from whence they were distilled" in the introduction to his *Curious Distillatory; or, The Art of Distilling Coloured Liquors, Spirits, Oyls, etc. from Vegitables, Animals, Minerals and Metals.*

In *Mysteryes of Nature and Art* (1634) John Bate describes colors that "are either merely tinctures of vegetables, or substances of minerals, or both: . . . Vegetables are rootes, juces, berries, and such like things as grow out of the earth. Minerals are such as are dig'd out of the earth, as earth, and stones, & c."

Until well into the seventeenth century, the power ascribed to colors was discussed in terms of psychological perception and a belief that they had material properties because they were obtained from plants, berries, roots, earth, stones, and minerals. In fact, the scholarly consensus was that the origin, effect, and meaning of colors, whether observed in nature or created on the painter's palette, needed to be discussed together because each shade was the result of a physical mixture of elements. As such, each was also suitable for painting. As the Italian artist and priest Matteo Zaccolini (1574–1630) points out in his 1618–22 treatise *De colori*, we need to imagine that the painter's palette is created from the same four basic elements that shape the entire universe. The earth with its minerals as the basis has produced the spectrum of colors through a combination with water, air, and fire. When a painter applies these colors to the canvas, he or she is handling the same substances and qualities prevalent in nature. As Zaccolini explains, it is as if natural materials, once they appear on the picture surface, transform from earth and minerals into something cosmic. Because the pigments of the painter are obtained from organic and inorganic substances in nature, they were thought of as both artificial and natural colors. The art-theoretical dialogue *Il Figino* (1591) argues that with the brush "the true can be imitated with the false, until the true is vanquished by the false, which now appears truer than the truth"—that is, "until fruits and flowers are but shadows of those depicted ['shaded'] with colors."

Pigment versus Color

The word "pigment" is derived from the Latin *pigmentum*, meaning "color," "makeup," or "spice, aromatic substance," and is etymologically close to the Latin verb *pingere* (*pictum*), meaning to paint or to decorate. *Pharmakeia* (φαρμακεία) is another ancient term for pigments in treatises on color, demonstrating a proximity between pharmacology and painting that also involved models of transmission, aesthetic infection, and/or healing. *Pharmakeia* are substances that are as useful as they are harmful and toxic, and it is interesting to see how the discourse on their medicinal use resembles the discourse of painters on the uses and effects of paints.

The close relationship between painting, cosmetics, and medicine will be discussed below. First, it is important to understand that pigments are colorants but should not be equated with the "colors" of objects. "Pigment" covers or colors materials. The term *color*, likewise derived from Latin, refers to the impressions induced in the viewer's perception by pigments—that is, a sensory experience. The Dutch painter and art theorist Gerard de Lairesse (1641–1711), for example, understood the colors (paints) on the canvas in two ways: as pigments to be mixed and as colors when viewed aesthetically. Color or paint material ("pigment," "colorant," "paint") and color perception ("color") are inextricably linked but by no means the same thing.

Color Today and in the Past

Any discussion of pigments must therefore address color. Nowadays, we would say that color is a sensation, a perception, and not a thing in itself. Our eyes register, and our brain constructs, color from a small part of the electromagnetic (EM) spectrum, the radiation that suffuses the universe. The EM spectrum spans a vast range of energetic radiation, from high-energy gamma rays to low-energy radio waves and beyond the two ends. The human eye is sensitive to only a tiny portion of this energy continuum, comprising wavelengths from about 390 to 750 nanometers (a nanometer is one billionth of a meter) and aptly referred to as "the visible." When the entire range of the visible spectrum reaches our eyes at the same time, we see "white," meaning no specific color at all. When the visible spectrum is scattered by a prism or water droplets, our eye/brain combination perceives the smaller, discrete energy ranges as different colors. We are able to perceive millions of shades of color and appreciate nuances and subtle differences between colors.

Pigments, on the other hand, are colored substances that absorb and/or reflect parts of the visible spectrum. White pigments do not absorb any part of the visible spectrum, while black pigments absorb it completely. Red pigments absorb all visible light except red light because they either allow it to pass through (transparent pigment) or reflect it (opaque pigment). Similarly, yellow pigments absorb the wavelengths in the blue portion of the visible spectrum and transmit or scatter all longer wavelengths (green and red) of the visible spectrum. This optical explanation of color phenomena gained acceptance by the end of the seventeenth century with the gradual establishment of so-called spectral color theory. For a long time, a different understanding of color prevailed, and we need to be familiar with it when looking at early modern artworks. Ever since antiquity, all colors were believed to come from a mixture of white and black (or, rather, light and dark) and to be linked to the four elements: water, air, earth, and fire. In medieval and early modern texts, the use of colors in painting corresponded to divine creation or the creation of the universe. Between light and darkness, colors shine like gems of varying purity. The resulting color values (hues) were understood as various levels of brightness that were explained by greater proximity to the poles of light or darkness. For this reason, the luminosity of colors was a factor in the evaluation of art, as the intensity and brightness of a color was understood as an indicator of the diaphaneity of the material. The purer and more radiant a hue, the less material-based it was in contemporary eyes. Accordingly, repeated attempts were undertaken to create hue scales and relate them to the color sequence of the rainbow.

Another concept of this earlier tradition was the assumption that color represents a stable property of things—a quality inherent in them. Within contemporary color theory, this concept was referred to as "real" or "proper" color (*colores proprii*), meaning that the colors perceived corresponded to natural bodies that possessed those colors. Pigment colors that were directly extracted from a plant or a mineral by grinding or distilling fell under this category. Following the logic of the period, colors are "real" if they represent qualities inherent in a physical object. In turn, "apparent" colors change their appearance depending on the position of the spectator and might not convey any information about the "real" color of the object at all. Apparent colors do not necessarily correspond to a physical object displaying those colors. Instead, they depend on the interplay between light and shadow and on the reflection of other colored objects surrounding them. For this reason, they belong to a temporal world that shifts its chromatic appearance by the moment. Albrecht Dürer's (1471–1528) *Self-Portrait* [FIG. 10] is perhaps the most famous example of the use of such a terminological distinction. He inscribed his painting at the top right: "This is how I, Albrecht Dürer from Nuremberg, painted myself with proper colors at the age of 28 years [Albertus Durerus Noricus / ipsum me proprijs sic effin / gebam coloribus aetatis / anno XXVIII]," thereby emphasizing the verisimilitude of his portrait. By contrast, the colors of the rainbow or the iridescent colors of bird feathers and butterfly wings appeared fleeting and ephemeral to the early modern eye. That is one reason why, in painting, intermediary figures such as angels, nymphs, and otherworldly messengers were depicted with *colori cangianti*, or iridescent colors. They are not of this world but instead move between different worlds, and this incorporeal or unstable state can be expressed through color.

Spectrum versus Pigment
The history of culture is always a history of color. Conversely, color is not universal but culturally and historically coded. Art historians examine the historical significance of colors through the study of, among other things, written sources in a variety of fields—recipe books, treatises on painting, optical treatises, natural philosophical writings, and literary texts. This knowledge is indispensable for the contextualization of artworks and leads to changed, and sometimes surprisingly new, perspectives.

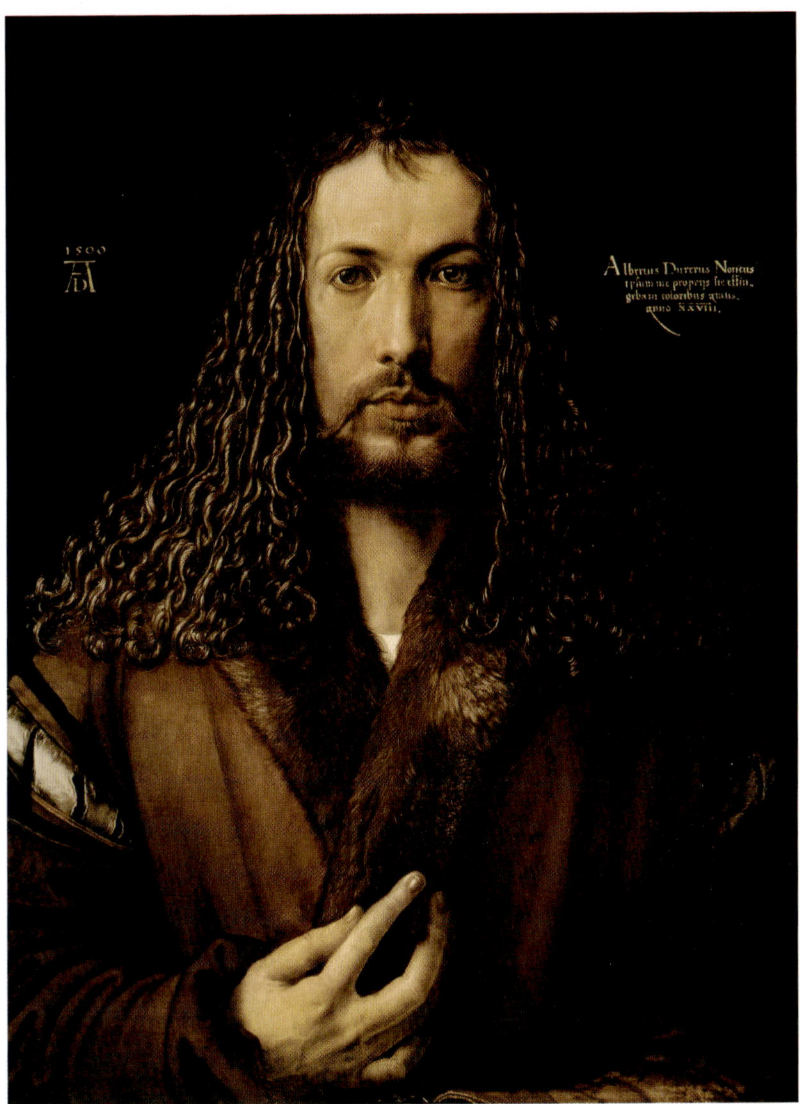

[FIG. 10]
Albrecht Dürer, *Self-Portrait with Fur-Trimmed Robe*, 1500. Oil on limewood, 67.1 × 48.9 cm. Alte Pinakothek, Munich (537).

It seems almost incomprehensible today that color was considered an integral part of the material world rather than a part of light. The colored appearance of an object (plant, animal, human being) provided information about a fundamental property of the object and lent it its individuality. Hence, Dürer wrote that he portrayed himself in "proper colors": painting produced physical equivalents of reality that were not subject to the vagaries of time. As long as the location of colored appearances was rooted in the physical world, such a claim would hold. But it changed the moment color shifted to the eye of the spectator, meaning the moment light was identified as the source of color. With the transition from a medieval to a mechanical natural philosophy, colors came to be considered light-induced sensations in the brain of the beholder. René Descartes (1596–1650), for example, remarked in 1637 on the senselessness of distinguishing between real and disembodied colors since all colors represented nothing but phenomena and were equally true and false. The hierarchy changed accordingly, and the spectral colors gained conceptual primacy over object, or "real," colors. Drawing on these theories, which inextricably linked the study of color to the study of light, Newton established a color theory on the sole basis of experiments on the refraction of light. In 1704 he published his *Opticks* as a summary of decades of research. The critical experiment presented in this work (Newton himself used the phrase "experimentum crucis") disproved all previous theories of color. When passing through a prism, sunlight was refracted into the spectrum. The experiment showed that it could then be recomposed into white light. Newton concluded that white light was not simple and homogeneous, as previously believed, but instead composed of colored rays of light. His definition of color had considerable consequences as each color appears solely as the result of a selective reflection of white light. Objects, therefore, must obtain their colors by reflecting certain rays of light while absorbing others. Accordingly, permanent object colors result exclusively from the varying reflective and refracting behaviors of their surfaces. Now color was created through surfaces off which light—which contains the entire color spectrum—is refracted and reflected. However, the role of light in color theory conflicted with artistic concerns about the materiality of paint and the laws of physical pigment mixtures.

Art versus Nature

For many centuries, a central concern of painters was creating shades of color that were as pure and luminous as possible and that matched the radiance of the rainbow. At the same time, they wanted to achieve a wide range of shades and nuances, either by using different colorants or all sorts of color mixtures. The two concerns were difficult to reconcile because in the eyes of contemporaries any attempt at mixing colors clouded their purity and was understood as a process of contamination, a "fading" or "deflowering."

The antagonism between the luminous spectral colors and the artificial pigments that imitated them defined early modern art in a variety of ways, especially in the development of still-life and landscape painting. The relationship between nature and art was central to these two genres since the latter was understood as a "second nature." This relationship, which was also a competitive one, is obviously of particular interest to art historians. The two models of "natural" and "artificial" coloring are often chiastically intertwined in art theory. On the one hand, nature is said to work like an artist because it colors and paints things. On the other hand, the artist resembles nature in his ability to deceptively imitate its colors with pigments. It is easy to see how the two concepts are closely correlated, not least because seventeenth-century color theory, as long it was concerned with physical or pigment colors, focused on material processes of mixing and coloring.

In Cornelis de Heem's (1631–1695) *Still Life with Parrot and Basket of Fruits and Flowers* [FIG. 11], for example, the artist engages with the theme of the bird onomatopoetically, imitating nature in a parable of mimetic visual forms. A large parrot with iridescent glowing plumage sits on a basket that has tipped over due to its weight, scattering its contents of colorful flowers and fruit on a tabletop. What draws the viewer's attention, however, is not only that the bird's splayed-out tail feathers are painted with loose brushstrokes and that the movement of the artist's hand can be traced via paint but also that the stripes of feathers extend across the width of the canvas like a rainbow. The light does not illuminate the feathers and the flowers from the outside but rather is inherent to them. The pictorial field glows and is transformed into a vibrating particulate universe made of light particles or pigments. Pigment and color are interrelated, as light passes through the painterly field as a coloring force, taking on a material form. Such a visualized connection of color corresponds to the blooming and waning spectrum of the rainbow. The seventeenth-century theorist Gerard de Lairesse accordingly advised flower painters to arrange the colors on the canvas so "that by the placement of one next to another a welcome blend of color is produced, one that is pleasing to the eye and satisfies it: this includes placing strong and flaming ones side by side with weak ones in such a way that they represent a charming rainbow."

Natural and Artificial Color

Color and pigment are central to understanding the relationship between art and nature in early modern painting. The Dutch painter and art

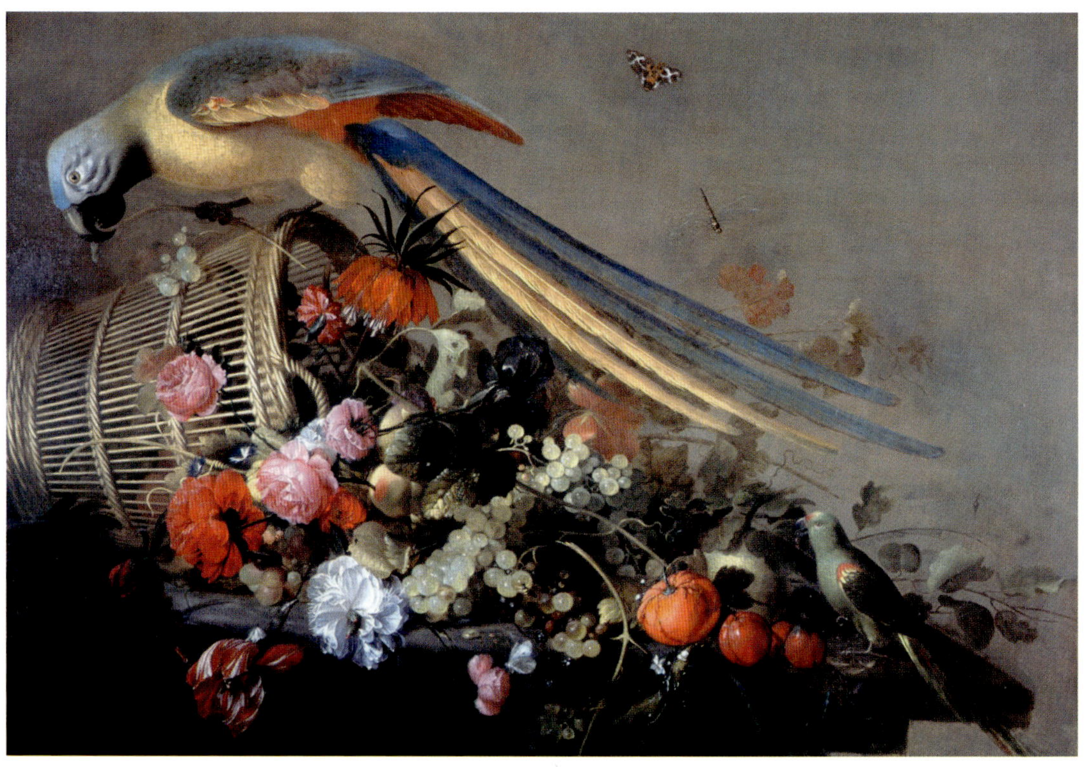

[FIG. 11]
Cornelis de Heem, *Still Life
with Parrot and Basket of
Fruits and Flowers*, ca. 1680s.
Oil on wood, 85 × 119.5 cm.
Galerie de Jonckheere, Paris.

theorist Samuel van Hoogstraten (1627–1678), a pupil of Rembrandt's, discussed this idea repeatedly, including in book 6 of his *Inleyding tot de Hooge Schoole der Schilderkonst* (Introduction to the Academy of Painting), which begins with thoughts on the importance of color in painting. As the author explains, color is understood to be like a colorful dress slipped over a body, giving the depicted object its vividness. But color is also the most immediate means of expression in painting when it is used directly, without drawing and without conforming to an outline. At this point, Van Hoogstraten makes an unexpected comparison, writing that to achieve two-dimensional areas of color, it suffices to press paint-covered leaves onto a canvas. The direct imprint of paint constitutes the lowest level of artistic representation, with the imprint functioning as a template devoid of the artist's hand. This discussion of natural matter inserted into painting is particularly interesting as it alludes to a pictorial genre that has become known in art history as *sottobosco* painting (after the Italian for "undergrowth"). The term refers to still lifes that depict subjects from nature that were dismissed as inferior for art, including insects, reptiles, snails, and plants such as mushrooms. Products of a mossy forest floor, these paintings were made using a painterly technique that involved applying viscous paint to a support and then pressing various natural objects such as leaves into it.

Such paintings were not only about faithfully imitating nature, as Van Hoogstraten explains, but the impression techniques were particularly suitable for the first stage of representing nature. The imprinted shapes of moss and leaves did not require any drawing or shading to model them but were "only concerned with color." On this ground, one could place all sorts of creatures such as snakes, lizards, tarantulas, or frogs. The next steps built up the painting to make it grow from the surface and appear three-dimensional. Van Hoogstraten instructs the painter to take the natural imprints and add a few more complex forms such as flowers or shells, the way they appear outdoors to the spectator and illuminated by a uniform light source.

Van Hoogstraten's excursus on the "underworld" is a reflection on the mimetic function of color. Even in its most basic application, an impression fulfills the task of imitating nature, but such means can be further enhanced by the ability of painting to deceptively imitate three-dimensionality through "rounding and shadowing." Here, too, pigments are used, but they do not simply serve to help nature imprint itself. Instead, they translate natural colors into artificial colors. In the works of *sottobosco* painting, however, the competition between artificial and natural colors also takes place elsewhere. Rather than painting the shimmering wings of butterflies, for example, some painters, first and foremost the Dutch artist Otto Marseus van Schrieck (ca. 1619/20–1678),

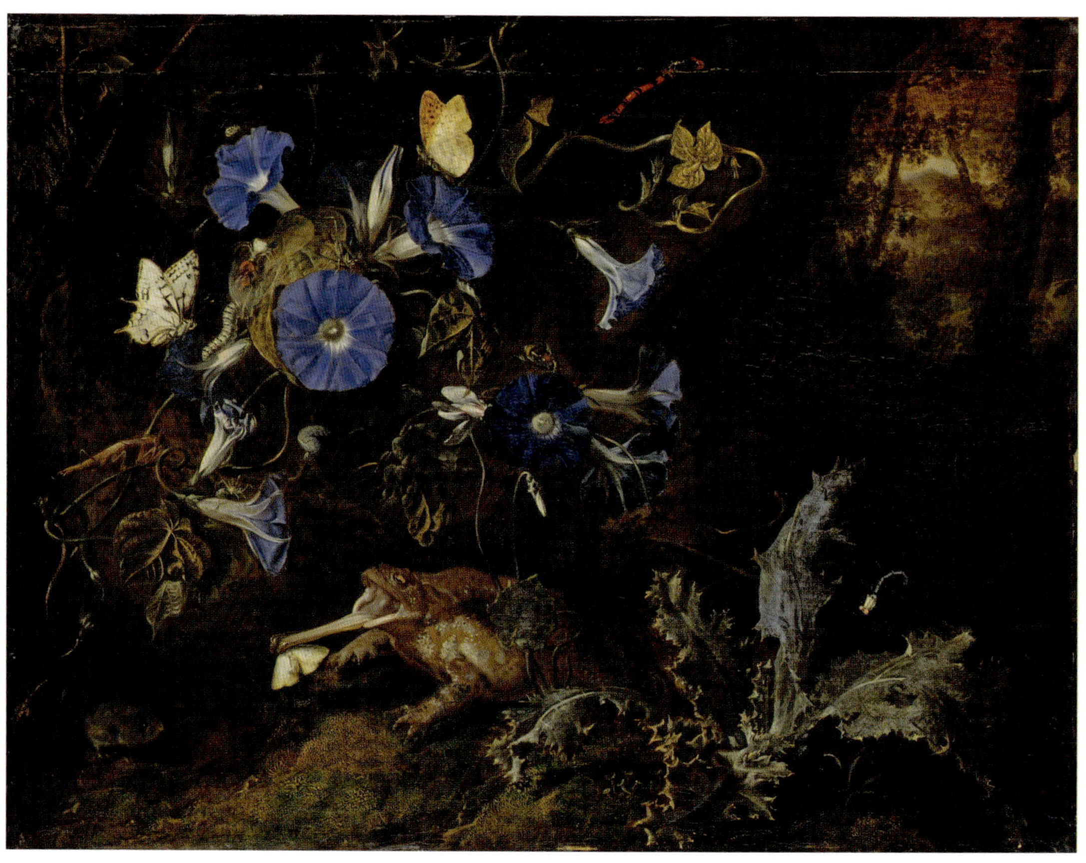

[FIG. 12]
Otto Marseus van Schrieck,
*Sottobosco with Toad and
Blue Convolvulus*, 1660.
Oil on canvas, 53.7 × 68 cm.
Staatliches Museum
Schwerin (G154).

applied the scales of actual butterflies onto the canvas. One of his followers, Elias van den Broeck (1649–1708), was later excluded from his painters' guild for so doing. The impressed butterfly wings in his paintings were said to be improper art because they did not involve interpretation. As *sottobosco* painting demonstrates, the application of color during this period was celebrated as a direct reflection of the natural world, yet the demonstrated mastery over color depended upon artificial means to realize the luminosity and opacity of nature's pigments [FIG. 12].

Pigments as *Pharmakeia*

The power of painting is based on the transformation of substances derived from nature into art, thus locating pigments at the intersection of nature and art. But the chain of associations by no means ends here. The term *pharmakon* was long understood to mean not only "medicine" but also "magic," "poison," and "color." In Florence until the end of the sixteenth century, painters belonged to the Arte dei Medici e Speziali (guild of doctors and pharmacists) because they bought their pigments from apothecaries: the guild's banner showed the Virgin and Child being portrayed by Saint Luke, who was a painter as well as a physician and could be appealed to as both. A fifteenth-century illumination [FIG. 13] shows the substances that could be bought in pharmacies and used as pigments by painters. The materials and colorants listed include mastic, plaster, pearl, coral, lapis lazuli, and a pigment known to artists as mummy brown that was popular well into the nineteenth century and was made from white pitch, myrrh, and the ground-up remains of ancient Egyptian mummies. Due to its transparency, it could be used for glazes, flesh tints, and shading. Historically, the demand for mummy brown at times exceeded the supply of real mummies. As a result, corpses of recently deceased slaves or criminals were occasionally used instead. Mummy brown declined in popularity in the late nineteenth century when knowledge of its composition spread among artists. Thus, the Pre-Raphaelite artist Edward Burne-Jones (1833–1898) is said to have solemnly buried his tube in his yard when he discovered the true origin of the pigment. Such references to the close relationship between original raw material and artistic use are important when we discuss the pharmaceutical and sometimes even magical components of individual ingredients.

Let us return to the Baroque painters of the "underworld." They sought to reconcile color and object at the pigment level, and they were enthralled by the idea of depicting stone with stone, earth with earth, and plants with plants—the poisonous mushroom cap with toxic pigment, the sky-blue flower with lapis lazuli. In the aforementioned painting by Van Schrieck, a plump toad crawls from a burrow, the thickly applied

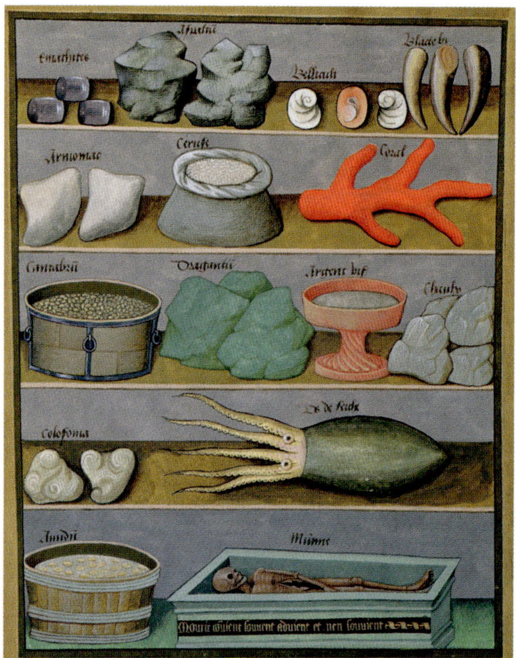 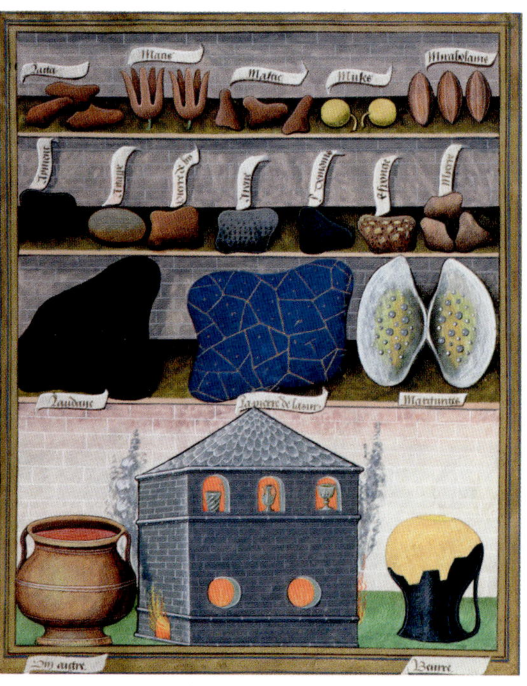

[FIG. 13]
Examples of *pharmakeia,*
in Matthaeus Platearius,
Liber de simplici medicina,
ca. 1470. Ink and tempera on
parchment. National Library,
St. Petersburg, Russia.

pigment acting as a generative matrix from which the creature emerges. Not only does the toad burst forth, but so does the blue morning glory used as a counterpoint in its splendor and beauty. The flowers show the various stages of blossoming and wilting, opening and closing like umbrellas. In between, two butterflies flutter with iridescent wings that were impressed, while a third has become the toad's prey. In this way, the painting conjures up the magic of a creation that begins in heavy matter, works its way out of it, and can rise to ethereal forms.

In this context, it is instructive to see how the painter used the expensive pigment lapis lazuli amid the brown paint made of earth pigments. For millennia, this stone was believed to have healing properties. As legend has it, lapis brought the blue of the sky down to earth and with it the divine light. Lapis lazuli was used to treat melancholy and depression, and in ground form it was used for medicinal purposes and as a cosmetic agent. It was also an expensive pigment in tempera and oil painting. It is, therefore, significant that Van Schrieck chose the most expensive lapis lazuli to paint the blue morning glory hovering cautiously over the toad, applying the pigment in pure form, almost like a glaze. The blue flower is a striking motif, especially given that Van Schrieck hardly ever used lapis again. Also consider the remarks in *De natura fossilium* by Georgius Agricola (1494–1555): "Lapis lazuli resembles the Heavens because of the golden points which represent the stars." Thomas Nicols (b. 1620), paraphrasing Boethius (ca. 480–524/26), states that lapis stones are of a dry nature, "and the very best of these are very comfortable to the eyes, if they be often looked on." Lapis even withstood the stiffest test: "If this stone being put into the fire doth not change its colour, it is called *Lapis Lazuli fixus*, of which is made that precious blue colour called azure." Dioscorides (d. ca. 90) recommended it as an antidote to snake bites and that "it is good in all melancholy diseases." He then adds a recipe by Antonius Musa Brassavolus (1500–1555), apothecary of Ferrara, describing pills of ground lapis lazuli, camphor, anise, cinnamon, and other purgative ingredients.

In the tradition of painting, the luminous blue color was used to depict the cloak of the Virgin. It may have had an apotropaic association, for according to the lapidaries, the main property of lapis lazuli was to protect its wearer and ward off harm, covering him or her with a protective coat, as it were. Perhaps it would be merely speculation to associate the blue morning glory with Marian symbolism, had Van Schrieck not also repeatedly chosen Saint Mary's thistle as a protagonist of his paintings. Butterflies circle in spirals around its spiky leaves, which were used in ancient and early modern pharmaceutics as an antidote for the thistle's sting, while snakes lie in wait on the forest floor or slither down a rock. The juxtaposition of toad and blue morning glory allows a literal and a figurative reading. It constitutes and shows, presents and represents, the antagonistic forces of nature that visibly express themselves by means of color. Based on this interpretation, it is now equally important and appropriate to say that "the petals of the morning glory are blue" and "the petals of the morning glory are painted with lapis lazuli." Anecdotal evidence suggested that just looking at the stone's color was good for the eyes and could help heal a sick body. Especially in times of the plague, possible processes of transmission between mind and body were discussed, and it was considered likely that healing and harmful impressions could reach the inside of the body both through the eye and through the power of imagination. Hence, it could make a difference what colors or materials one surrounded oneself with, for these were understood to be medicinal substances that could affect body and soul.

Pigments and Alchemy

We see how closely the material and immaterial aspects of color can be associated. This symbiotic relationship is similarly reflected in the interdisciplinary cooperation between conservation science and art history. Based on the technological identification of pigments used, scholars obtain information about the materials, while a historical study of sources can help to reconstruct the symbolic values contemporaries attributed to those materials. This close association becomes particularly evident when the chemical processes involved in producing colors became a topic of painting. Many painters made their own paints, not only by crushing and pulverizing pieces of rock in a mortar or on a muller or rubbing stone but also by distilling or synthetically producing colorants.

Ever since the Italian painter and biographer Giorgio Vasari (1511–1574) called Jan van Eyck (ca. 1380/90–1441) an alchemist and described his "invention" of oil painting as the result of chemical experiments, Netherlandish art and Venetian art were discussed in terms of alchemy. Dutch theorist and painter Karel van Mander (1548–1606) wrote that the Van Eyck brothers "examined many kinds of colors and, for this purpose, studied alchemy and distilling." Alchemy was close to a process of art-making that focused on the manufacturing, mixture, and application of paints, the luminosity and "vividness" of colors. It relied on the specific properties of *colori* in painting rather than on *disegno*, drawing and contouring.

A pigment that played a special role in alchemy was vermilion (cinnabar or minium). To prepare it, two basic elements were used—mercury and sulfur—allowing any adept to understand that their connection was the union of the two opposing principles of man and woman or of form and matter. In the process of preparing the philosopher's stone, the man usually refers to sulfur, which is married

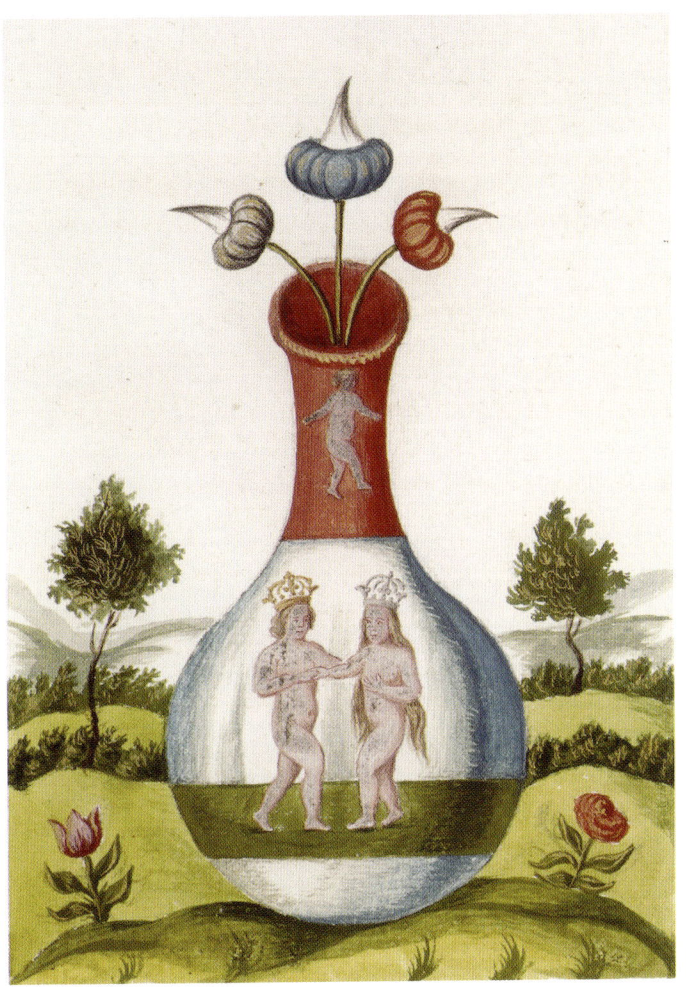

[FIG. 14]
"Solutio Perfecta,"
in Georgius Aurach,
Pretiosissimum Donum Dei.
Bibliothèque Nationale
de France, Paris (MS 975).

to mercury, the woman. The understanding of the chemical process as a marriage that initiates procreation and birth goes back to an ancient alchemical tradition. In terms of color symbolism, the wedding is said to be a mixture of black and white. When understood as a marriage, not only of ultimate principles but also of the actual chemical substances sulfur and mercury, then vermilion is born from it as a pigment.

Ever since ancient times, colors have been regarded as indicators of animating power, and color changes have been understood as the result of changes within substances. In alchemy, substances were primarily identified by their color, and color changes represented the various stages of the magnum opus [FIG. 14]. The transformation of the elements resembled a path from darkness to luminous silver or to the red color of gold, depending on whether only white elixir (silver) or the more valuable gold was to be obtained through the transmutation of a base material. According to one model, this transmutation was performed in seven color gradations. The starting point was usually blackness (*nigredo*), which was equated with an original state of matter, the *prima materia*. Once the process had passed through various color stages, understood as an iridescent yellow-green-white "peacock's tail," a reddening (*rubedo*) signaled the successful passage of the original substances into a refined state. This process involved further differentiating the color sequence that had been described since ancient Greek alchemy as blackening (*melanosis*), whitening (*leukosis*), yellowing (*xanthosis*), and reddening (*iosis*). The importance attached to the colors of the alchemical process became evident in the elaborate color schemes used to symbolically illustrate the various stages of the magnum opus. Particularly common was the performance of a transmutation in seven stages, where the changes could sometimes be monitored through the glass wall of a flask or alembic called *vas hermeticum*.

Alchemical theories of color, often represented in the form of a bouquet of flowers in a vase, help to contextualize still-life painting of the same period. The painter and alchemist Johannes Goedaert (1617–1668), for example, may have produced some of his pigments himself as an end or by-product while doing alchemical work. In Goedaert's *Flowers in a Porcelain Vase*, wilting leaves at the bottom of the bouquet vary from brownish green to yellow—a color today echoed in the painted decor of the ceramic vase, though it was probably blue at one time and now has a tinge of gold due to the age-related change of the colorant [FIG. 15]. In the middle of the bunch, next to the magnificent tulips, a horned violet protrudes, its color now radiating from a yellow center to a blue-violet edge, resembling a small flame. The blue violet played an increasing role in the coded language of seventeenth-century alchemy, as it was supposed to illustrate the animation of minerals in analogy to vegetation.

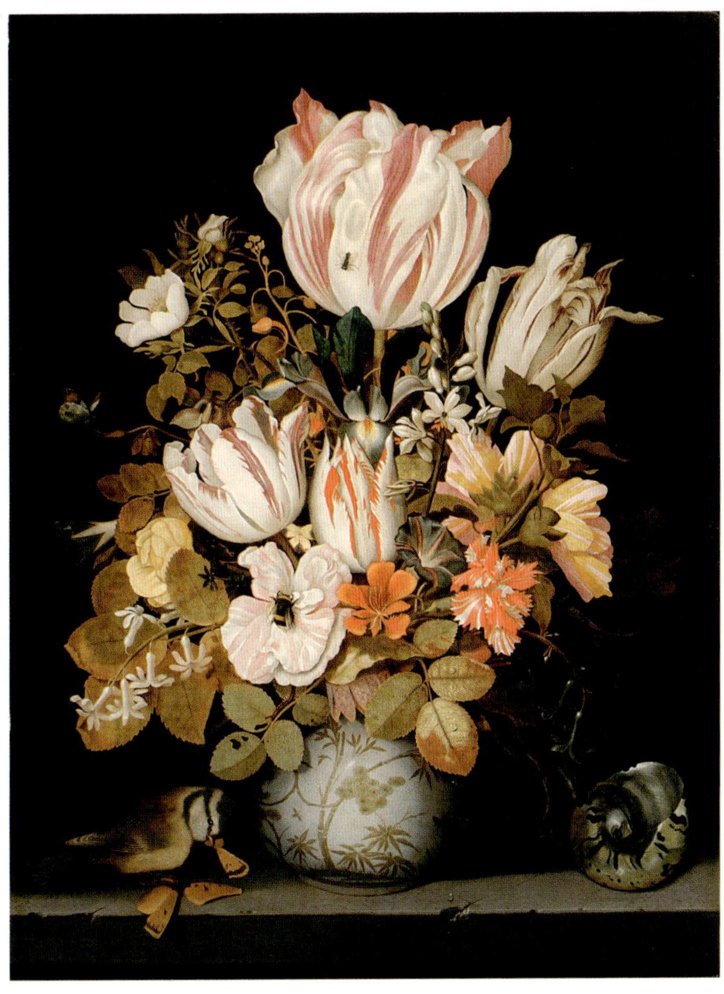

[FIG. 15]
Johannes Goedaert, *Flowers
in a Porcelain Vase*, ca. 1650.
Oil on wood, 50 × 37 cm.
Private collection.

Pigments and Cosmetics

As mentioned earlier, pigments were obtained from apothecaries and closely related to medicine. For this reason, apothecary bills are an important primary source for research into the trade in colorants and artists' materials. The salutary and harmful properties of pigments are an integral part of their history and enrich our reading of paintings and other artworks in significant ways. One major topic arising due to the affinity of pigment and medicine that deserves a chapter of its own is the use of colorants in painting and cosmetics. Much has been written about this subject, and it is fascinating to see how the same paint materials served both to create beauty and to defy the impermanence of the human body.

This dual role of pigments becomes particularly evident in portrait painting. During the Elizabethan era, for instance, an extremely pale face achieved through various cosmetics and substances served to identify members of the aristocratic classes. Elizabeth I (1533–1603) wore a heavy coat of leaded makeup making her face flawless. According to historians, however, it was precisely this lead—and other highly problematic cosmetics—that led to her death. In October 1562 Elizabeth became seriously ill with smallpox, and she started using a powder of lead white and vinegar that allowed her to hide the various scars that smallpox had left on her face. Lead irreversibly damages the skin and causes hair loss. Over the years, the queen's face was eaten away by makeup, but Elizabeth responded by applying more and more powder to cover both the smallpox scars and those caused by the lead. As if that were not enough, the makeup reportedly was not removed in the evenings during this period but worn for as long as a week at a time, with some lead occasionally being added. When it had to be removed, the coat was so thick and compact that it had to be removed with mercury. Lead powder is not the only toxic cosmetic Queen Elizabeth used to look the way she wanted. Her beauty routine included mercury-based lipstick that gave her lips their bright red color. Elizabeth also often used egg white to glaze her face, which helped hide wrinkles and gave her a smooth complexion but at the same time made it impossible for her to move her face. Another cosmetic trick involved painting blue veins on the skin to make it appear even more transparent. As a blush, Elizabeth used cochineal, which was applied to the entire cheek and the lips. A derivative of cochineal is still used in cosmetics. Elizabeth also applied so-called lamp black to draw dark eyebrows [FIG. 16].

Ceruse was blamed for the death of Maria Coventry, Countess of Coventry (1732–1760), who used the pigment frequently and died aged just twenty-eight from complications from blood poisoning caused by lead makeup products. She was well known among London society as a victim of cosmetics. Other beauty products of the period also contained high

[FIG. 16]
Unknown artist, *Queen Elizabeth I* (*"Darnley Portrait"*), ca. 1575. Oil on canvas, 113 × 78.7 cm. National Portrait Gallery, London.

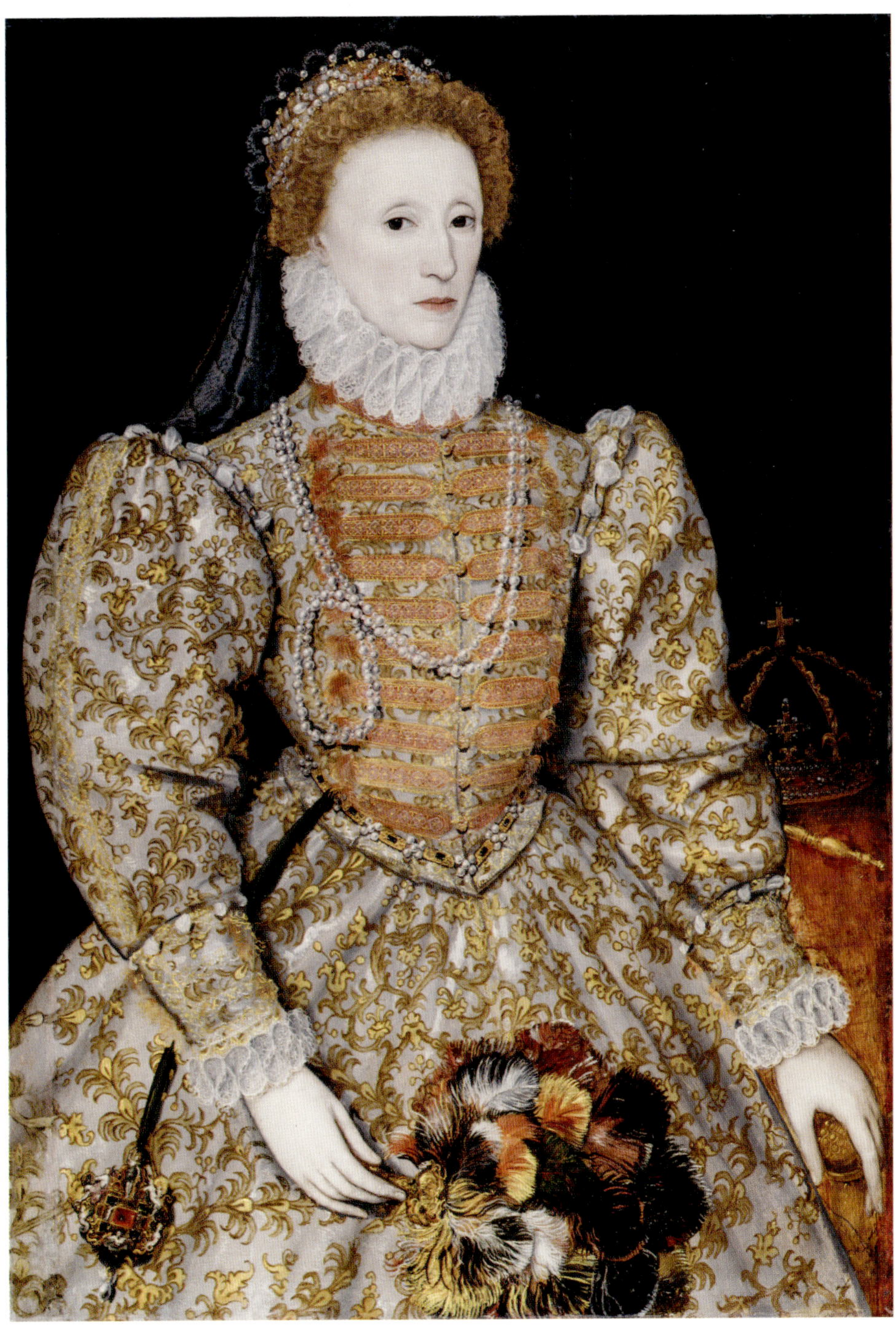

levels of mercury and arsenic. There was a close relationship between cosmetic colorants and those used in painting. For instance, the same pigments Elizabeth used to paint her face were employed by painters to create her portrait. The connection is obvious: pigments are *pharmakeia* and cosmetics because they are artificial colorants used to beautify nature, add a veneer to it, or make it last.

In Japan artists used lead white almost exclusively until the fourteenth century, when so-called shell white, or *gofun,* came to be used as a pigment. It was made from oyster shells and took ten or more years to produce. The hard shell consisting of calcium carbonate crystals and the protein-collagen mixture conchin needed to be weathered before it could be crushed and ground. The white from the sea also became popular as a face powder and for makeup and ended up replacing the toxic lead white in cosmetics, though in Japan this use was not banned until 1934 [FIG. 17]. Numerous other examples could be cited to illustrate the close connection that can be drawn between the chemical properties of pigments, their technological analysis, and their use in art history, as further explicated in Anne Lafont's essay on skin color in this volume.

The Aging of Color

While colors in cosmetics are meant to rejuvenate or preserve facial appearance in cosmetics, a reverse process has also been described by Barbara Berrie in this volume. Some organic colorants such as red lake that were used in portraits to redden cheeks have faded completely over the years, leaving pale faces. The portrait of Ginevra de' Benci by Leonardo da Vinci (1452–1519) is one work that may have fallen victim to the aging process of colors [see FIG. 24]. Some portraits of Elizabeth have been subject to this kind of color change as well, as discussed by Berrie. In the so-called *Darnley Portrait* [FIG. 16], for example, microscopic analyses have shown that the queen once had rouged red cheeks. Elizabeth's now extremely pale skin would have appeared much rosier had the red pigments not faded over time. Technical analysis showed that other colors in the painting have also deteriorated. The golden-brown pattern on her dress, for instance, was originally crimson and gold, so it had a completely different effect.

Other pigments and colorants are also subject to marked changes and therefore influence our perception of paintings. In his didactic poem of 1604 *Den grondt der edel vrij schilder-const* (The foundations of the noble and free art of painting), Karel van Mander addresses the durability of pigments and their positive and negative properties. He warns the inexperienced painter against using lamp black, red lead, Spanish green, and orpiment. The latter is toxic because it contains arsenic sulfide, and Spanish green or verdigris can change and darken over time. Van Mander

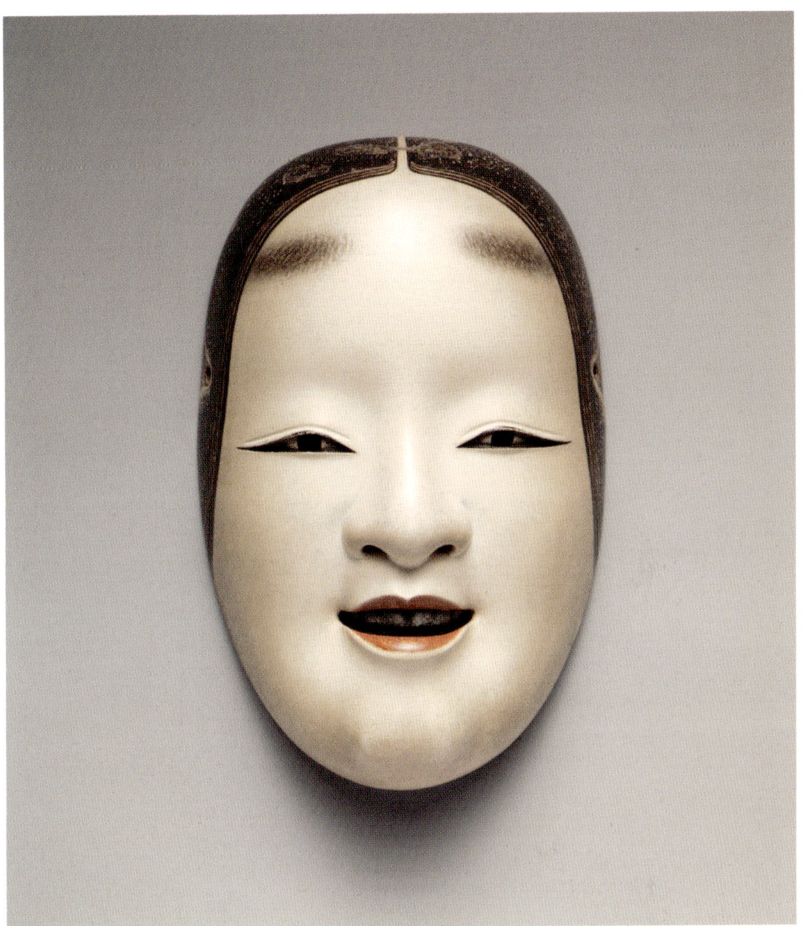

[FIG. 17]
Unknown artist, *Noh Mask of Woman*, 18th–19th century. Polychromed wood, 21.11 × 13.34 × 7.3 cm. Minneapolis Institute of Art, Mary Griggs Burke Collection, Gift of the Mary and Jackson Burke Foundation.

cautions that, because of the instability of some pigments and the risk of contamination by other pigments, painters must always keep their brushes clean and tidy. As sources testify, it was not uncommon for a painter to have poisoned himself by thoughtlessly licking the tip of the brush that had residues of lead white or orpiment stuck to it. According to a famous episode related in Van Mander's lives of the artists, Hendrick Goltzius (1558–1617) had put orpiment into his mouth as a child and was saved only because his father "scraped out his mouth" as best he could.

Orpiment is a yellow pigment that was frequently used in still-life and landscape painting to create various shades of green when mixed with blue pigments such as smalt or azurite. As David Bomford reminds us in writing about pigment changes, this range of shades could also be expanded using yellow glazes. Green leaves, for example, were created by glazing yellow over blue, which had the disadvantage that the yellow lakes were of organic origin and were therefore not lightfast, causing them to fade and leave blue rather than green treetops, meadows, and leaves in the paintings. Van Schrieck repeatedly used "Dutch pink" (*schiet geel*) in his nature pieces to create the greatest possible variety of greens, but these glazes have long since faded and the effect of green foliage has been irreversibly lost. Paintings age just like a human body or a face. In this sense, all colorants are subject to the wear and tear of time and change their appearance due to chemical or physical processes, be it because of environmental influences that affect them superficially or substantially, or as the result of a human environment that uses, scuffs, alters, damages, adds to, or removes. In a way, pigments are applied onto the canvas or other support like makeup, making every painting in the first place a portrait of its time—all images are essentially faces or physiognomies that have aged, losing or changing color.

Pigment Science

Barbara H. Berrie

Pigments color the natural world: earths, leaves, flowers, skin, and hair. We use pigment to decorate and enliven our surroundings and many things we use such as cloth, paper, ceramics, plastic, and glass; even our food gets a lift, though it is not always healthy, from added pigments. Some people use pigment almost daily to smooth or alter the surface of their skin with makeup or permanently with tattoos. Pigment is everywhere, and the pigments used to color the world are derived from both natural and artificial sources.

Pigment is made with materials from the animal, vegetable, and mineral kingdoms. Red cochineal, for example, is prepared from bugs that live on the nopal cactus. Tyrian purple is extracted from sea snails. Indigo blue and yellow weld are made from plant extracts. Pigment is prepared from minerals such as the intensely yellow orpiment (arsenic sulfide, As_2S_3) and the sapphire-like copper carbonate called azurite (copper hydroxy carbonate, $Cu_3(CO_3)_2(OH)_2$). Earthy deposits provide colors across the spectrum. We synthesize inorganic (metal-ion containing) and organic (carbon-oxygen based) pigments, and while some of them have analogues in nature, others are entirely novel compounds. Artists use pigment as dry powder, as in pastels, but most often it is mixed with a binder (also called a vehicle) to make paint [FIG. 18]. Pigment is incorporated into lime frescoes, concrete, paper, glass, plastics, and just about anything that can be colored. In the past, pigment was made in workshops and alchemists' crucibles. Today, it is manufactured in industrial plants and is a billion-dollar enterprise.

As a child, I was fascinated by the idea that minerals taken from the ground could be used to make wonderful paintings that depict our world with such fidelity, a world that natural light renders visible and changeable. With nothing more than colored paint, artists provoke memories and emotions. As a chemist working in a museum, I use my scientific education and my "analytical" eye to identify pigments and

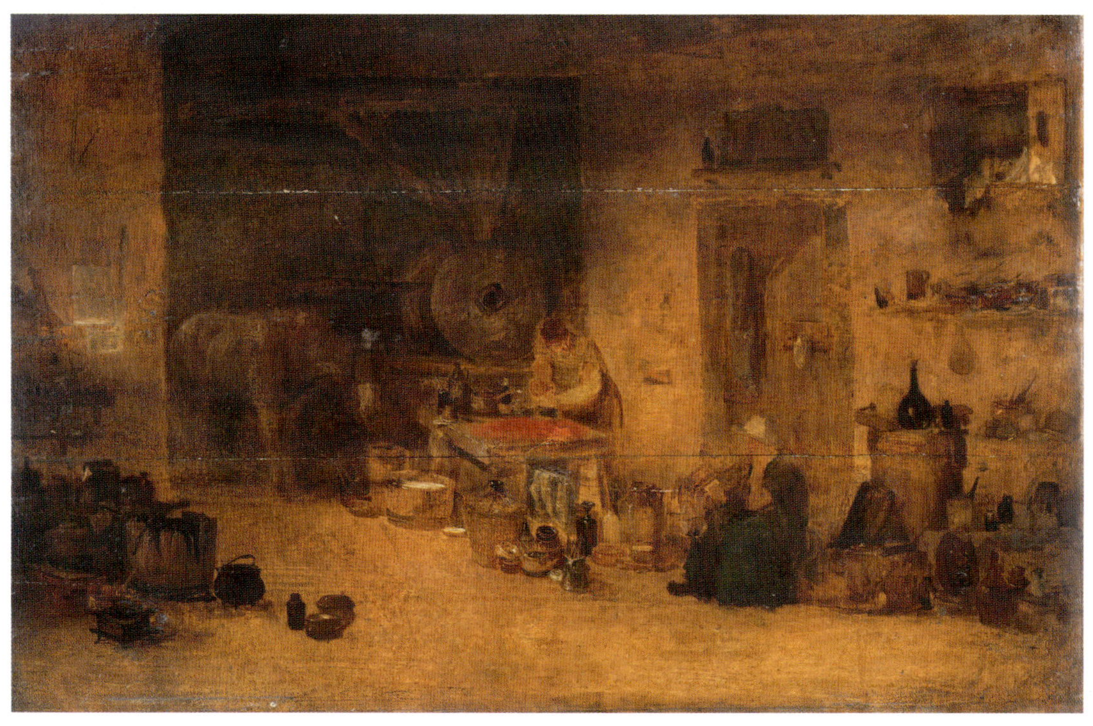

[FIG. 18]
J. M. W. Turner, *An Artists' Colourman's Workshop*, ca. 1807. Oil on wood, 62.2 × 91.4 cm. Tate, Accepted by the nation as part of the Turner Bequest 1856 (N05503).

learn how painters mixed and layered them to create compositions and surfaces that delight the eye and engage the imagination. My work has given me a deep appreciation for artists' inventiveness and their marvelous skill in choosing pigments and mastering their properties to depict light, texture, objects, and mood. I have also come to realize that color makers, and not only artists, are engaged in intellectual and creative work that shapes how the world is perceived.

Identifying pigments provides answers to questions about the role of color in artifacts and works of art and our perception of them. Developing the history of pigment allows us to recognize moments of technological inspiration, invention, and artistic innovation. Detailed analysis reveals artists' careful choices from a broad, nuanced palette of color. Meaningful links between the materiality of pigments and the history of color are created when we combine art history, economic history, history of technology, and art conservation with pigment identification. Conservators use the information to assess the extent of change that has already occurred and to choose appropriate pigments for their own conservation and restoration treatments. Comparison between analytical results and descriptions of colorants in ancient texts, painting treatises, contracts, and receipts for commissions of artworks provides us with a better understanding of the value of specific pigments and their use at different times and places. Discovering how pigments were employed reveals artistic exploration of color and colorants and relationships between material and color.

Pigment-Making

Some friable rocks can be powdered using nothing more than fingertips to make pigments, but most rocks, soils, and earths need to be worked up more laboriously. The processes used from prehistoric times until the nineteenth century were important, though they are rarely employed today. They have arcane-sounding names: comminution, sedimentation, levigation, lixiviation, and calcination. Comminution is simply the crushing of minerals or rocks to make them into small pieces suitable for further processing. Sedimentation is a process akin to panning for gold, using water to obtain the colorants in natural earths by separating the heavier colored minerals from the lighter clay in soils. Levigation removes unwanted minerals in a heterogenous rock or soil by grinding the solid in a lot of water and then decanting the liquid that has particles suspended in it from one basin to another until a slurry of the desired pigment remains. Pigment is graded by particle size using this method since finer particles stay suspended longer and are slower to settle and can be poured off. The fraction with the largest pigment particles has the deepest, most intense hue, while the finest particles have a paler appearance. Ultramarine, azurite, malachite, and the glassy blue smalt were available in many grades based on particle size. Artists working in oil, tempera, or watercolor extend their color palette by taking advantage of the range of tones and hues that varying particle size offers and exploiting other physical attributes of pigment particles, including color, shape, and opacity in their paint [FIG. 19].

Lixiviation removes water-soluble impurities as part of the purification process of pigments. It was used during the work-up of lead white, one of the oldest pigments, which was manufactured by corroding plates of metallic lead using vapors from fermenting dung or pots of vinegar (acetic acid). The seventeenth-century English miniaturist Edward Norgate (1575–1650) advised artists to treat impure, darkened lead-white pigment by means of lixiviation, going so far as to note that it should be rinsed until the wash water tasted sweet not salty! A sweet taste may have been due to a common impurity in lead white, lead acetate, which was called sugar of lead, though Norgate was likely using the word sweet to suggest pure.

Calcination was important for expanding the range of colors for artists and artisans by roasting readily available raw materials or pigments. Green earths and raw umber acquire a deeper, warmer hue during heating; yellow ochers that contain limonite (a rock comprising hydrated iron (III) oxides) or goethite (α-FeO(OH)) yield the red pigment hematite (Fe_2O_3). It is possible to prove that prehistoric color makers used calcination to make red iron-oxide pigments. Calcining iron-containing compounds such as green vitriol (hydrated iron (II) sulfate, $FeSO_4 \cdot 7H_2O$, also known as copperas) rather than iron-containing (ferruginous) earths give a range of brighter, purer colors and provide more consistent hues than natural earths. These artificial equivalents of ochers and siennas were desirable when oil painting was fully embraced in Europe in the mid-sixteenth century since the fine texture (small particles) provides paint useful for translucent glazes to modify the hues of underlying layers.

Depicting black, dark objects or spaces so that they appear naturalistic to the eye is not easy because there are always small amounts of color that must be expressed. Carbon-based black pigments are made by burning all sorts of organic materials to give soots, chars, and charcoal. Ancient names indicate the many sources of raw materials, including lamp oil, paper, resin, peach pits, vines, horns, bones, and ivory. Sooty, oily blacks are preferred for printmaking, while other carbon blacks are prized for watercolor paints and ink washes. Ivory black had the reputation for being the best of all for oil painting. In 1555 the German scholar Johann Neudörffer said that it was blacker than any black. Calcium phosphate remains in the char that forms after horns, bones, or ivory have been calcined. It can be detected using various instrumental methods and thus

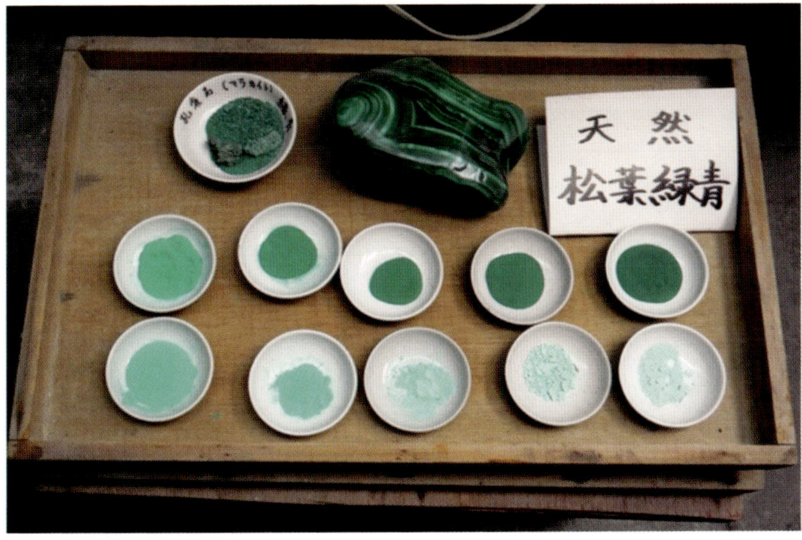

[FIG. 19]
Shades of malachite,
Ueba Esou, Kyoto. Different
particle sizes of ground
malachite give different
hues and shades.

reveals the provenance of the starting material. From finding calcium
phosphate in black paint, we discovered that many artists often used these
sorts of blacks to great effect to paint hair, fur, and various kinds of dark
silks and velvets. Charcoal, usually made from willow tree or sometimes
grapevine twigs, has a bluish undertone that is evident when it is mixed
with lead white and red lakes to make purplish colors.

Painters have used other deeply colored brown and gray substances
to render the warm or cool aspects of darkness and black. Black chalk,
mummy, asphalt, coal, graphite, manganese oxides, stibnite (antimony
sulfide, Sb_2S_3), pyrite (lead sulfide, PbS), iron filings (Fe), and metallic
bismuth (Bi) are mentioned in treatises. Black pigments are difficult to
characterize let alone visually distinguish. However, the diversity of black
pigments mentioned in treatises reminds us that the assumption that
artists and artisans in the past had access to fewer pigments than we
have today is not entirely correct, and the analyst must always be on the
lookout for unexpected pigments. Discoveries of unusual pigments—of
all colors, not only the blacks—are a stimulus to keep an open mind about
what we might find when analyzing pigments.

Lead white and verdigris, as Karin Leonhard describes, are made by
corroding lead and copper. Pigment makers could tweak the methods to
suit their circumstances, giving rise to variations in the product. There are
ancient recipes for verdigris that include damp cloths and salt in addition
to the required vinegar. These modifications would create a galvanic
pile to hasten the corrosion processes. While today the word "verdigris"
is associated with copper acetate compounds, in the past it likely referred

to a mixture of impure compounds that might include a suite of copper hydroxychlorides such as clinoatacamite, atacamite, or paratacamite ($Cu_2Cl(OH)_3$). The copper hydroxychlorides, whether manufactured or naturally occurring, range from turquoise to deep green. Perhaps the names in old treatises, such as Spanish green or salt green, signify differences in color that analysis will help understand.

The use of complex chemical synthesis to make new pigments can be traced back more than five thousand years. Pigment manufacture in pre-classical Egypt was associated with glass- and ceramic-making to create a blue pigment, calcium copper silicate (cuprovariate, $CaCuSi_4O_{10}$). It is possibly the first inorganic pigment made using a chemical synthesis. No ancient written recipes for calcium copper silicate survive, but analysis of the pigment found on objects and a description by the first-century BCE Roman architect and engineer Vitruvius give us clues about how it was made. Likely, a mixture of calcium-rich sand and copper or bronze filings was combined with a flux to reduce the melting point of the sand. This flux was probably natron, a naturally occurring deposit of sodium carbonate and sodium bicarbonate. The mixture of sand, filings, and flux was roasted to make the pigment. Small chemical variations identified among samples supplement the sparse written record we have of ancient chemical technology and manufacture of this pigment.

From a technical point of view, Han blue ($BaCuSi_4O_{10}$) and Han purple ($BaCuSi_2O_6$) are like Egyptian blue, though their histories are different. In place of calcium (from sand) in Egyptian blue, the Han pigments contain barium, which was obtained from deposits of the minerals baryte (barium sulfate, $BaSO_4$) or barium carbonate ($BaCO_3$). The pigments were first identified on objects from the Han dynasty (206 BCE–220 CE) and objects from its Warring States period (475–221 BCE), hence their contemporary names. Han purple was identified on warriors in the famous Terracotta Army, created in 210–209 BCE in Xian for the first emperor of China.

The desire to synthesize blues was perhaps to augment the color palette since naturally occurring blue minerals are rare and blue paint cannot be made by mixing other colors. Even with many from which to choose, finding new blue pigments is tantalizing. In 2009 the excitement surrounding YInMn blue (yttrium indium manganese oxide ($Y_{(1-x)}InMn_xO_3$)), hailed as the first new blue in two hundred years, is a sign of our fascination with the nuances of color and with invention. YInMn is a subtly different hue from other blue pigments, and this small difference has captivated the art world [FIG. 20].

Plant extracts have bright and subtle pigments. The technology no doubt came from dyers using mordants to fix color to textiles. The chemistry is complex, and it is intriguing to imagine how dyers discovered ways to make pigments from roots, leaves, and blossoms. Our ability to

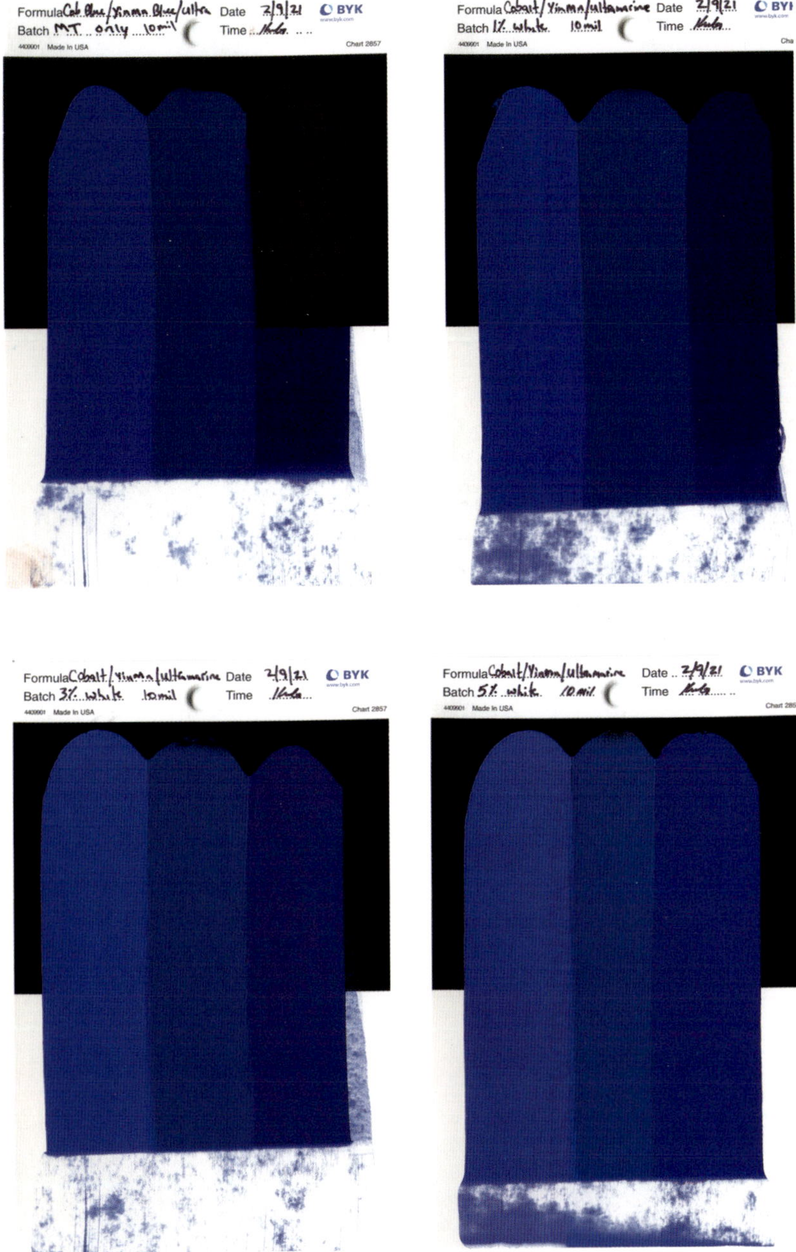

[FIG. 20]
The new blue pigment YInMn is not the same color as ultramarine or cobalt blue. Artists appreciate the nuanced difference.

appreciate how early the expertise evolved is hampered for two main reasons. First, the natural chemicals in the pigments are not stable, so little remains after a few centuries. Second, our ability to identify these molecules has developed only recently, and we are therefore just beginning to recognize the important role of natural organic pigments in coloring the ancient world. For example, a painted quiver from the Egyptian Middle Kingdom (2121–1981 BCE) is one of the oldest objects on which we have found the pigment made from an extract from madder root.

In the late nineteenth century, a plethora of synthetic organic pigments appeared. These pigments, which usually do not occur in nature, were prepared from petrochemicals. They were called coal tar or aniline colors because these by-products of coal distillation were the starting material for making certain pigments. The first commercially influential synthetic organic pigment was made in 1856 by William Henry Perkin, only eighteen years old and working in his parents' house during his college break. He was trying to synthesize the medicine quinine—a treatment for malaria—when he accidentally made a violet compound. When Perkin realized the value of his discovery, he obtained a patent for a pigment he named mauveine in 1865. By the beginning of the twentieth century, hundreds more new pigments had been patented. Inventive names such as emeraldine (green), aurine (golden orange), azuline (blue), and eosin (the color of a rosy dawn; [FIG. 21]) alluded to their appearance. Their brilliant colors, useful physical properties, and compatibility with synthetic binders gave artists the freedom to experiment. The novel synthetic organic pigments were less expensive than inorganic pigments. Not only were the starting materials inexpensive, but the pigments' high-tinting strength also made them strong colorants, so a little went a long way. The fine particle size, intense chroma, and dispersibility of these new pigments revolutionized printmaking. Since the pigments were cheap and easy to use, the cost of making posters decreased and multi-colored advertisements appeared everywhere, creating a new colorscape. With the introduction of these pigments, the era of the complete industri-alization and globalization of color had begun.

Before the nineteenth century, there were few violet or purple pigments. Tyrian purple was laboriously prepared from a gland in sea snails (gastropods) from the genus *Murex* and it was rare and costly. Violet and purples made from plants and lichen were available, though the colors were notoriously short-lived and not useful in oil. Painters relied instead on mixing and layering red and blue pigments. Since red lakes fade over time while blue pigments do not change much, purples shift to blue and reds become pale pink.

In the late Victorian era, admiration for Perkin's mauveine was intense and there was a "mauve craze," or *violettomania,* that lasted decades.

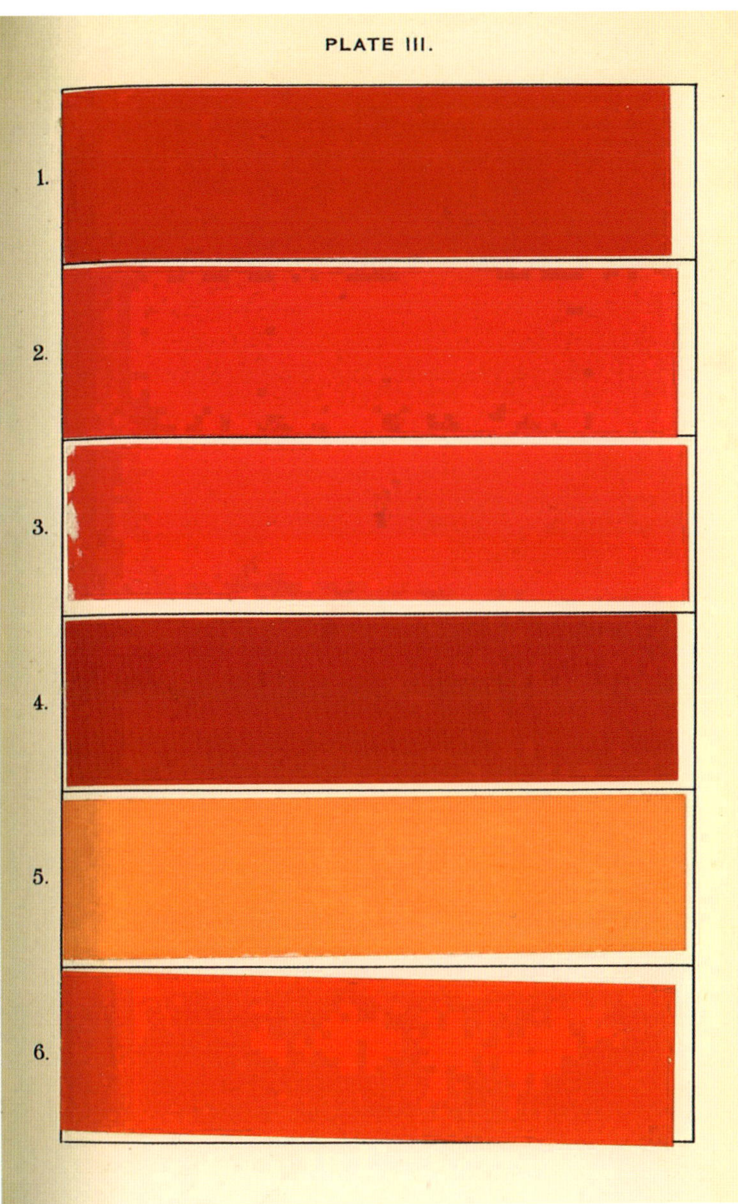

[FIG. 21]
Color swatches of variants of the synthetic organic pigment eosin, a brominated derivative of the yellow dye fluorescein. In Francis H. Jennison, *The Manufacture of Lake Pigments from Artificial Colours,* 1st ed. (London: Scott Greenwood, 1900).

After flooding the textile market, violet, lavender, and lilac hues appeared everywhere in painting; even black was painted using a deep purple. Connoisseurs offered withering criticism of this new aesthetic, yet these violets and purples changed the spectrum of artists' palettes. Since these colors were often prepared from mixtures of stable blue and unstable red pigments, the prevalence of violet and purple in Impressionist painting has been muted due to fading reds. In the second half of the nineteenth century, stable purple pigments and inorganic cobalt violets, both the phosphate and the poisonous arsenate versions, became available. They were extremely expensive and in short supply but nevertheless were coveted. Today, paintings made using the cobalt colors have areas of warm violet tones, while the original violet and purple hues have become blue when artists used mixtures of blue with fugitive reds. Residual traces of fugitive reds have been chemically identified in many nineteenth-century paintings, including works by artists who considered themselves colorists—for instance, Vincent van Gogh (1853–1890) and Winslow Homer (1836–1910). We may never be able to appreciate the full extent of *violettomania* and the presence of violet and purple in Impressionist painting since we cannot accurately account for the red pigments that have disappeared.

In their search for ways to take their art in novel directions, artists often adopt new colors, experimenting with all sorts of pigments. Quinacridone pigments, intensely colored reds, magentas, and golds were developed in the 1950s for their outstanding light stability and suitability for car finishes and exterior house paints. Artists quickly recognized their value for outdoor murals, prints, and painting. They added metallic, sparkly finishes, "light-dark flop," "flip-flop," or two-tone effect pigments that change color depending on the angle from which you look at them. They also added fluorescent colors, which fostered intense visual sensations. DayGlo fluorescent pigments, for example, were made in the 1930s for advertising posters. But military uses of DayGlo during World War II catalyzed developments and broadened the range of colors available. Mid-twentieth century artists such as Frank Stella (b. 1936), Andy Warhol (1928–1987), and Carla Accardi (1924–2014) used luminescent pigments aimed at vibrant eye-popping compositions. Analysis of their pigments helps us to understand these experimental, innovative adoptions. When the effects are no longer visible, the analysis will allow for an understanding of the creative impulse that prompted using such materials.

Trade and Commerce

Long before the Industrial Age, commodities associated with color-making were traded and transported over long distances. Analysis of the pigments in artworks has given us information about the local, trans-continental, and intercontinental movement of materials in ancient and historical times that is difficult to obtain in other ways. The detailed mineral composition of the ocher pigments found in prehistoric wall paintings shows that they were sourced mainly from regional locations. In some instances, however, the ochers were brought from hundreds of miles away, reminding us that a pigment with a specific color or association might have had extraordinary value of which we are no longer aware. Ultramarine is an archetypal example of the extensive trade in color. Its source, lapis lazuli, was mined from the Sar-e (or Sar-i) Sang deposit in the Badakhshan district of modern-day Afghanistan for seven thousand years. The pigment name, derived from *oltre* (over) *marine* (sea), tells us that ultramarine came from over the sea, though its journey was over mountains, too. It traveled along the Silk Road with many other goods, including other pigments as well as artistic motifs and ideas. Imported lapis lazuli was used in Egypt, Sumeria, and Mesopotamia to make small figurative and decorative objects thousands of years ago, but current analytical evidence suggests it was rarely used this early as a pigment. Making the pigment required laborious workup of the blue stone, employing more than the simple physical methods of pounding and levigating. It entailed kneading the pulverized rock with things like honey or resins and lye (potassium hydroxide, KOH) to refine lazurite $((Na_7Ca)(Al_6Si_6O_{24})(SO_4)S_3 \cdot H_2O)$ from the other minerals in the rock to obtain the pure, intensely blue pigment. Ultramarine has been found in fifth-century CE wall paintings in India and in seventh-century CE wall paintings in the Mogao Caves, a complex of 492 Buddhist grottoes on the Silk Road in Dunhuang, China. An early occurrence of ultramarine, unexpectedly mixed with Egyptian blue, another pigment that was rare at that time, is in eighth-century CE wall paintings at San Saba in Rome. Typically, the earliest occurrences of lapis lazuli in places far from the original mines are in illuminated manuscripts made in England and in Western Europe about 1000. More analyses will help us to continue to develop the history of trade of lapis lazuli and other pigments.

It is remarkable how far and wide pigments moved. From historical patterns of pigment usage, we see the influence of supply and demand and the effect of geopolitical events on trade and manufacture that impacted artists' access to pigments and raw materials. Analysis of the impurities in pigments shows how sources of raw materials were interrupted and new trade routes and treaties were established. Changes in the nature of the trace elements in cobalt-blue pigmented glazes on Italian ceramics in the early sixteenth century and the isotope distribution in lead white in seventeenth-century Dutch painting are among the many clues that analysis provides about the disruption of established supplies for pigment production. Trade with the Indian subcontinent provided colorants, many from native plants and trees. While indigo and the red pigment lac have a long history of trade, other pigments, including gamboge, Indian madder, and Indian yellow, have shorter histories, only centuries long. The overlap of exchange with the different areas of color-making and commerce is extensive since pigments and their raw ingredients were used for dying cloth and as agents in alchemy among other lucrative uses.

There is a long history of pigment and bodily adornment. In Egypt in the Badrain era (ca. 4000 BCE), men and women outlined their eyelids with *udju* made using malachite. This green pigment came from the Timna mines just north of the Red Sea, where copper and turquoise were mined. Hathor, the Egyptian goddess of mining, was known as the mistress of turquoise. The copper mines at Timna were especially associated with the goddess, who was thought to offer spiritual protection and through her agency it was transferred to malachite. Green paint, identified as malachite, was used around the eyes and for the brows in a representation of King Mentuhotep II (ca. 2051–2000 BCE) on a fragment of a limestone relief [FIG. 22]. The relationship between the color and its spiritual significance might be important in similar instances.

Products had to be authentic and unadulterated to be valuable as medicine and pigment. Visual appearance and physical characteristics were the main criteria for judging quality. A tinge of gray in lead white or of black in vermilion spoiled their appeal and cheapened their value since it signaled poor quality. The demand for purity and consistency of compounds for medical uses encouraged manufacturers to employ careful processing and ensure quality control. Medical grades of pigments were exactly what artists needed to make reproducible batches of paint— essential for the consistent execution of paintings. Venice's reputation for good pigments was due not only to its being at the crossroads of trade routes but also owing to its production of materials of exceptional quality such as lead white and vermilion that were used not only as pigments but also as lucrative medicines and cosmetics.

Color Degradation

Most paint colors degrade over time, losing brilliance and intensity or becoming browner. These changes can spoil the intended color balance and relationships in paintings, and they can ruin carefully planned juxtapositions of hue and flatten the appearance of objects. Alteration of colors can hinder our recognition of their symbolic meaning. The impermanence of pigments has vexed artists and critics for a long time. David Bomford discusses this history in his essay on seventeenth- and

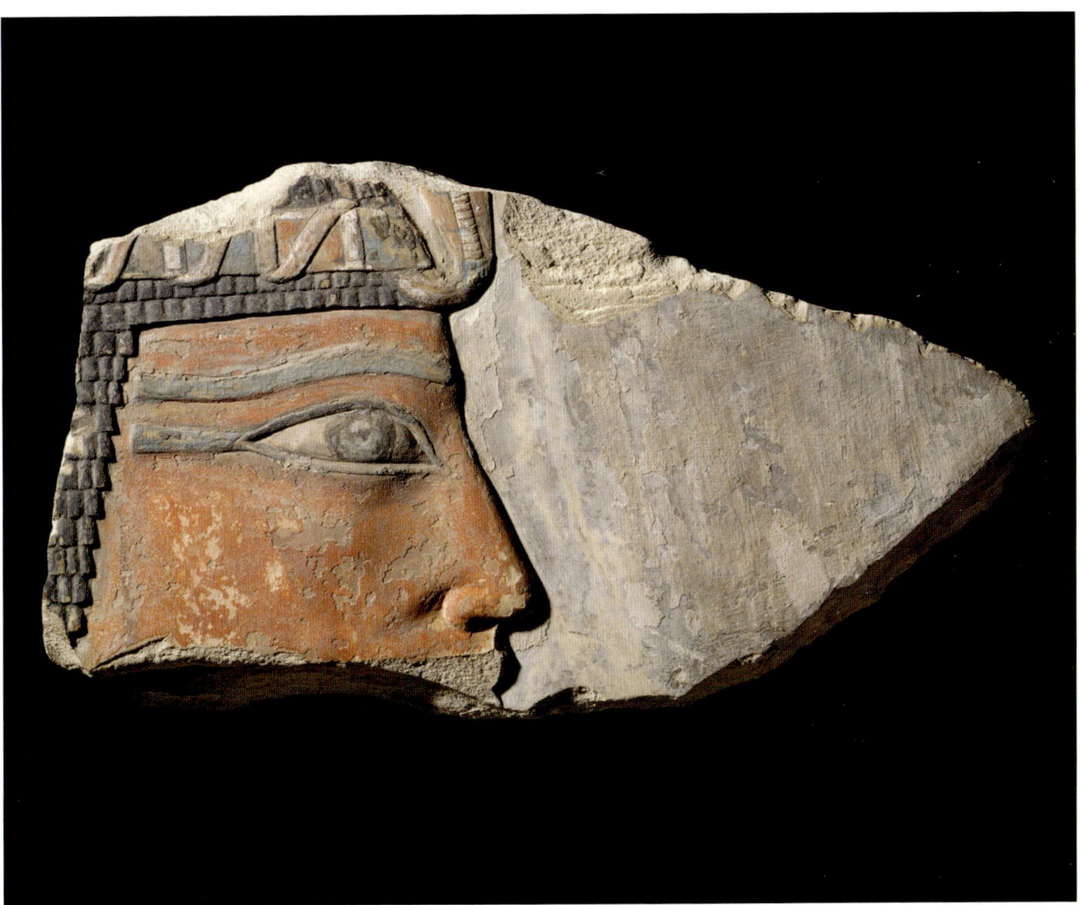

[FIG. 22]
Relief of King Nebhepetra-Mentuhotep II, 2061–2010 BCE, Egyptian Middle Kingdom, Dynasty 11. Findspot: Deir el-Bahri, Egypt. Limestone, 35 × 25.5 × 12 cm. Museum of Fine Arts, Boston, Egypt Exploration Fund by subscription (06.2473). In this portrait of King Mentuhotep II as in life, malachite was used to paint green eyeliner.

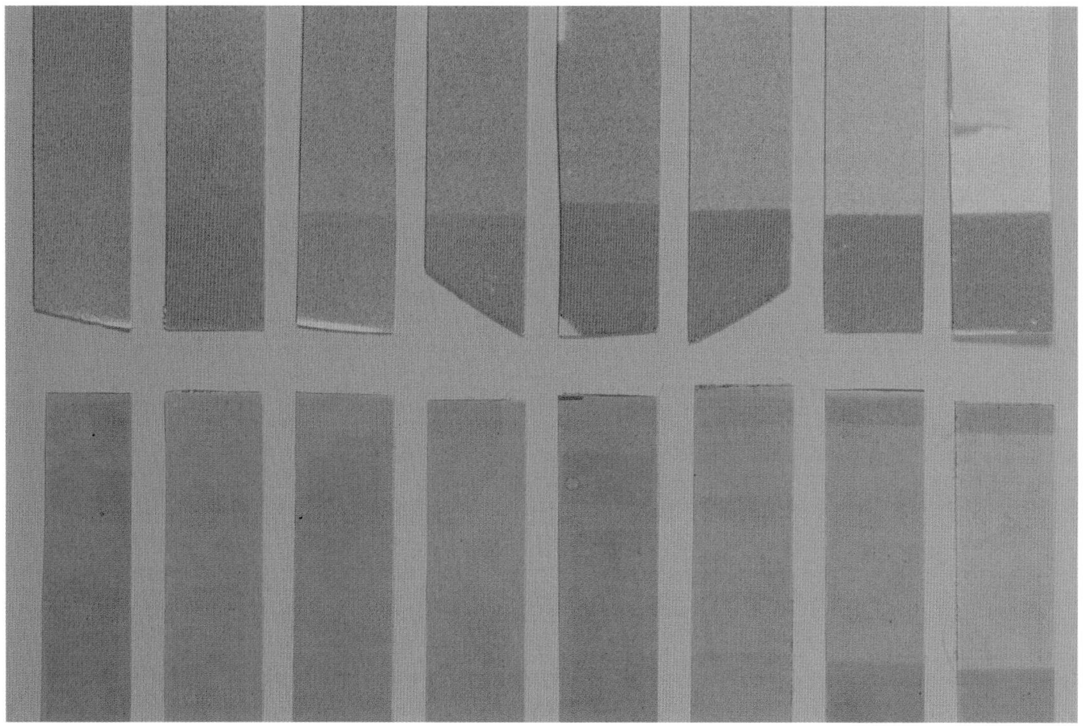

[FIG. 23]
The effect of light on cochineal is seen using artificially accelerated aging. Painted watercolor swatches were placed in an instrument called a weatherometer that approximates many years of natural exposure to light in only hours. The swatches on the bottom row are made using the pigment carmine formulated without mordant and the swatches on the top row are alum-lake carmine watercolor. The swatches were removed from the light chamber after 1, 3, 6, 9, 11, 19, 30, and 70 hours of exposure. After 70 hours the carmine still had some color, but the alum-lake carmine had completely faded.

eighteenth-century painting in this volume. Change occurs because pigment molecules are reactive, most often slowly but sometimes quite quickly. They undergo oxidation (from oxygen in the air), hydrolysis (reaction with water), and photochemical reactions (on exposure to light [FIG. 23]). Paint is a dynamic system. Pigments react with one another, the binding medium, the substrate, or even paper. Scientific investigation has shown that certain forms of chrome yellow in an oil turn a muddy olive color upon light exposure. The reaction has dulled the yellow sunflowers in Van Gogh's paintings and dimmed sunny highlights in many nineteenth-century Impressionist paintings. Research into the color change of verdigris and the related bottle-green pigment called copper resinate, made by dissolving verdigris in resin, indicates that reactions with the binding medium coupled with oxidation cause discoloration. The reactions turn green colors to ocherous browns. This sort of degradation is frequently noticed in trees in paintings. In the portrait of Ginevra de' Benci by Leonardo da Vinci (1452–1519), the juniper trees have become brown [FIG. 24]. Other factors such as impurities that promote reactions that lead to degradation, biological activity, or human intervention all cause change in the colors of pigment and paint. Many organic pigments, natural lakes, and synthetic colorants are prone to fading on exposure to light. Since they lose color so quickly, these pigments are described as fugitive colors. The earliest synthetic organic pigments are notoriously fleeting, fading rapidly due to photooxidation. Fluorescent pigments lose their color and "pop" quickly. Special care must be taken when exhibiting works that have these pigments, or only traces of chemical markers will remain to convey the extra brilliant pigments that once were there.

There are many other factors that can contribute to shifting tonalities of color in a painting. Varnish, for example, is often an obvious source of discoloration, as can be seen in the photomicrograph of the blue paint in a sixteenth-century Netherlandish oil painting [FIG. 25]. At one point, a conservator attempted to restore an area of paint loss but used a shade of blue that matched the discolored paint beneath the thick yellow varnish. Since the paint used in old restorations has itself often changed and is mismatched to the current appearance, conservators often remove it if possible. Art conservators do not aim to compensate for color changes occurring in original paint, though this practice was once acceptable. Conservators generally do not use the same pigment as the artist for several reasons. Inpainting—filling in areas of loss—is done using materials that can be readily removed. Also, conservators select pigments and binders that are extremely stable and unreactive, so their work is lasting. Therefore, the binding medium, which has an influence on appearance, is usually a stable polymer, and it is often different from traditional artists' paint, either old or contemporary.

Methods for Pigment Identification

Analysis of pigment cannot be done reliably by the eye or by taste as Norgate suggested. Conservators are physicists, chemists, and materials scientists who understand the chemistry of pigments and the history of their use. Although we employ sophisticated instrumentation, pigment identification begins with close visual observation. The condition, age, appearance, and authorship of an artifact give clues about what pigments might be present. Knowledge of the history of pigments and artists' techniques helps scientists choose the best analytical tools. Using more than one method provides complementary information to identify pigments with confidence. Conservation scientists have two broad categories of analytical methods: spectroscopic and chromatographic. Spectroscopy measures how pigments interact with the electromagnetic (EM) spectrum, not only the small part of the spectrum that we see with our eyes—that is, the visible region—but also higher and lower energies extending far on either side of the visible region. Spectroscopic methods examine minute samples, and they can be deployed in non-sampling and noncontact modes. Imaging methods for chemical analysis are constantly improving, providing more complete information on how artists used pigments. Despite the phenomenal advances in chemical imaging over the past decades, small samples are nevertheless required to obtain specific information about the detailed nature of pigments and their chemical state. The amount of paint required depends on the nature of the pigments. Since modern instrumentation is sensitive, samples that are almost invisible to the naked eye are often adequate. Sometimes, only a few particles taken by grazing a needle across the surface of the paint are enough for optical microscopy of many crystalline mineral pigments. Cross-section samples show us how layers of paint were applied, revealing how an artist used layering to build color (see [FIG. 27]). Further, we can identify the pigments used in each layer. Cross sections are obtained using a surgeon's scalpel or a needle to pry out a tiny fragment, almost always from a crack in the paint or next to an old loss. The sample needs to be no bigger than half a millimeter to contain an amazing amount of information. The fragment is embedded in a small block of plastic resin that is cut and polished to show the stratigraphy of paint layers, revealing how the artist worked.

Chromatographic methods separate the molecular components of complex colorants such as natural pigment made from plant extract or early synthetic organic pigments. Chromatography is coupled with mass spectrometry, a technique that breaks individual molecules into fragments from which we learn about the molecular arrangement of the original compounds and their identity. Chromatographic methods always require a small sample, which is a drawback because it demands physical

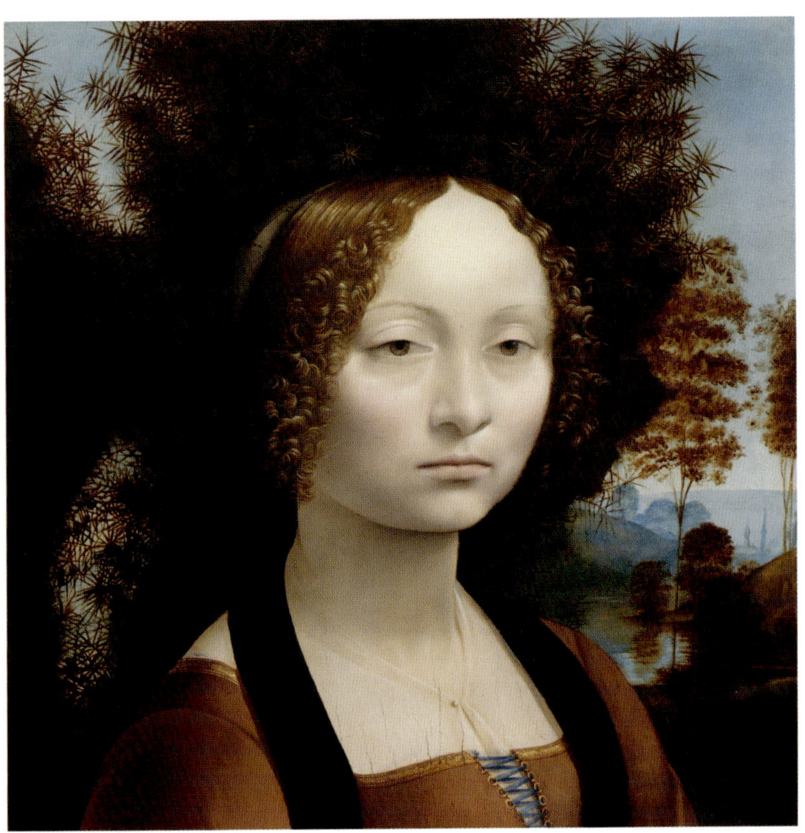

[FIG. 24]
Leonardo da Vinci, *Ginevra de' Benci*, ca. 1474–78 (obverse). Oil on panel, 38.1 × 37 cm. National Gallery of Art, Washington, D.C., Ailsa Mellon Bruce Fund (1967.6.1.a). The copper-green pigment used in the trees has become brown.

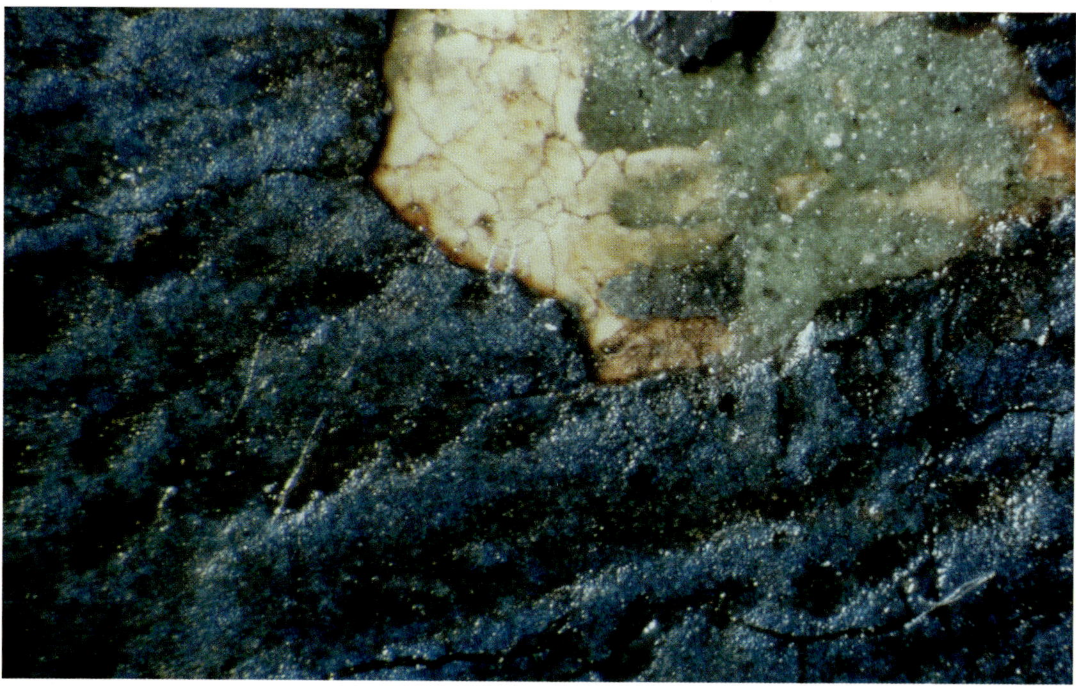

[FIG. 25]
A microscopic view of the surface of the Virgin's robe in *The Saint Anne Altarpiece* by Gerard David (ca. 1500/1520; National Gallery of Art, Washington, D.C., Widener Collection, 1942.9.17.b). The area shown is about 1.5 inches long. A small loss of paint reveals a traditional white chalk ground (pale yellow color) and the end of a stroke of black underdrawing just visible at the lowest point of the loss. There are remnants of old green restoration paint in the loss. When the paint was applied, it would have matched the blue color covered by yellowed varnish. A tiny cross section was taken from the edge of this large loss.

interference with the work. Nevertheless, it provides detailed information and is especially useful for identifying organic pigments. Identification of an organic pigment using chromatography might require micrograms of paint about one-fifth the size of the smallest pinch of salt. These samples are obtained by lightly dragging a surgeon's scalpel or a needle across the paint surface.

To study these samples of pigment, conservators and technical scientists depend on increasingly advanced imaging technology. Imaging methods were first used to reveal artists' sketches hidden under finished paintings. Now, spectral signatures associated with individual pigments can be mapped over the pictorial composition, and these maps can be superimposed on the visible image to show where and how an artist used certain pigments throughout a work of art. Imaging methods not only provide extraordinary visualization of data, but they also guide the selection of sites for sampling to aid in answering specific questions about the pigments and how they are mixed and layered.

Optical Microscopy

Stereomicroscopy is a good starting point when looking at pigments. At high magnification it is possible to see individual particles of some pigments on a painted surface. Relying on a long tradition from mineral analysis, transmitted polarized light microscopy of dispersed paint scrapings was one of the first methods conservation scientists used to identify pigments. Optical microscopy is employed less often due to the development of today's highly sensitive instrumental methods, but it is invaluable for getting a general sense of how many different pigments are in a mixture, thus making it easier to interpret the results from other analyses that cannot spatially resolve the intimate mix of colorants. It can be valuable to find mineral pigments when they were used in small proportions in complex mixtures. For example, orpiment was not expected to be in late eighteenth-century wall paint in a tavern in Williamsburg, Virginia, since contemporary books on painting and house decorating deride orpiment, also called King's yellow, as foul-smelling, sick-making, and incompatible with other pigments. Nevertheless, it was easily identified using polarized light microscopy of a tiny scraping of the paint from the interior [FIG. 26], though the elements it contains, arsenic and sulfur, had not been detected using instrumental techniques.

Optical microscopy of cross-section samples is ideal for seeing how artists use paint layering and to discern later interventions. Although close inspection of painted surfaces at high magnification is useful, samples from a painting show much more than is visible from surface examination. Cross-section samples include priming and other preparatory layers, sketches, and washes used to build form before the paint layers, final glazes, and highlights are applied. The cross section from a sixteenth-century Venetian painting [FIG. 27] shows that the artist worked directly on the fabric support and developed the color of the sky using azurite that had been sorted into batches of different particle sizes. The paler layers applied first and lower in the stratigraphy have fine-sized particles of azurite mixed with lead white. The hue was varied by sweeping a stroke of paint mixed from the same azurite and lead white with a yellow lake. The artist then applied more paint made using lead white and azurite with larger particles to deepen the shade of blue. A final layer of paint is present, made using midsize azurite particles. This layer may have been applied a little later since there is a discrete boundary between it and the underlying layer, a finding consistent with the fact that we know the painting was substantially modified from its original state by the artist.

Scanning Electron Microscopy with Energy Dispersive X-Ray Analysis

Scanning electron microscopy (SEM) coupled with energy dispersive X-ray (EDX) analysis (also called energy dispersive X-ray spectroscopy, EDS) is often used to analyze pigments in samples of dispersed pigments and in paint cross sections. EDX analysis, like X-ray fluorescence analysis, which is described next, provides information on the elements present in a pigment. The samples are placed in a vacuum chamber on the electron microscope and imaged using a beam of electrons that scatter off the sample in various ways. These electrons form an image of the sample. Denser pigments that have heavy elements such as lead and mercury appear bright because more electrons bounce off them. The shapes and the sizes of pigment particles are easily visualized. Some of the electrons interact with atoms or ions in the pigments forcing them into higher energy-excited states, which then emit characteristic X-rays via fluorescence when relaxing to the ground state. The energy of the fluorescence tells us which elements are present, helping us identify the pigments. Individual pigment particles are easily seen and analyzed using SEM-EDX. Data can be obtained from a single pigment particle, or an entire sample can be scanned to generate maps of the distribution of pigments in different paint layers.

Van Gogh placed his palette at the bottom of the composition in *Self-Portrait* [FIG. 28]. Four daubs of paint are set out in pairs of complementary colors—yellow and blue, green and red. Using SEM-EDX we learn that pigment particles in a small scraping of the pink paint contain chlorine, bromine, or iodine [FIG. 29]. These elements indicate the red paint is a mixture of the synthetic organic pigments eosin (Geranium red), erythrosine (rose Bengal), and possibly phloxine as well, all from the chemical class xanthenes and probably combined by the colorman

[FIG. 26]
Particles of orpiment are identified in a small sample of wall paint from Wetherburn's Tavern in Williamsburg using transmitted plane and crossed polarized light microscopy.

[FIG. 27]
Cross section from the sky of Jacopo Tintoretto's *Doge Alvise Mocenigo and Family before the Madonna and Child* (ca. 1575; National Gallery of Art, Washington, D.C., Samuel H. Kress Collection, 1961.19.44) shows the artist painted directly on an unprimed canvas. He used azurite graded into three different particle size ranges to paint several layers. Length of the sample is 0.7 mm.

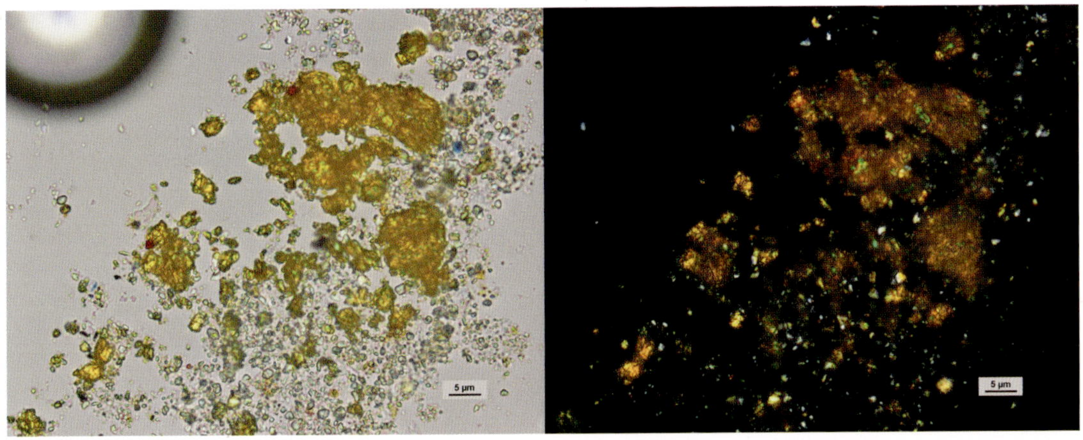

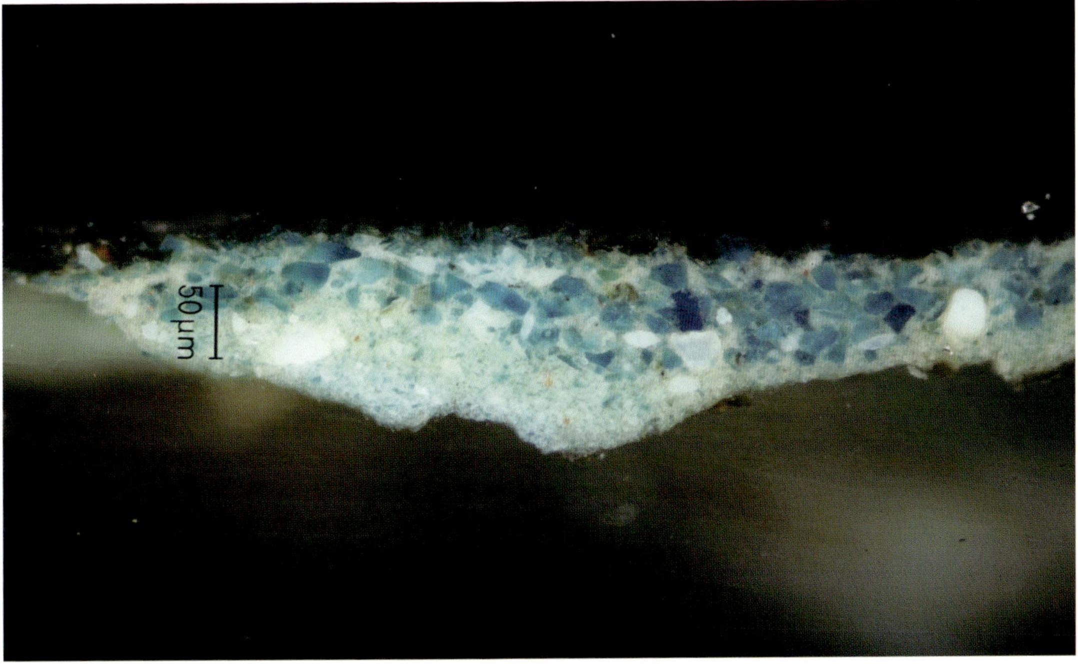

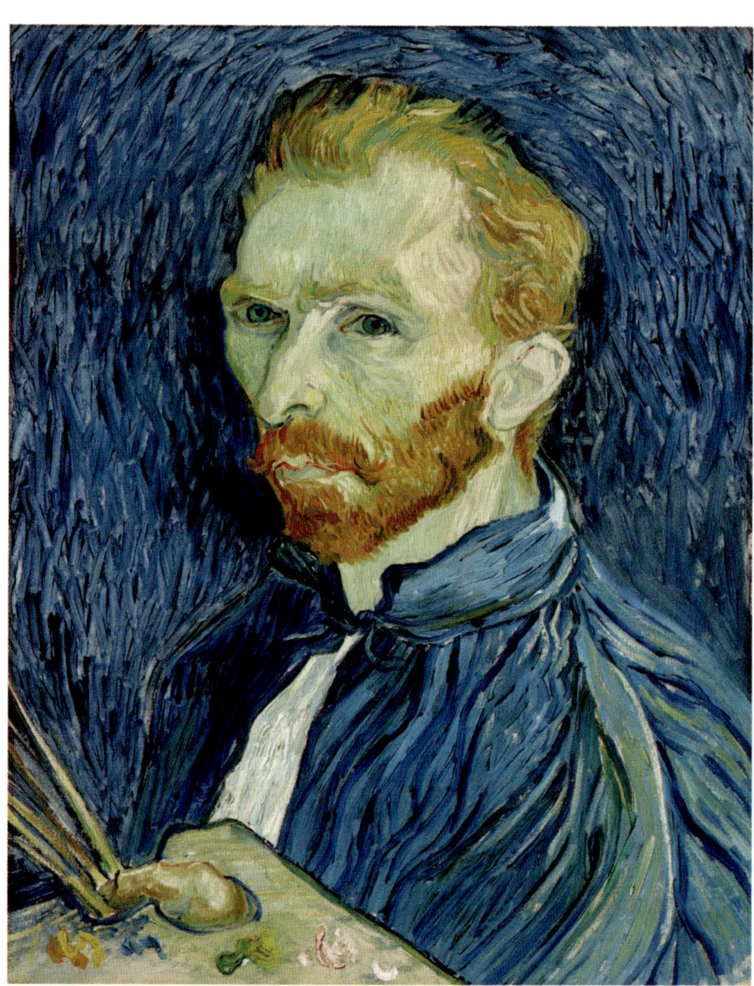

[FIG. 28]
Vincent van Gogh, *Self-Portrait*, 1889. Oil on canvas, 57.8 × 44.5 cm. National Gallery of Art, Washington, D.C., Collection of Mr. and Mrs. John Hay Whitney (1998.74.5).

[FIG. 29]
Scanning electron microscopy with energy-dispersive X-ray analysis. A tiny scraping of pigment from the pink daub in Van Gogh's *Self-Portrait* contains the pigment zinc white and particles that contain chlorine, bromine, or iodine, indicating the presence of the fugitive red synthetic organic pigments eosin and erythrosine.

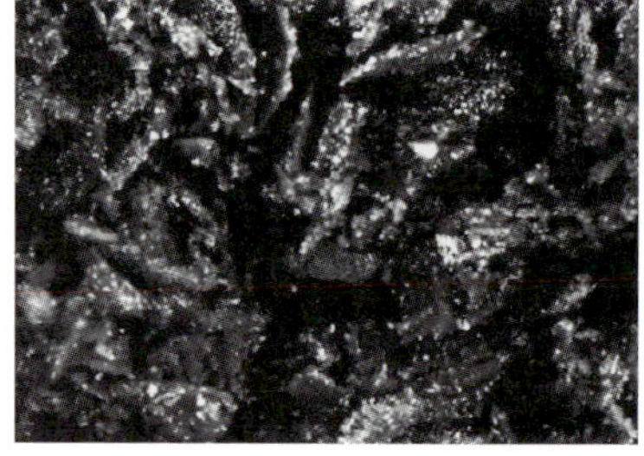

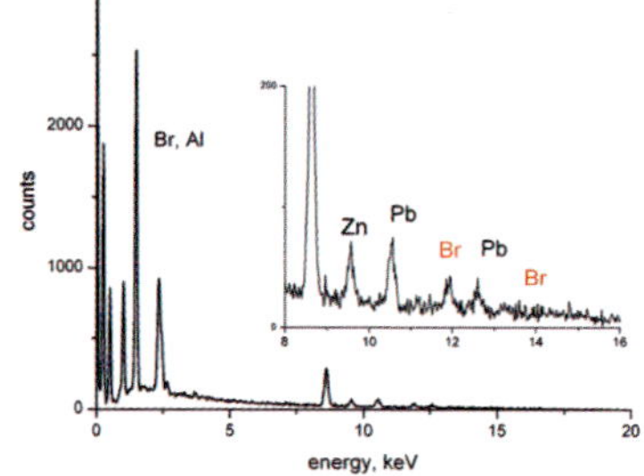

who made the paint. Although such mixtures have always been in the colorman's repertoire, we often forget they mixed pigments to make uniquely colored paints. The iodine in rose Bengal has only been found using SEM-EDX, but we are reminded to consider its presence no matter whether it is detectable or not. These xanthene pigments give a strong color since they have a high tinting strength, but all are extremely light sensitive and fade quickly. When first painted, the colors on the palette in Van Gogh's hand must have been intense. Not only was the pink paint probably a brilliant red, but the chrome yellow was likely brighter. The daubs of colors were an emphatic visualization of the artist's written descriptions of complementary color pairings for symbolic and visual effect. These pairings are still apparent but less stridently now due to color change. The results from analysis of the pigments reinforce Van Gogh's thoughts, described in his letters, about the suggestive power of intense color.

X-Ray Fluorescence Analysis

X-ray fluorescence (XRF) analysis, also called X-ray fluorescence spectrometry or X-ray fluorescence spectroscopy, is used to aid pigment identification by determining the element composition using information like EDX analysis. XRF relies on a beam of X-rays that excite atoms or ions in pigments into a high energy state. They then fluoresce, emitting X-rays that have energies that are characteristic of specific elements. Based on the elements found, we can infer which inorganic pigments are present. The XRF technique was adapted in the late 1970s to examine cultural heritage objects without having to remove samples. Instead of working with samples in a vacuum, the changes in the design of the instrument allowed measurements to be made directly on objects. To distinguish this new methodology from the typical way of working, the technique was called "air-path XRF." Since air absorbs low-energy X-rays, certain elements that are common in pigments, such as oxygen, sodium, magnesium, and aluminum—important constituents of organic pigments, glasses, and earths—are difficult to measure, but the technique is extremely valuable for identification of many inorganic pigments and is employed frequently by conservators and heritage scientists. While the earlier movable instruments are large and heavy, handheld devices that have high sensitivity have been developed and are used for fieldwork and increasingly in museums [FIG. 30].

Micro-XRF (or μXRF) analyzes spots that are less than a micrometer in diameter, just a little more than the width of a human hair. This tiny spot size is useful for examining fine lines in drawings and manuscripts and spots on small or complex objects and for scanning paintings at high spatial resolution. Scanning XRF systems have been developed by putting

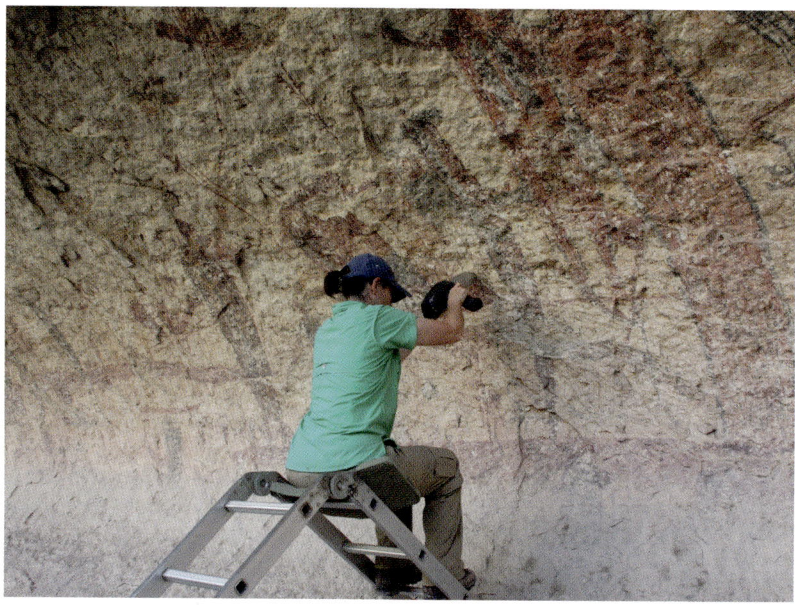

either an XRF instrument or a work of art onto a motorized easel. As the easel moves, spectra are collected continuously all along the sweeping motion to create 2D maps of the elements in the paint that can be interpreted to show where different pigments were used [FIG. 31].

Since air-path XRF tells us only the elements in the paint, and not all of them, we use other evidence, including color, to infer the pigment composition. Some pigments are easy to identify using only XRF, though it can be a challenge to find pigments that are in low proportions in mixtures. Nevertheless, XRF is a powerful tool for the identification of many pigments that contain metallic elements and is valuable and widely used in combination with other techniques.

Vibrational Spectroscopy

The atoms and groups of atoms in molecules are in constant movement, vibrating, bending, stretching, and wagging as the molecule absorbs heat (infrared radiation) from the environment. The movement of bonded atoms has a frequency that tells us about the kinds of bonds present and something about how they are arranged. We can collect a spectrum of the absorption through infrared and use it to identify many pigments. Three techniques applied frequently in cultural heritage science are Fourier transform infrared spectroscopy, Raman spectroscopy, and infrared reflectance spectroscopy. They have various ways of being deployed and have strengths in different applications.

Fourier Transform Infrared (FTIR) Spectroscopy Fourier transform infrared (FTIR) spectroscopy can be used in noninvasive and noncontact modes. Most FTIR spectrometers operate in the part of the EM spectrum called the mid-infrared region (between 1000–2500 nm or 4000–400 wave numbers), where the fundamental vibrational modes of molecules occur. The absorbance peaks are sharper and overlap less than in the shortwave region used for spectral imaging applications, where combination and overtone (harmonic) vibrations occur, so it is easier to discriminate among spectra of similar compounds. A sample is often required, though conservation scientists are working to apply non-sampling methods. FTIR is not useful for detecting pigments that are simple oxides—for example, hematite (Fe_2O_3) or minium (red lead, Pb_3O_4)—but it is well suited for analysis of organic molecules and complex inorganic compounds such as lead white or azurite. Some pigments can be identified with certainty using infrared spectroscopy. Non-sampling methods using techniques that take advantage of external reflectance or diffuse reflectance from pigments are increasingly employed, though obtaining high-quality spectra is dependent on the characteristics of the surface of the object.

Raman Spectroscopy Raman spectroscopy gives information on molecular structure like that provided by Fourier transform infrared spectroscopy. Raman spectroscopy is versatile and sensitive. It is used to identify inorganic pigments that cannot be detected using FTIR. It can be used in sampling and non-sampling modes and even to analyze individual particles if they are large enough, since the technique uses a laser that can be focused through a microscope to look at very small spots. The pigments in miniature portraits by Nicholas Hilliard (ca. 1547–1619) were analyzed without having to touch the small precious objects [FIG. 32]. Raman spectroscopy showed that Hilliard used pigments we expected to see except that arsenical yellow and orange pigments were also found. This finding is surprising because Hilliard explicitly notes in his treatise on painting that orpiment, verdigris, and other ill-smelling and ill-tasting pigments, which include the fugitive natural organic pigments made from toxic berries and lichens, are "naught for limning."

Pigments that fluoresce under laser illumination, and there are many, are difficult to examine using Raman spectroscopy, but a sophisticated technique called surface-enhanced Raman spectroscopy (SERS) increases the Raman spectrum compared to the fluorescence. SERS has been used to confirm that the organic red pigments that Winslow Homer used for his watercolor paintings were based on cochineal, for example. Scientists using Raman spectroscopy discovered that the French miniaturist Jean Bourdichon (1457 or 1459–1521) chose a variety of pigments to create images that shimmer under certain lighting. Iridescent metallic bismuth

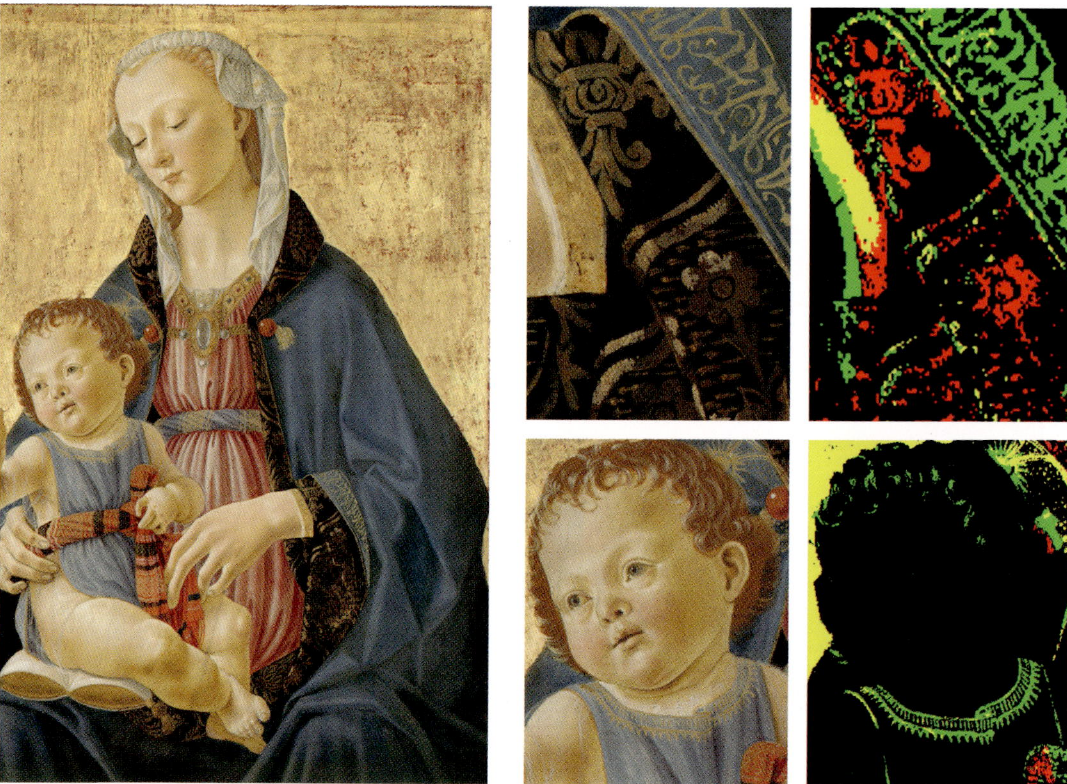

[FIG. 31]
Scanning micro-XRF analysis.
Domenico Ghirlandaio,
Madonna and Child, ca.
1470–75. Tempera on panel
transferred to hardboard,
70.8 × 48.9 cm. National
Gallery of Art, Washington,
D.C., Samuel H. Kress
Collection (1961.9.49).
Element maps obtained
from area of the detail show
the distribution of gold,
Au (yellow), lead, Pb (green),
and tin, Sn (red). Ghirlandaio
used three different materials, gold foil, and the
pigments lead tin yellow and
mosaic gold (tin sulfide) to
depict the gold embroidery
on the Virgin's robe.

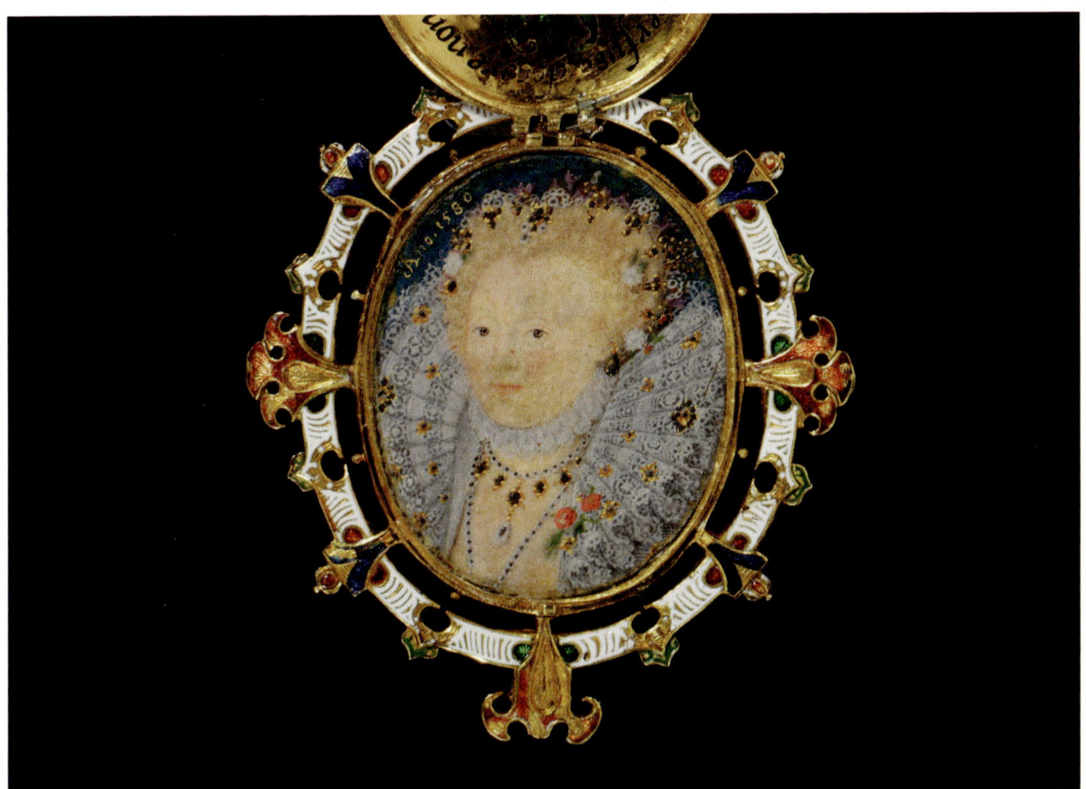

[FIG. 32]
Nicholas Hilliard, *The Heneage Jewel* (*The Armada Jewel*), ca. 1600. Pendant in enameled gold, table-cut diamonds, Burmese rubies open to show portrait miniature of Elizabeth I (1533–1603), with hinged locket inner side with Tudor rose encircled by leaves and inscription; 7 × 5.1 cm. Victoria and Albert Museum, London, Given by the Rt. Hon. Viscount Wakefield CBE, through Art Fund (M.81–1935).

provided a deep gray, and yellows and other colors were enlivened by the presence of sparkly pigments including iron pyrite, shiny hematite, and mosaic gold in addition to the more typical paint in miniatures, shell gold.

Infrared Reflectance Spectroscopy

As we have seen, spectroscopy in the visible and infrared regions of the EM spectrum provides information about molecular groups and chemical structure that is complementary to data obtained using XRF. Reflectance spectroscopy was transformed for pigment identification in artifacts by implementing the use of fiber-optics cables that allowed conservation scientists to measure light reflected from small spots on objects so that pigments could be analyzed without contacting the surface. This technique has been described as fiber-optic reflectance spectroscopy (FORS). In its original application, the detectors were sensitive to visible light and a little beyond into the near infrared, but recent instruments have detectors that measure a broad part of the EM spectrum, so it is much easier to differentiate pigments that have similar reflectance in the visible spectrum of light even if they have different chemical compositions. Novel mathematical algorithms, developed using artificial intelligence and machine learning, help deconvolute the reflectance spectra of mixtures of multiple pigments to aid in the interpretation of the complex spectra from pigmented surfaces.

Chemical Imaging

Reflectance spectroscopy can be deployed over large areas and in small spots for pigment analysis throughout entire works. Recently, major advances in imaging, many borrowed from the field of remote sensing and imaging, have allowed us to measure reflectance at high spatial resolution—that is, to create an array of spectra at many closely spaced points—from large painted areas, even in inaccessible places such as wall paintings and frescoes high in buildings. Measurements of the intensity of reflectance from narrow regions of EM spectrum to create a large data set are collected, which allows identification of the pigments and visualization of where they were used. The terms "multispectral" and "hyperspectral" imaging have been used in the context of pigment studies. Multispectral imaging typically refers to measuring the reflected radiation (energy) over eight to fifteen narrow bands of radiation within the visible region and the entire infrared region, while hyperspectral generally refers to capturing reflectance spectra in many narrow wavelength bands over a wide range of the EM spectrum.

Conservation scientists identified the pigments in wall paintings in Cave 465 in the Mogao complex of grottoes in northwestern China using multispectral reflectance spectroscopy [FIG. 33, left]. Most scholars think the paintings were made during the Yuan dynasty (1279–1368).

[FIG. 33]
A remote spectral imaging system is being used to collect, from the ground, images of entire wall and ceiling paintings to identify the pigments. A small area of the wall painting is shown with reflectance spectra of a set of colorants that describe the pigments in this detail, and mapping the distribution of the spectra helps visualize the strokes of paint that have become indistinct.

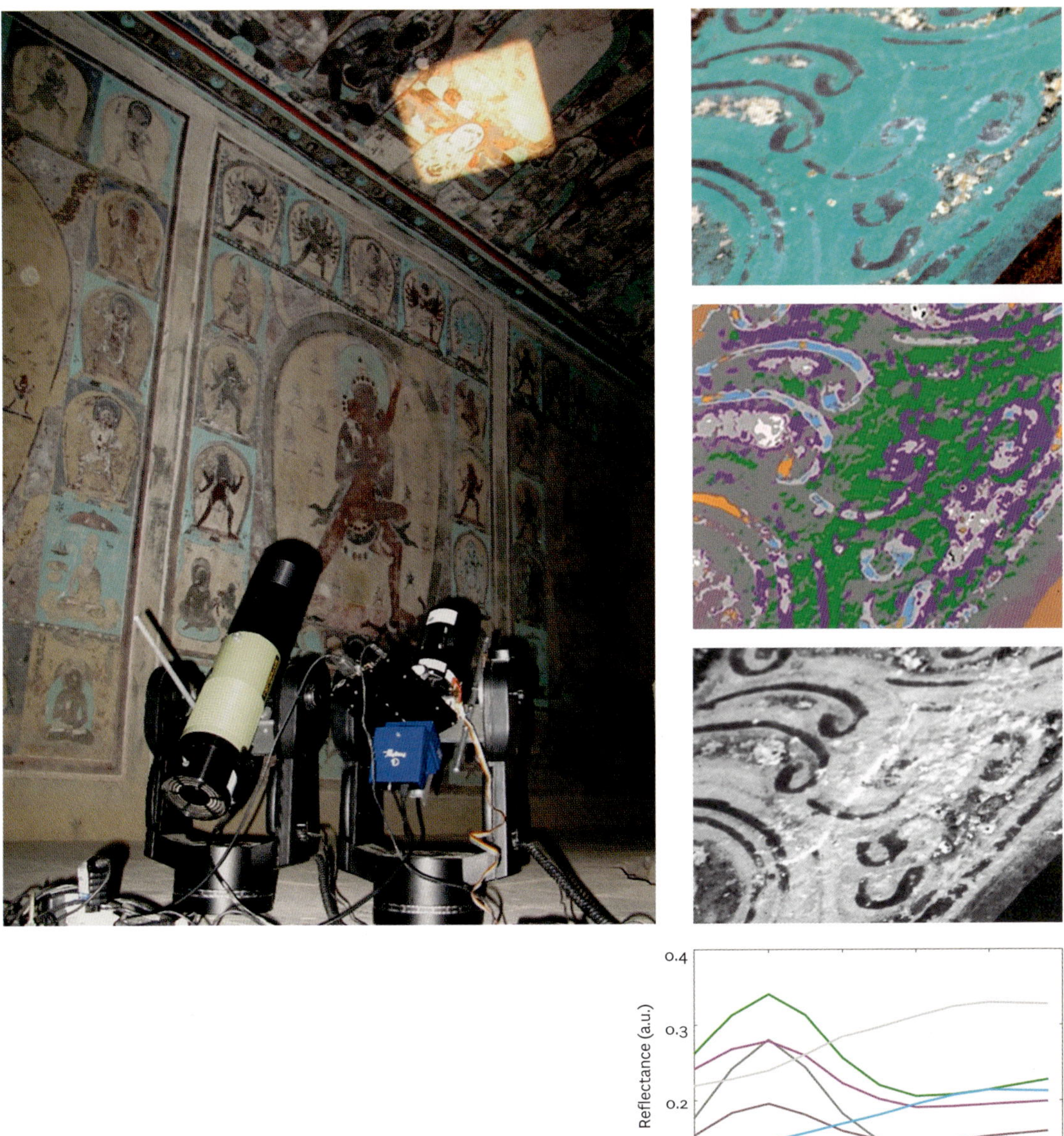
Reflectance (a.u.)
0.4
0.3
0.2
0.1
400
500
600
700
800
900
λ (nm)

Reflectance was captured as a large data cube, and the extracted spectra suggest the paint is generally just a few distinct pigment mixtures that provide a range of hues and tones. Some of the strokes are now barely visible due to change over time, but they can be visualized in images created by statistical processing of the spectral reflectance data cube [FIG. 33, right]. Other analytical methods used in closer proximity to select parts of the wall paintings confirmed the identification of pigments. The painters used indigo and azurite separately and in mixtures for the variety of blues. Ultramarine was not on their palette. Green paints were made using a copper chloride salt, atacamite, or a mixture of indigo and orpiment. Some of the browns and blacks that we see are due to conversion of red lead (lead oxide, Pb_3O_4) into black lead dioxide (PbO_2, plattnerite). The pigments in the paintings in Cave 465 are typical of Tibetan artists and consistent with the art-historical attribution of the wall paintings. Imaging the distribution of pigments allows us to see details of the brushwork and the colors of the decorative scheme that are partially obscured due to deterioration and alteration, giving us insight into the original appearance of the paintings.

The luminescence of certain pigments can be visualized using light at specific wavelengths and special detectors to reveal invisible traces of paint. Scientists discovered strong emission from Egyptian blue on sculptures from ancient Greece and imperial Rome, leading to the realization that most of them had once been brightly painted. The emission from red lakes and Egyptian blue are readily perceived and distinguished to show how these pigments were used separately and mixed to make a variety of hues [FIG. 34]. A few pigments can be confirmed by their luminescence, but currently these visualizations show where different pigments were used rather than give specific information on chemical identity.

X-Ray Diffraction

Many pigments, both natural or manufactured and organic or inorganic, are crystalline. Crystals have a regular arrangement of ions called a lattice, which diffracts a beam of X-rays in a unique pattern that is a fingerprint of the pigment. The technique usually requires a powdered sample of a pigment, hence the full name of the technique as used in pigment studies is powder X-ray diffraction (PXRD). The sample size required is dependent on the pigment since the diffracting power is determined by the atomic weight of atoms in the crystal lattice—the heavier they are the better they are at diffracting X-rays. Although many synthetic organic pigments are crystalline, they are often mixed with inorganic extenders and fillers that dominate the diffraction pattern of samples from paint, so they are difficult to detect using this method. PXRD was used to discover that lead white is rarely a single compound but frequently contains

[FIG. 34]
Detail of a Romano-Egyptian panel painting depicting Nemesis holding a staff in her right hand, ca. 40 BCE–113 CE. Hide glue paint on sidr wood (*Ziziphus spina-christi*). (left panel) Visible light photograph; (middle panel) ultraviolet induced visible fluorescence imaging; (right panel) visible light-induced infrared luminescence imaging in combination with some infrared reflected light.

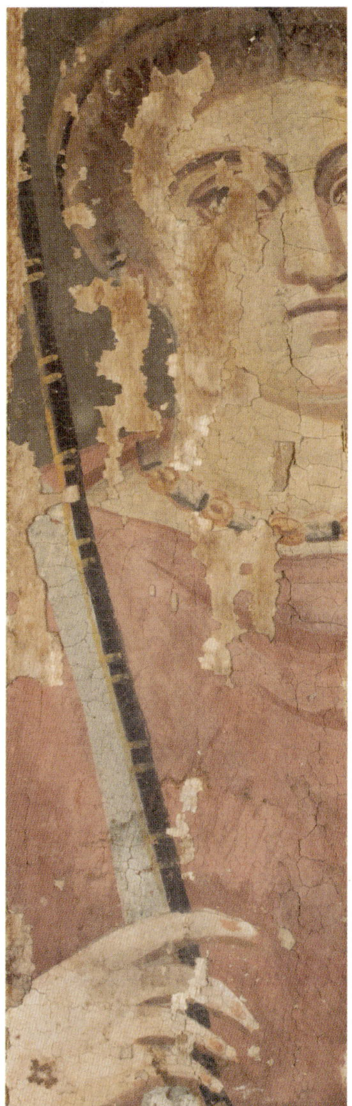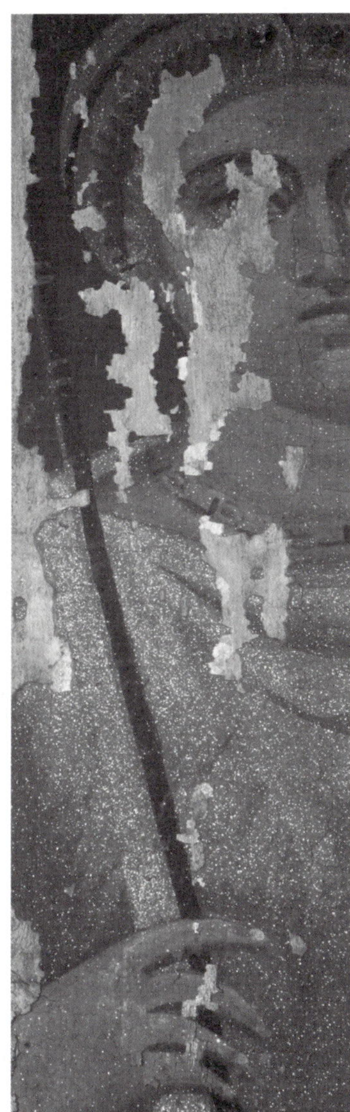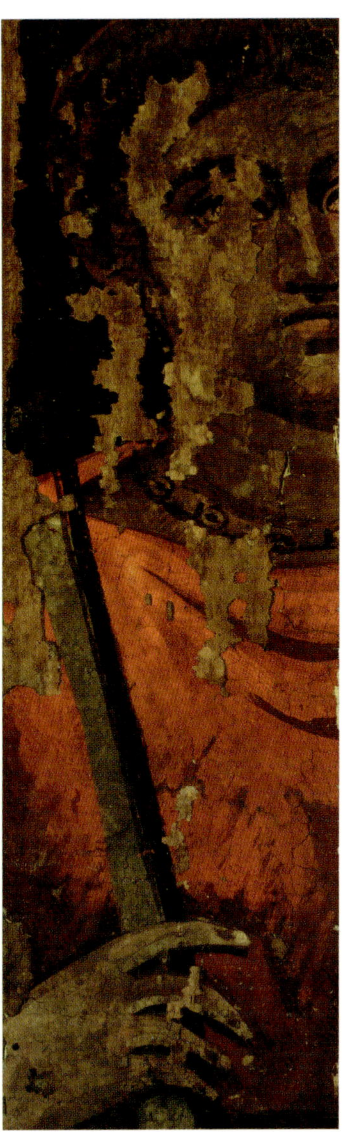

varying proportions of several lead carbonate compounds in different states of hydration. Research is ongoing to understand how the variety of compounds reflects the diverse procedures used in manufacturing the pigment. XRD has been adapted for non-sampling configurations, but at this time few institutions have the capability. Instruments that simultaneously collect information on the crystalline structure of samples and the element composition using X-ray fluorescence analysis are even more useful for pigment identification, demonstrating that employing more than one analytical method is valuable for pigment characterization. PXRD used in a non-sampling stand-off mode revealed there are two sorts of lead white in the complexion of Johannes Vermeer's *Girl with a Pearl Earring* [FIG. 35] and how they were applied. PXRD also shows that there has been chemical alteration in the paint, with both lead white and chalk changing to form other compounds that contain sulfur. These changes might be due to reactions with residual alum that was used to make the red lake pigments and offer further evidence that the purity of pigments is a factor in their long-term stability.

Chromatography

Chromatographic techniques use sophisticated chemical and instrumental methods to analyze insoluble pigments by means of chemical modification (derivatization) and high-tech columns to separate the molecular components of natural and synthetic organic pigments. Mass spectrometry (MS) is employed in tandem with chromatography to characterize molecules following their separation. MS is a complex procedure involving ion fragmentation, measuring the mass of the fragments, and determining how they formed from the whole molecule. Reverse construction allows scientists to determine the original molecule.

High performance liquid chromatography (HPLC) with MS requires a small sample that must be chemically derivatized to make the pigment soluble. Our confidence in the chemical analysis and the interpretation of the results are constantly advancing as our capabilities and knowledge grow. Since the coloring agents (chromophores) from different plants can be similar, chromatography is required to establish a lake pigment's exact molecular identity. Based on the small chemical variations in the natural pigments that depend on their source, the results can tell us if local or imported colorants were used. In some cases, it is possible to determine if a red-lake colorant comes from European (*Porphyrophora polonica*), Asian (*Porphyrophora hamelii*), or New World (*Dactylopius coccus*) insects. The first two live on the roots of plants; the third, which lives on the fleshy leaves of nopal cactus, supplanted the European and Asian sources in the mid-sixteenth century. This kind of information improves our understanding about the influence of trade on artists' palettes.

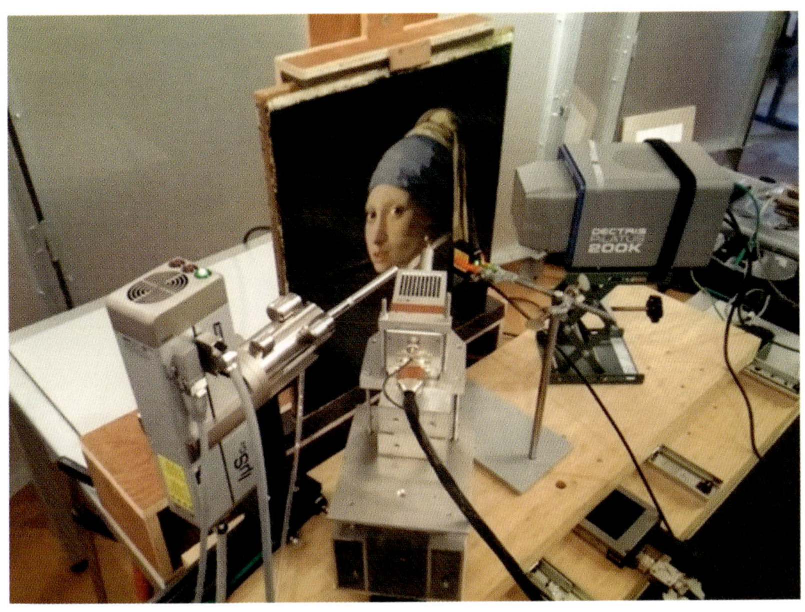

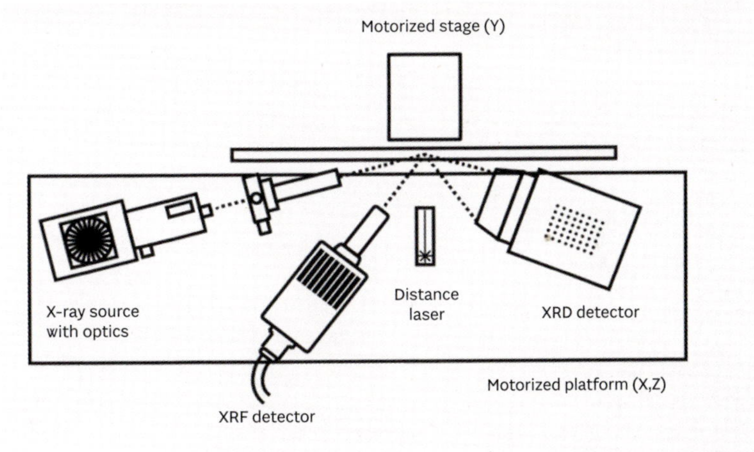

[FIG. 35]
Johannes Vermeer, *Girl with a Pearl Earring*, 1665. Oil on canvas, 44.5 × 39 cm. Mauritshuis, The Hague. The painting is being examined using X-ray powder diffraction and X-ray fluorescence analysis simultaneously. A beam of X-rays is aimed at a small area. Two different detectors measure X-rays coming from the surface. One measures the energy of characteristic X-rays, which gives information about the elements present, while the other measures how X-rays are diffracted, thus identifying the crystalline pigments.

What Pigment Analysis Reveals

Using chemical analysis, we are sometimes able to obtain information on the raw materials used to make pigments. Detailed information about the molecular makeup of complex molecules in an organic pigment can point to the botanical origin of the species used to make it and thus its geographical origin. Pigment identification pushes us to consider if the appearance of a painted object has been impacted by changes. From analysis, we learn how accomplished (or not) a color maker was from signs of deterioration and impurities associated with pigments. Impurities also provide insight into historical manufacturing processes. Using pigment identification, we often learn that painters do not follow their own advice. For example, orpiment, an extremely toxic pigment that was difficult to use, was widely disparaged, yet we find that artists and artisans used it again and again. We discover that the pigments chosen to depict specific things such as grass or pale complexions are remarkably consistent across vast distances and times. We also discover, however, moments of innovation in the history of color-making and art-making that have had a radical and long-lasting influence such as the invention of mauveine or the synthesis of cobalt violets.

Pigment identification helps to determine authenticity. If pigments are used in atypical ways or if anachronistic pigments are present, such findings allow conservators to distinguish repairs and additions to an original work. We can check the veracity and usefulness of treatises and texts as sources for information on pigment identification. We have learned that these accounts do not always reflect contemporary practice but are instead often repetitions of earlier, sometimes much older texts. The art historian must help determine if we can use treatises as reliable guides. Results from instrumental analysis can be vague and incomplete. We are, however, rapidly becoming more sophisticated in our understanding and interpretation of technical and textual information.

The identification of a pigment depends on several factors related to its chemistry, state of preservation, the presence of interfering compounds, and the relative difficulty of characterizing some classes of molecules. The conservation scientist must take care to understand the limitations of the different analytical methods because small but historically important components in paint mixtures can elude detection, especially when chemically altered through aging. The analyst's curiosity and determination are important for the precise and reliable characterization of pigments. Scientists and art historians should look at data without preconceived notions, being mindful of the changes in our knowledge and thinking as we learn more about the history of pigment. The unwritten history of pigment is preserved in artifacts, and the emergence of sophisticated analytical instruments for pigment analysis in combination with historical analysis allow us to "read" this history and gain insight into how pigments, technology, and artistry are woven together. The improvements in our capabilities using non-sampling methods have relied on the knowledge developed from analysis of materials removed from cultural objects. It is no longer appropriate to take large samples, since analytical science has improved significantly. Nevertheless, the results of past analyses paved the way for the interpretation of data obtained using non-sampling methods.

Only the most inert colorants on the most stable supports such as rock walls and stones have survived thousands of years without change. Still, I am often amazed at how much remains. Paintings in many mediums have survived, and we can easily appreciate their color even now. Although the most stable pigments influence the current appearance of art and our conclusions about what artists used, they are evidence that the story of color-making and pigment has a remarkable constancy. It is surprising to discover how many different materials have been used as pigments and how quickly artists adopt new ones. Connecting chemical identification and art-historical analysis fosters our appreciation of how pigments contribute to the aesthetic effects achieved in painting. Pigment analysis informs us about conventions and norms of color and trade. It reveals the availability of materials in specific regions, which is dependent on economic and geopolitical events. Pigment identification sheds light on how ideas spread. We have more insight into the original appearance of art and artifacts prior to any deterioration, and our awareness of the cultural and aesthetic value of color and colorants grows exponentially the more that we understand about pigment.

Case Studies in
Pigments

Pigments in Baroque and Rococo European Painters' Palettes

David Bomford

The first time one sees a painting being cleaned, as the original colors emerge from dark clouds of dirt and discolored varnish, the revelation of color is unforgettable. I have never lost my excitement at seeing the details of an artist's original composition reemerge in all their brilliance. Studying brushwork and examining the freshly revealed surfaces is like looking over artists' shoulders as they work. Only later in my career did I realize that the original appearance may not be fully evident, even in a cleaned painting, as the carefully calculated tonal equilibrium of individual painted passages fall out of balance over time. To look beyond present appearance is an essential component of technical art history, and it is key to understanding the original effect of an artwork and the ways in which that first impression has degraded over time. I will discuss some pigments in painters' palettes in the seventeenth and eighteenth centuries and use examples to consider common changes that occur in the appearance of paintings so that contemporary viewers may understand that the works they encounter in a museum are often as much products of time as of an artist's brush.

Between 1600 and 1800 strongly colored, high-tinting pigments became readily available, leading to the emergence of a new palette for European painters. Some of these were more intense varieties of ancient pigments, formulated using new sources, while others were novel discoveries. These pigments provided more choices in the primary colors—red, blue, and yellow—colors that cannot be made by mixing. New pigments allowed artists to explore an augmented and intense palette that became a hallmark of Baroque and Rococo painting in Europe. In *A Personification of Fame* [FIG. 36], for example, Bernardo Strozzi used these pigments to create a vivid, expressive composition.

Several events led to this new palette. Raw materials became more abundant from exploration of the Americas, and exploitation of natural resources for color-making increased in Europe. Simultaneously, scientific

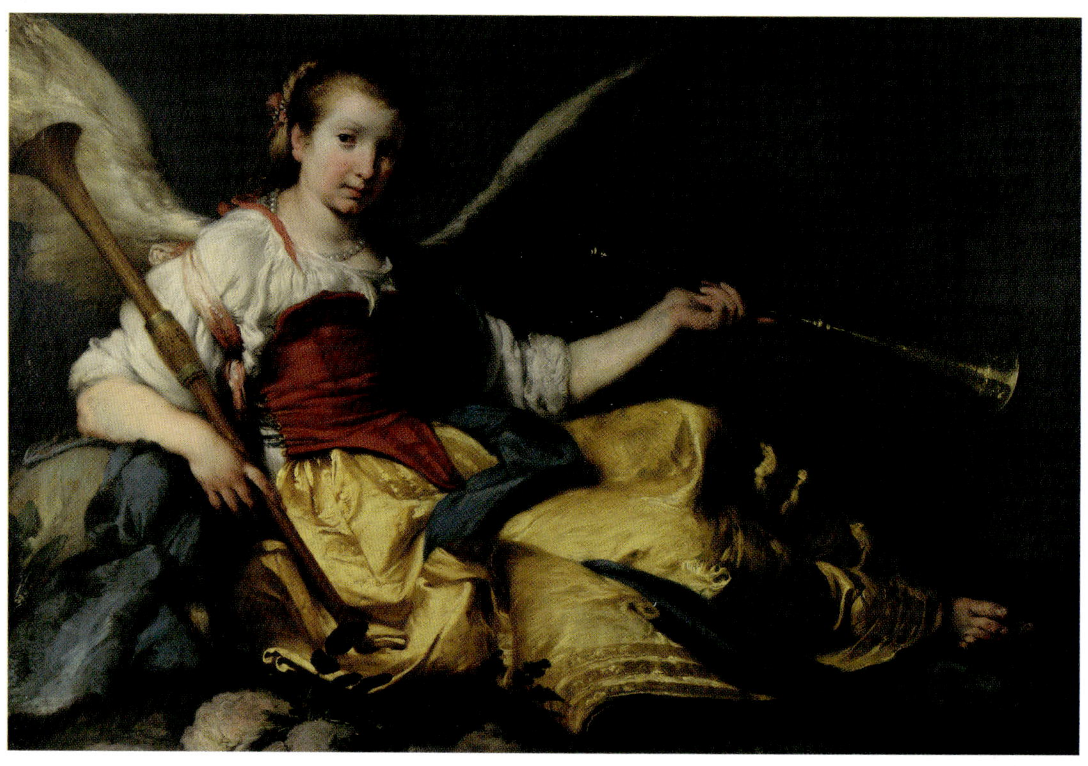

[FIG. 36]
Bernardo Strozzi,
A Personification of Fame,
probably 1635–36. Oil on
canvas, 106.7 × 151.7 cm.
National Gallery, London,
Bought, 1961 (NG6321).

and technological advances encouraged experimentation in pigment-making. Colonization and the subsequent, unprecedented volume of trade between the Americas and European centers of commerce, including London, Amsterdam, Seville, Genoa, and Venice, brought tons of raw materials to be worked up for the color trade. Among these, there were two new sources for red dyes and pigments: brazilwood and cochineal. The colorant brazilwood lent its name to the Portuguese colony Brazil, a source in the late sixteenth century for the eponymous pigment obtained from a tree that grew abundantly there. The trees were felled by enslaved people and shipped to Europe. In Amsterdam, the supply of logs was prepared for pigment and dye-making by prisoners at the Rasphuis, where they rasped the timber into shavings from which the colorant was extracted. Cochineal, exported from Mexico beginning in the early sixteenth century, has a hue like other red lakes such as kermes and lac, but it is brighter and more intense and therefore was highly prized. At the beginning of the seventeenth century, a chance discovery that cochineal reacts with tin salts to make a scarlet color gave artists a high-keyed red pigment that also proved impermanent.

The Spanish artist and writer Francisco Pacheco (1564–1644) declared he was fortunate enough to have a supply of early modern "Santo Domingo blue," a copper pigment, now known to be azurite, obtained from the Latin American colonies. In *El arte de la pintura,* he describes it as making a brilliant, permanent paint in purified linseed oil when used thinly. Other European artists were often obliged to compromise, since blues were either too expensive, difficult to obtain, or poor in quality. The glassy blue pigment smalt was used, but it was unsatisfactory both in handling and in durability. If finely ground, smalt would lose its color and become pale. For a sufficiently strong tone, it had to be used as a coarse dispersion in oil. In consequence, smalt paint tended to have excess oil that continued exuding from the surface after it had been applied. Treatises recommended using an absorbent underlayer, blotting the surface to soak away the surplus oil or laying down a tinted layer first then sprinkling coarse, dry smalt on top. While none of these solutions solved the fundamental problems with smalt as a pigment for oil painting, many painters continued to favor it. By the mid-seventeenth century, smalt almost completely replaced azurite, indigo, and natural ultramarine in painters' palettes. Azurite was in short supply, and contemporary commentators deemed it too greenish for skies. Indigo was a poor pigment in oil, producing a dull blue that was chosen mainly for under-painting and painted sketches. Ultramarine was extremely costly. In turn, the preparation of smalt was not difficult. By this time, ores from mines in Germanic regions provided large quantities of the raw material for the cobalt that colored glass. Huge amounts of smalt were produced across

Europe, as the Dutch in particular set up glasshouses and manufactured smalt for domestic use and international trade. Deep-hued, high-quality smalt was made for easel painters, and it almost matched the color of ultramarine. Since it was a fraction of the cost, despite the challenges of using it in oil, it became ubiquitous in the Baroque palette.

In the eighteenth century, Prussian blue would transform the market for blue pigments. First made in Germany, it gained an important role within a few decades, replacing the mineral pigments ultramarine and azurite and the glassy smalt. Prussian blue's hue and high tinting strength made it useful for painting skies and seas as well as for rendering fabrics of all sorts. It was valuable in mixtures with yellows to make a wide range of greens for depicting vegetation and with reds to make purples and violets.

During the seventeenth century, a variety of pigments prepared from oxides of the elements lead, tin, and/or antimony gave artists a wide choice of yellows. Richard Symonds, an English traveler in Rome (1650–51), noted that the Italians had three or four yellows to choose from—some redder, some yellower. Since yellow is an artists' primary color, these compounds provided a variety of hues that could be adjusted by adding other pigments. Mixed with blue or red, these pigments gave artists rich, intense color. The wide range of both high-keyed and naturalistic greens that was possible using the new pigments is readily seen in flower and still-life paintings and landscapes. The gamut of hues that could be made employing the new pigments is also evident in the rendering of the textures and colors of voluptuous fabrics. These pigments allowed artists to combine an exploration of light and shade with subtle use of colors to paint naturalistic landscapes and still lifes as well as dramatic narratives.

During the seventeenth century, the failings of the copper-green pigment verdigris (copper acetate) were well known. As Margriet van Eikema Hommes points out in her important survey *Changing Pictures*, artists became wary of it, and its use as a key color declined. Theorists such as Gerard de Lairesse (1641–1711) and Joachim von Sandrart (1606–1688) drew attention to its harsh tonality and declared it too "cruel" for depicting beautiful landscapes. Painters decided that they could achieve a variety of green tones by mixing or layering blue and yellow pigments instead. The new yellows were useful, though the use of organic yellow lakes, as we will see, led to a series of problems.

At the moment of making, the physical qualities of paint are perceived and utilized in particular ways to express the artist's intention. In general, however, the artist cannot predict how his or her work will age and whether the original concept will be preserved. A work constructed in color is peculiarly vulnerable if relationships of tone and hue are altered by time and circumstance, particularly if choreographies of color—so carefully, deliberately, and artfully contrived—are mutable. Certain pigments or paints change in color and character as they age, and therefore the appearance of a painting might be subtly or significantly altered in irreversible ways. When looking at the art of the past, the possibility of such shifts in hue or tonality must be borne in mind.

We have to imagine that artists from this period took a calculated risk to achieve the results they desired. If they used only materials that they knew to be permanent, they would be left with a palette too restricted for their needs. In addition, there were economic considerations: durable pigments of sufficient strength might be expensive, so cheaper substitutes, reasonably satisfactory in the short term, would be bought instead.

The technical history of art is the study of the dialogue between the imagination and skills of the artist and the ability of materials available at the time to realize the artist's concepts in a tangible form. The combination of pigment identification and consulting contemporary artistic treatises is an avenue into the mind and the practice of the painter. Nevertheless, while the treatises tell us what pigments are likely to have been used, the recipes were often reproduced from other sources and do not contain information about idiosyncratic uses. The treatises also seldom address problems of availability that occur owing to a variety of circumstances, technical and geopolitical.

The pigments that were most problematic were red and yellow lakes, vegetable or animal dyes precipitated onto insoluble powders to make beautiful translucent glazes when used in oil. There are many instances of fading or diminished reds in seventeenth-century painting such as in *The Rape of Europa* [FIG. 37] by Guido Reni (1575–1642).

Artists were aware of the potential problems of fading pigments, and technical treatises recommended ways of combating future alteration. The celebrated *Arte de la pintura* (On the art of painting), written by Francisco Pacheco (1564–1644), father-in-law of the painter Diego Velázquez's (1599–1660), and published posthumously in Seville in 1649, discusses not only iconography and the lives of artists but also materials and methods, including pigments. Pacheco advises mixing a certain amount of lead white with a questionable pigment to protect it and to counter any darkening that might result from its disappearance. Carlo Cesare Malvasia (1616–1693), the Italian biographer of the artist Guido Reni, claims that Reni used large quantities of lead white in his later works to preserve the colors. While Reni's late white style as a stylistic or technical choice remains a matter of debate among scholars, the argument focuses our attention on the artist's choice of pigments and demonstrates the value of understanding technical art history when addressing philosophical questions such as "late style."

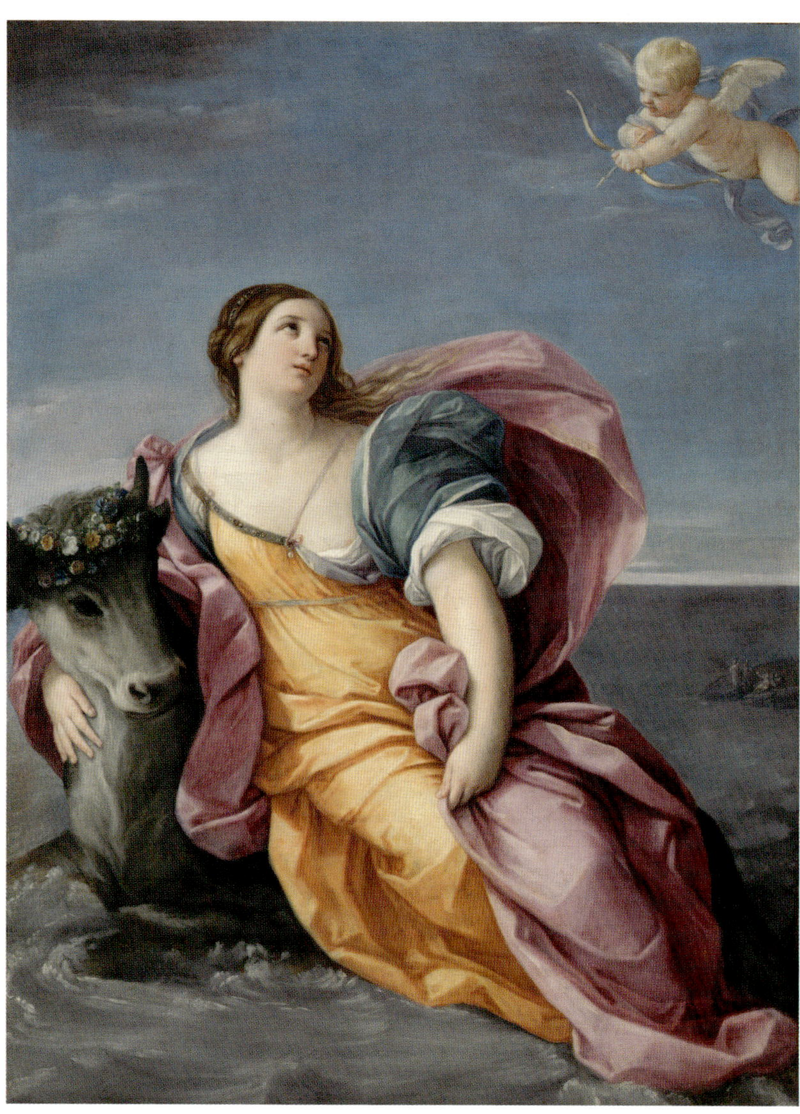

[FIG. 37]
Guido Reni, *The Rape of Europa*, 1637–39. Oil on canvas, 177 × 129.5 cm. National Gallery, London, Presented by the Trustees of Sir Denis Mahon's Charitable Trust through the Art Fund, 2013 (NG6642).

It was well known that exposure to light that was a major cause of pigment change. Treatises such as Antonio Palomino's *El museo pictórico y escala* (1724) suggest placing paintings in sunlight to bleach an oil medium that tended to yellow the surface. Yet he also recognized the danger of losing color from vulnerable paints as a possible drawback to this practice. Thomas Gainsborough (1727–1788) depended on fugitive red lakes in his work. Some of his paintings diminished in intensity as carmine lakes, based on cochineal, lost their color. In Gainsborough's portrait of *Dr. Ralph Schomberg* (ca. 1770; National Gallery, London) the sitter wears a pinkish brown coat in which a red glaze was applied unevenly over a light brownish yellow underpaint. The red in the thinner areas has faded and all but disappeared but has largely retained its color in the thicker parts, leading to an unintended patchiness in the overall tonality. Moreover, there is a correlation between the lightness of the underpaint and the apparent amount of fading. The deeper red is preserved not only where it is thickest and over a darker underlayer, but also where it passes under, and is protected by impasto, applied on top. Under close examination, it is possible to see remnants of stronger color in the shadow of the upper paint.

The eighteenth-century English painter most notoriously indifferent to sound practice and stable materials was Sir Joshua Reynolds (1723–1792). Due to risky choices of mixtures of pigment and medium, some of his works took months to dry and began to crack and shrivel within a relatively short time. He was interested in the immediate effect and the apparent richness of his materials upon completion and experimented on his canvases with unconventional materials: a beautiful dark, translucent brown might be chosen for its sumptuous color, regardless of its inherent instability. Reynolds wrote about technique, but his knowledge did not seem to deter him from making ill-advised decisions in his own work. For the faces of several of his portraits, he used fugitive red lakes, the properties of which surely must have been known to him. Today, those sitters look out at the world with deathly white features. Later in his career, Reynolds made some attempt to correct his propensity for using fading flesh tones, which were already the subject of contemporary comment. In a few late works, he used nonfading vermilion and red earths instead of carmine, but he continued to flirt with unstable colors right to the end.

Yellow lake pigments are even more prone to fading than red lakes. Color loss has a prominent effect in Dutch flower paintings in which green leaves were created by mixing blue and yellow or glazing yellow over blue. The disappearance of the yellow, either by fading or perhaps aggravated past cleaning methods, is a phenomenon encountered throughout Old Master collections. One well-known example is *Flowers in a Terracotta Vase* [FIG. 38] by Jan van Huysum (1682–1749). When the discolored varnish and grime were removed from the painting's surface and bright blue foliage emerged, it prompted an interesting debate concerning cleaning, changing materials, and artistic intent. Before cleaning, the change in the color of the leaves could hardly be detected since the yellow varnish had replaced the missing yellow tone and caused the leaves to appear similar to their original color. After removing the varnish, the alteration to Van Huysum's green became fully visible, which raised the question of which is closer to the artist's intent: The picture before cleaning with its color relationships subdued by the yellow varnish but more or less intact or the picture after cleaning with its true colors glowingly evident but unbalanced by the unnaturally blue foliage?

The painting could have been cleaned and restored differently to arrive at a compromise solution for the loss of the yellow pigment. It could have been partially cleaned, leaving a thinner layer of yellow varnish, which would have compensated for the faded yellow while allowing the true colors to show. Or it could have been selectively cleaned so that the yellow varnish was retained on the foliage but removed everywhere else. Another alternative would have been to clean it fully and then put a yellow glaze back on the blue foliage to compensate. So, there are various choices in treatment that lead to different aesthetic outcomes. Thus, every cleaning and restoration is a critical act of interpretation that depends on understanding the chemistry of pigments.

The fading of yellow lakes is obvious in a case such as the Van Huysum but is more difficult to detect in other circumstances. In the calm, poised interior scenes of Vermeer, for example, we often encounter a beautiful pale yellow in the garments of some figures. It consists largely of the stable pigment lead-tin yellow, but it is only by microscopic studies that substantial amounts of chalk are also detected. This occurrence is due to the presence of a yellow lake, now completely colorless. The implication is that Vermeer originally intended these areas to be a stronger and warmer yellow than they now appear.

Fading is the main color change that occurs with these unstable yellows, but there is another phenomenon that occurs with certain painters. The landscapes of Claude Lorrain (1600–1682) and Aelbert Cuyp (1620–1691) are especially prone to *blanching* in the green areas. This phenomenon is a combination of loss of color with a hazy, whitish appearance that may be highly localized in specific features such as leaves and plants or spread across entire sections of the composition. The change is likely light induced or influenced by exposure to the atmosphere as suggested by unaltered strips of paint in areas that were protected by the frames.

Cuyp's *Large Dort* has been studied extensively at the National Gallery, London, and the color degradation mapped across its surface. The mechanism of blanching in paint is still not entirely understood, but it

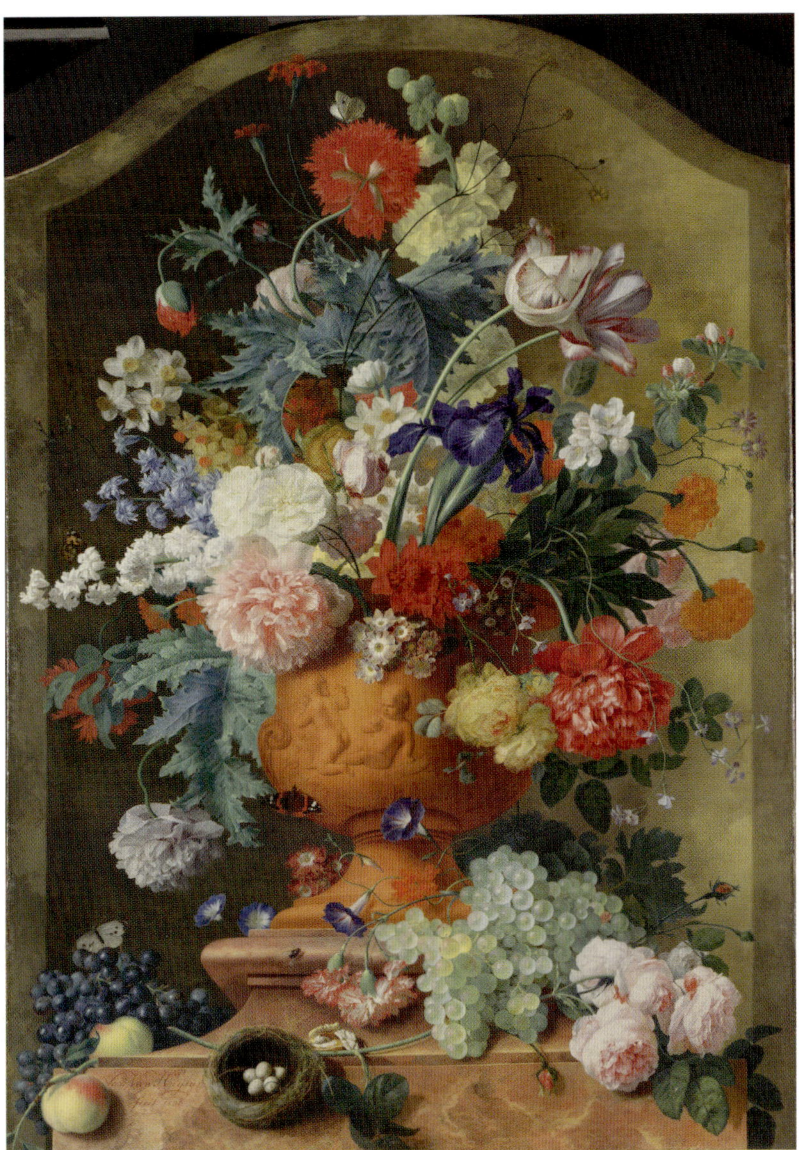

[FIG. 38]
Jan van Huysum, *Flowers in a Terracotta Vase*, 1736–37. Oil on canvas, 133.5 × 91.5 cm. National Gallery, London, Bought, 1869 (NG796).

seems to accompany certain pigment and medium combinations. To make his green paints, Cuyp used the unusual blue pigment vivianite, a rather rare iron mineral ($Fe_3(PO_4)_2 \cdot 8H_2O$) sometimes called blue earth, mixed with a chalk-based weld-yellow pigment. Vivianite is not stable and weld lake is highly fugitive, so the chances of such a green surviving were low. However, the blanching or whitening of these areas is due to something more than simple fading or color change. Likely, we are seeing the white chalk base, left behind as the yellow disappeared. In addition, micro-cracks and fissures developed within the paint layers in these parts, and by the scattering of incident light, the paint appears gray and hazy. This effect has been known for some time, and restorers in the past attempted to counteract it by rubbing oil and varnish into the surface to fill the tiny cracks. This treatment can only be partially successful if the cracks are near the surface, and, in time, it leads to more problems as the added oil and varnish darken.

The blue pigment smalt, as already noted, is not permanent. A long-term problem is that as smalt-containing paints age, they lose color as a result of deterioration of the unstable glass network. In addition, the low refractive index—essentially, the high transparency—and diminishing tinting strength of the cobalt glass allow darkening of the oil medium to play a greater part in the overall tonality. The visual trajectory of deterioration over time is a gradual loss of the blue, ending up as a dull, grayish, cloudy brown. In *Madonna of the Stars* [FIG. 39] by Tintoretto (1518–1594), the effect of the juxtaposition of a blue or purple mantle and the intense yellow mandorla that surrounds the Virgin is completely lost due to the degradation of smalt.

Rembrandt used smalt extensively in his later paintings. It is often difficult to realize that deterioration has taken place because the dull brown of the degraded pigment tends to blend in with the typical Rembrandt tonality. Many of his paintings are, however, considerably less colorful and detailed than they appeared originally. Rembrandt's *Homer* is severely affected by the deterioration of the smalt paints. Although thickly applied light paint areas of his face, his right hand, and the golden yellow of his shawl are reasonably well preserved, the rest of Homer's garment and his cap now appear an almost monochrome brown with most of the detailing lost. These areas show little contrast with the background, and the spatial illusion in the painting is difficult to read.

Wherever smalt was used—skies, drapery, landscape—the artist's original intention has been compromised. Subtle or bright colors have been reduced to drab monochromes in many cases. In many canvases by Paolo Veronese (1528–1588), from a slightly earlier period, the skies, originally pale blue, have become pale brown, and the brilliance of one of the great colorists in European art can no longer be seen fully. This

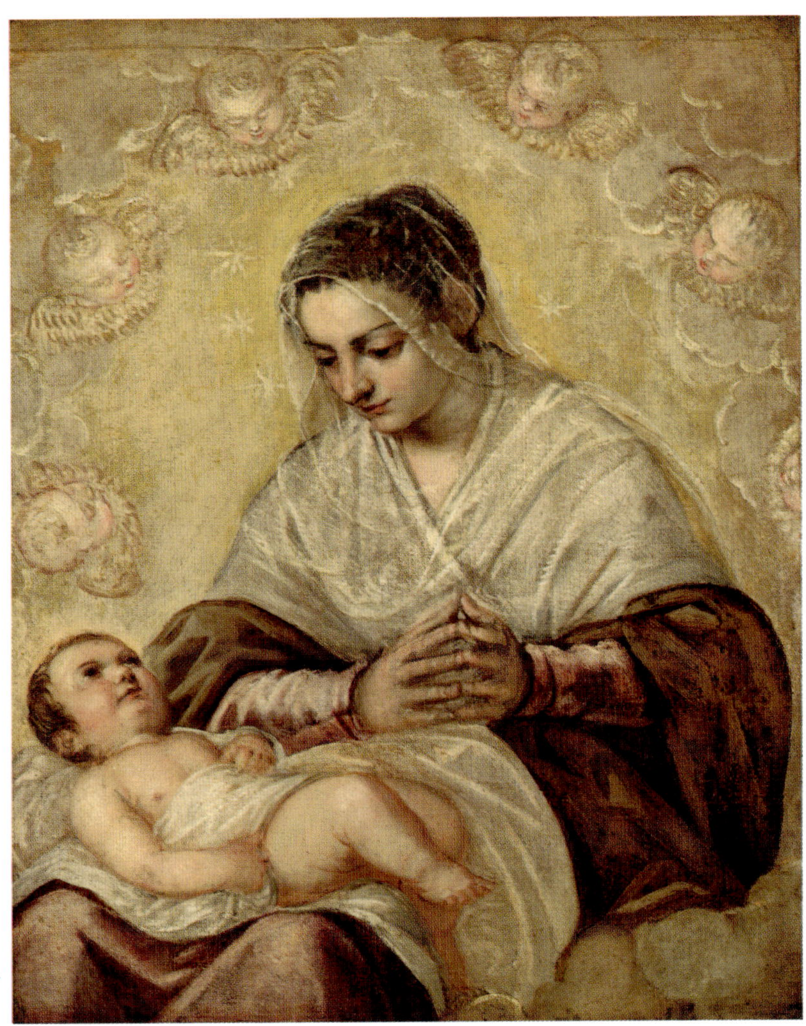

[FIG. 39]
Jacopo Tintoretto and
Workshop, *The Madonna
of the Stars*, ca. 1575/85.
Oil on canvas, 92.7 × 72.7
cm. National Gallery of Art,
Washington, D.C., Ralph
and Mary Booth Collection
(1947.6.6).

pervasiveness of fading is so widespread that it has led art historians to wrongly assume that it was a deliberate device by the painter to imitate the paler color of frescoes and flatten perspective within the compositions. The actual loss of color became evident only when the pigments in these paintings were analyzed.

When first made in the early eighteenth century, Prussian blue was hailed as the answer to the various drawbacks of blue pigments available in the seventeenth century. With its high tinting power and translucency, it became the blue pigment of choice for most European artists. Despite its clear advantages, however, it does change over time, turning yellowish when used in pale mixtures, though altering less than smalt or indigo. Artists who chose it as the main blue in their palettes were Gainsborough, Canaletto, and Tiepolo. After using ultramarine in his earlier works, Canaletto turned to Prussian blue for his skies, and now many of them are slightly yellower and lower in key than when they were first painted. It is a subtle change that we are alerted to through technical examination and becomes particularly evident when studied in comparison to the early ultramarine-containing examples, such as the 1723 *Piazza San Marco* in the Thyssen Collection, in which the brilliance of Canaletto's sky retains its full intensity.

Studying works of art in multidisciplinary ways, including examination of their materials, especially pigment identification, deepens our understanding of them and how they might have changed. In the examples presented here, I have shown how knowledge of the pigments available to artists provides the viewer with an appreciation of the aesthetic milieu in which they were painted. When we know the pigments that were used and gain insight into their characteristics and histories, we achieve a stronger understanding of paintings in museums. The aesthetic approach to treatments is also changing because of technical studies that have broadened our knowledge of pigments as well as the ways artists mixed and applied them. Our willingness to accept change has increased, perhaps because we now know much more about artists' choices of specific pigments and are aware of how alteration occurs, and how complex, unpredictable, and inevitable it is.

Color Engenders Life: Pigment and Process in Prehistoric Rock Art

Carolyn E. Boyd

During the Middle Ages in Europe, skilled artists created masterworks using paint recipes that carried significance beyond that which was visually perceived. The unseen message in the medium had its origins in the materiality of the paint. Spiritualized materials composed of the four elements that shaped the universe of the medieval world—water, air, earth, and fire—produced an array of colors, the origins of which instilled life and agency in the paintings. Artistic participation in divine creation, however, predates the Middle Ages by millennia.

Five thousand years ago, in the arid canyonlands of southwest Texas and Coahuila, Mexico, hunter-gatherer artists created some of the most complex pictographic murals in the world. They wove together layers of black, red, yellow, and white paint to create pictorial narratives, ordered arrangements of earth colors codified on rough limestone walls. In Indigenous realities, such painted images are not passive props. They are reservoirs of potency actively engaged in creation—past, present, and future.

High on a canyon wall overlooking the Pecos River near its confluence with the Rio Grande, a small rock-shelter houses one of the finest and best studied murals in the region—the White Shaman Mural [FIG. 40]. Here, hunter-gatherer artists related a creation narrative that has endured in the myths and histories of Native America for thousands of years. This essay explores how color, the materiality of the paint, and the image-making process not only encoded the mural with meaning but activated the characters in the narrative it embodies.

The White Shaman Mural belongs to a prehistoric rock-art tradition referred to as the Pecos River Style (PRS). It is stylistically homogeneous with universal themes, a conventionalized graphic vocabulary, and a consistent artistic expression. Over three thousand years, beginning about 3640 BCE, artists from a hunting and gathering society created at least three hundred murals along the Rio Grande in the region known as the Lower Pecos Canyonlands. The murals are ambitious in scale

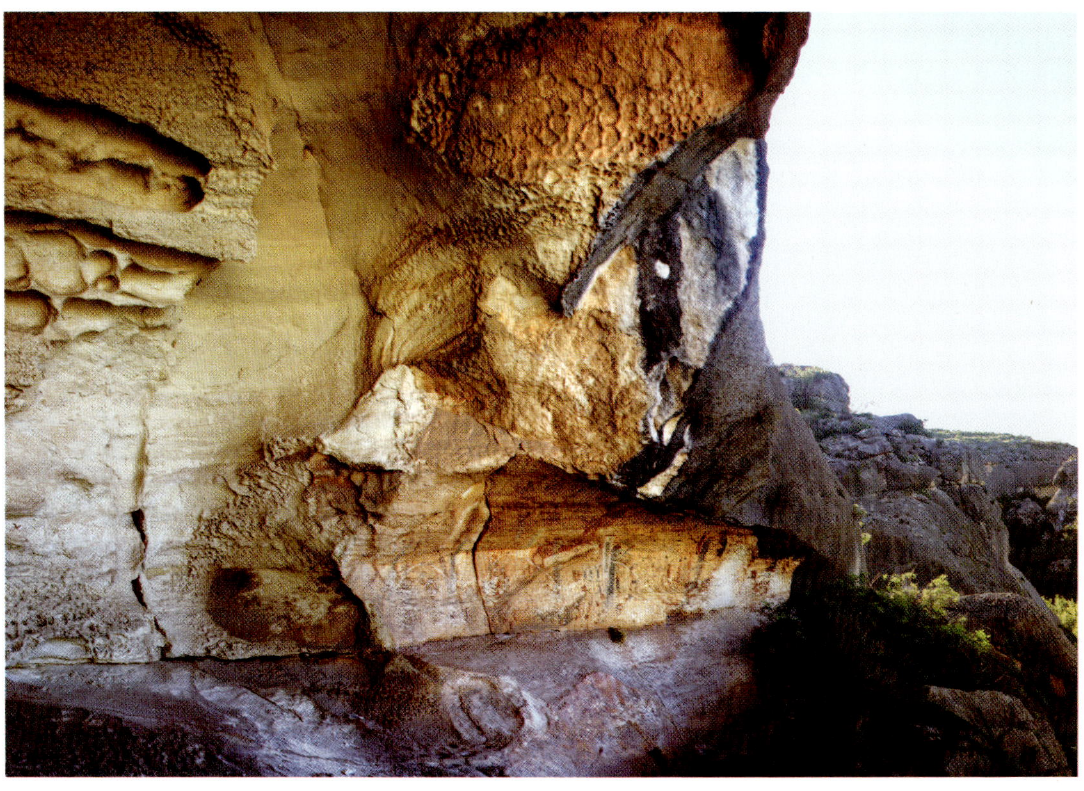

[FIG. 40]
Rock-shelter housing the
White Shaman Mural.

and deliberate in execution. Recent investigations into the use of color and the technical history of these artworks are challenging preconceptions regarding hunter-gatherer complexity and the function of art in Indigenous America. Recognizing their outstanding contribution to history and culture, the United States designated the region the Lower Pecos Canyonlands Archaeological District National Historic Landmark in 2021. The White Shaman Mural, stewarded by the Witte Museum of San Antonio, Texas, is one of the preeminent sites within the district.

Art of the Lower Pecos Canyonlands

The region is situated at the eastern edge of the Chihuahuan Desert. The northern half of the region lies in southwest Texas and the southern half in Coahuila, Mexico. Near the region's center, the Pecos and the Devils Rivers converge with the Rio Grande. The dramatic landscape is incised by deep and narrow canyons containing hundreds of dry rock-shelters. Within these rock-shelters archaeologists have discovered an extraordinary account of hunting and gathering lifeways that began about thirteen thousand years ago and endured until European contact. Deeply stratified and well-preserved archaeological deposits contain artifacts of stone, bone, and plant fiber. Above the deposits, painted along rock-shelter walls and cliff overhangs, lies a rich record of polychromatic mural art.

In 1931 artist Virginia Carson participated in an archaeological expedition sent to the Lower Pecos by the Witte Museum to produce artistic reproductions of the pictographs. She describes PRS murals as masterpieces of beautifully proportioned and arranged images. A few years later, professional draftsman and artist Forrest Kirkland provided the first formal analysis of the paintings, including a discussion of color harmony, picture arrangement, rhythm, movement, and action. Like Carson, he recognized the murals as complex compositions, suggesting that moving a single figure or symbol would upset their delicate balance and detract from their artistic merit.

A few years after Carson's work documenting the murals, George C. Martin led an expedition to excavate the deposits of nine rock-shelters just a few kilometers southwest of the White Shaman Mural. In Cave No. 5, Burial No. 9, Martin found remnants of an artist's tool kit, including a mano and a metate (mortar and pestle) coated with red pigment, a "stylograph" made by inserting a piece of manganese ore into the marrow cavity of a deer bone, a lump of processed black paint formed from manganese oxide pigment mixed with a binder, and a paintbrush made from the fibrous leaf of a yucca plant. In nearby shelters, he recovered other grinding stones used for processing pigment, similar drawing implements, processed lumps of paint, and a flat limestone slab, which he maintains was a palette smeared with red paint on one side and black on the other.

These items, and likely many others, formed the tool kit used by hunter-gatherer artists to create the White Shaman Mural. The same hands that fashioned the stone and bone tools found in the deposits deftly painted sophisticated narratives on rock-shelter walls and along cliff overhangs, transforming the region into a pictorial landscape.

The murals range considerably in size and complexity. Some are quite small, less than a meter in length and height, and contain only a few figures. Others consist of hundreds of figures and are 150 meters long and 15 meters tall. At least half the murals reach heights greater than 3 meters from the shelter floor and required a ladder or scaffolding to produce. Perched on these supports, artists used pigment crayons to sketch out and organize the elements in their compositions, employing many of the tools used by artists through the ages to complete the pictures such as brushes, straightedges, stencils, and oil paints. Oxalate mineral crusts now obscure many of the once-vibrant images, creating the illusion of colors faded through the millennia. Beneath the layers of oxalate minerals, however, the paint remains vivid. The natural crusts encapsulate the paintings, protecting them from exposure to wind, sun, and rain, and cements them to their limestone support.

The compositions are made up of conventional symbols that serve as graphic abstractions of divine and mortal beings, things, places, sensations, and experiences. Human and animal forms provided a framework upon which artists added semantically charged visual attributes. Animal forms consist mostly of deer, felines, birds, and serpents; however, it is the human, or "anthropomorphic," figures of shifting shapes, colors, and sizes that dominate the murals, both in numbers and meaning. Artists carefully chose from a palette of earth colors to create these figures, painstakingly bedecking them with headdresses of varying types, adornments attached at the wrist, elbow, waist, or hip, and paraphernalia, including atlatls (spear throwers), darts, staffs, and rabbit sticks. These attributes function like a graphic vocabulary, and their arrangement in the mural, not unlike syntax, conveys meaning. Selecting from this wide range of meaning-filled pictographic elements, the artists of the White Shaman Mural created a creation narrative that relates events leading to the birth of the sun and the beginning of time and delineates key features of a ritual reenactment of this cosmic event.

The White Shaman Mural

The White Shaman Mural is housed in a rock-shelter stretching twenty meters across and eight meters deep [FIG. 40]. The artists selected the wall of a west-facing alcove within the shelter as their canvas. The paintings are located above a slick bedrock bench that provided a workstation for them. Red pigment stains the shallow grinding depressions in the bedrock

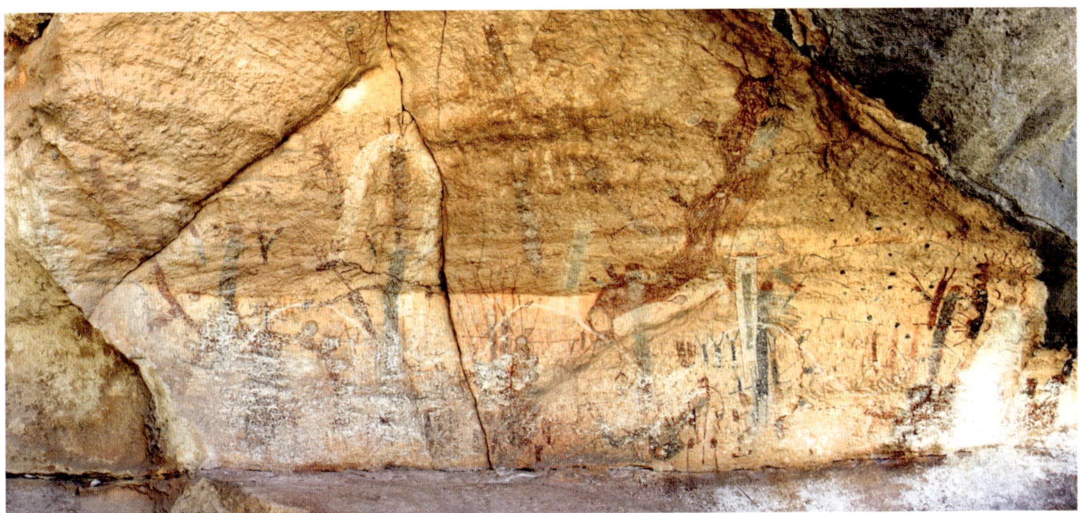

below the paintings. Even standing on the bench, the artists required scaffolding or a ladder to reach the upper registers of the mural.

The painting is eight meters long and four meters high and contains 117 figures in black, red, yellow, and white [FIG. 41]. Five black anthropomorphs with red heads are spaced evenly across the length of the mural. Each one carries two black objects with red tips. A crenellated arch painted in black, red, and yellow anchors the left end of the mural and a red and black crenellated bar anchors the right end. Two deer overlie the crenellated bar on the right end. Another deer is painted above the crenellated arch at the left end. A long, wavy white line terminating in black runs the length of the painting, connecting the five black anthropomorphs and their associated imagery. Using various conventions, the artists linked the five black anthropomorphs with other more complex figures in the mural. A red inverted anthropomorph overlies the black anthropomorph on the right end. Moving left, a striking white headless anthropomorph connects with the second black anthropomorph. Continuing to the left, a large snakelike shape painted vertically at the center of the mural overlies the third black anthropomorph. A white band runs along the side of the fourth black anthropomorph before arching over its head and connecting with a dual-antlered figure below. A series of parallel lines links the fifth black anthropomorph with a small antlered figure emerging from the crenellated arch. Variously depicted anthropomorphs plunge headfirst toward the row of black anthropomorphs below. Each is impaled by a spear. Just left of center, a long red line runs vertically across the mural. A small yellow circle envelops the top of the line, and at its base a large yellow circle surrounds an enigmatic figure bedecked with antenna-like

[FIG. 41]
White Shaman Mural.

protrusions and lobes along its body. Well-formed black dots of varying sizes are scattered throughout the mural and adorn many of the figures. The artists arranged these figures and others into a sophisticated composition that researchers have recently begun to interpret. Although the people who created the mural are no longer with us, ethnographic and ethnohistoric accounts of Indigenous peoples in the American Southwest and Mesoamerica provide clues to the mural's meaning.

Drawing on archaeological research, iconographic analysis, and insights from ethnohistory, linguistics, and semiotics, researchers identified patterns in the mural that equate to the mythologies of Uto-Aztecan–speaking people in Mesoamerica, most notably the ancient Aztec and the present-day Huichol. These patterns led to the interpretation of the White Shaman Mural as a creation narrative. The imagery relates the sun's daily cycle and its apparent path along the ecliptic throughout the year. It documents the changing seasons, the beginning and ending of ages, and the mythic pilgrimage and sacrifice that gave birth to the sun and time.

Beyond its portrayal of real-world cosmological events and cycles of nature, the mural articulates the ongoing transformations of people throughout their lives. The mural also provides a prescription for ritual reenactment of the cosmic event that realized the sun and time. According to Huichol myth, before time began, ancestral pilgrims traveled through the underworld to the primordial mountain. They carried the fire that would fuel the sun and light their path through the dark, watery underworld. Collectively, they represent Venus and the stellar sacrifice required for the sun's birth. The sacred deer guided them along the ecliptic to the mountain where they would emerge from the underworld and where their sacrifice would initiate the first dawn. Even today, the Huichol people in Mexico repeat this pilgrimage annually to ensure that the sun will continue to rise and set each day.

The White Shaman Mural creates a visible context within which the structure of the cosmos and its supernatural inhabitants can be seen as tangibly present. Thousands of years ago, the imagery was more than a simple graphic representation of forager cosmovision; it instructed, informed, and socialized the community and members of the society. As will be discussed below, it is the mural's place on the landscape, the materiality of the paint, and the painting process that put the actors and the story into motion.

Places of Power

For Native American peoples, certain places in the landscape are of extraordinary spiritual significance. These are locations in which important events took place during the time of creation and continue to serve as portals between spiritual dimensions. Rock art has often been used by Indigenous peoples as a physical marker of their special relationship to this sacred geography and to the events that took place there. The creators of the White Shaman Mural chose its placement on the landscape accordingly.

The mural faces due west overlooking the Pecos River and the Rio Grande. Looking south into Mexico one can see the Planos del Coahuila and, rising out of the plains, the Serannías del Burro, an impressive mountain range with elevations exceeding 1,500 meters. Each evening, as the sun sets, the paintings are bathed in golden light, enhancing the red and yellow pigments. On a moonlit night, cool light subdues the earth colors but enhances the images painted white. On equinoxes and solstices, light and shadow created by the sun and the moon dance across the mural, interacting with the imagery to activate the story. For example, just before sunset on the spring equinox, an arch of light illuminates the crenellated arch while the rest of the panel remains in shadow. This motif represents the primordial mountain and birthplace of the sun. It is where the ancestors emerged from the underworld carrying torches to fuel the sun at the dawn of time.

Another interesting phenomenon takes place on the winter solstice. On this shortest day of the year, as the sun descends into the west, its light travels up the mural until it reaches the top of the headless white anthropomorph, where it abruptly stops. Through an interplay of light and shadow the sun decapitates it [FIG. 42]. This striking white figure represents the lunar deity who in myth was beheaded by the sun on the winter solstice. Her decapitation marked the end of her reign as the ruler of the nighttime of the year. With the sun in power, the days began to lengthen and the rains were released from the heavens. These documented interactions, including sounds, smells, and the night sky, demonstrate that the White Shaman composition is dynamic. It transcends the traditional bounds of painted images to engage the viewshed, light, shadow, and other natural phenomena, each intentionally integrated into the composition. Unlike art on display in museums, the White Shaman Mural is not "art out of place." It was painted here, to be experienced here, and to remain here. It is part of the landscape, and the landscape is part of it. The movement of the cosmos—sun, moon, and stars—infuses life into the narrative, and the cosmic events portrayed are played out in real time.

Materiality of the Paint

Native American peoples perceived a universe in which a vital life force or essence imbues all things, including rock art and its stone canvas. Both the imagery and the rock upon which it was placed were alive and

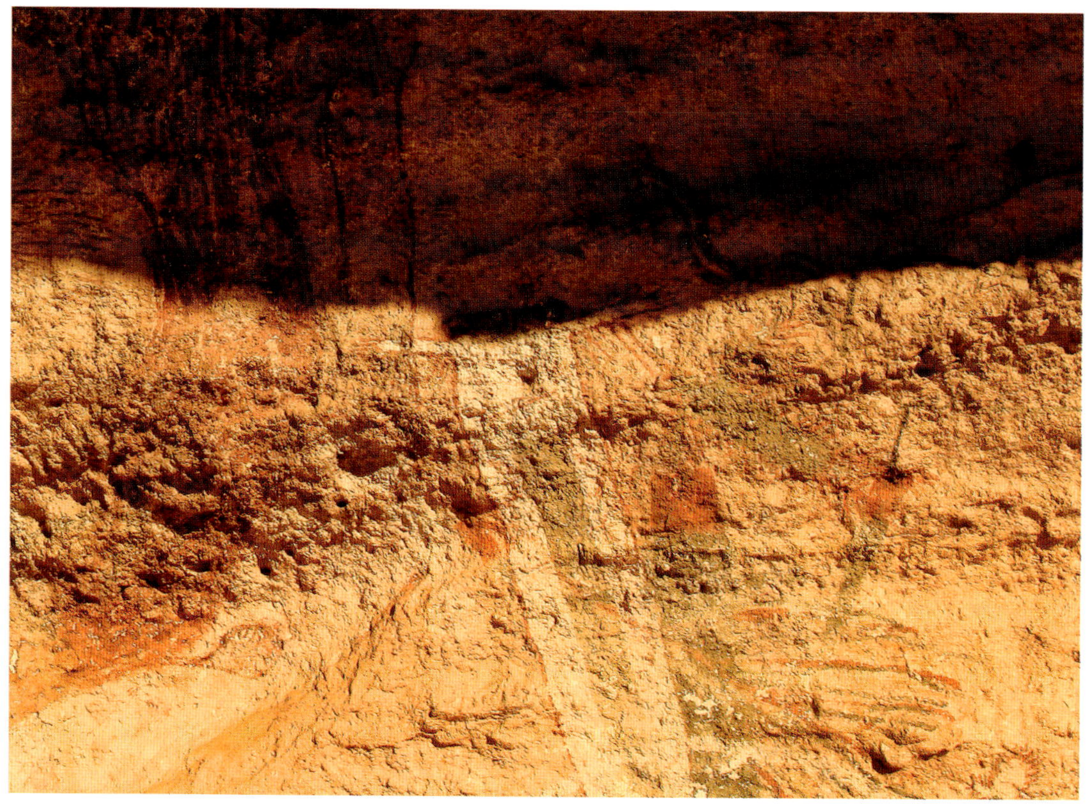

[FIG. 42]
Decapitation of the lunar
deity by the sun on the
winter solstice.

powerful. Out of respect, artists obtained permission from the rock before altering its surface. Deference entered every aspect of rock-art production. Paint-making involved two-way communication between the artist and the materials acquired to make paint. Whether mineral, plant, or animal, each was imbued with agency, power, and symbolism. The artist communicated their desires to the resource. If in agreement with their intended use, the materials would serve the artist by giving life to the images they created. Indigenous artists used a wide range of ingredients to make paint, each selected according to its rarity, religious significance, and intended use. Universally, the most powerful and sacred ingredient in paint is the color-producing pigment because color begets life. Color not only made visible the characters represented in the art but transformed them into living beings.

Colors are laden with potency and symbolism and are perceived as the words and magical songs of the gods. Colors are frequently associated with specific deities and spirit beings, natural phenomena, gender, locations, plants, animals, emotions, substances, souls, and the cardinal directions. Native Americans regard red pigment as medicine and one of the most powerful animating substances in the cosmos. In Mesoamerican cultures, red is equated with blood, life, spirit, fire, masculinity, day, and the crepuscular light of the sun on the horizon at dawn. In contrast, black is equated with water, death, matter, femininity, and the cold stars of the night sky. In the Maya language, black is a homonym for stars. Color symbolism for yellow and white is more elusive. Yellow may be related to human flesh, sunlight, and the sun-drenched earth. White is often equated with the zenith, Milky Way, spirit, clouds, vapor, sacrifice, transcendence, and transformation.

Color meaning is fluid, shifting according to context and the origins of the color-producing components in the paint. Pre-Columbian artists in Mesoamerica, like medieval artists in Europe, assigned value to colors according to the raw materials used in their production. These spiritualized materials possessed complex identities resulting from their animal, plant, or mineral origin. Meaning, therefore, was not limited to shape and color but extended to include the paint ingredients. Images were enlivened by the inherent, invisible force of the raw materials. For example, Aztec artists of the *Florentine Codex* used either plant or mineral pigments to produce paint of the same color, indistinguishable without chemical analysis. Their motivation for choosing plant-based or mineral-based paint went beyond obtaining a specific color. It was intended to instill the image with the hot, luminous solar force of organic materials (plants) or the cold, dark telluric force of inorganic substances (minerals).

In the Lower Pecos, researchers have conducted mineralogical, chemical, and elemental analyses to determine the color-producing agents in PRS paint. Using X-ray diffraction (XRD), they determined that the pigments are mineral based. Black paintings contain manganite and pyrolusite, with various iron minerals present. Although charcoal would have been readily available, PRS artists chose manganese as their source for black pigment. Red and yellow paints contain iron mineral pigments—primarily hematite and maghemite, with goethite, lepido-crocite, magnetite, and ferrihydrite also present. Subsequent elemental analyses using portable X-ray fluorescence (pXRF) spectroscopy confirmed XRD results, demonstrating that artists produced red and yellow paint using iron mineral pigments and black paint using manganese pigments.

Researchers used laser ablation inductively coupled plasma mass spectrometry (LA-ICP-MS) to source the minerals in red PRS paintings. Their preliminary findings indicate that rather than using readily available red minerals, such as red ocher and rhyolite stones, the artists extracted iron oxide from yellow siltstone pebbles found along canyon bottoms and processed them into red pigments. Producing red paint from yellow siltstones would have been a labor-intensive process that included grinding the pebbles into a powder, separating the iron-rich components from the quartz matrix, and building an earth oven. The yellow, iron-rich powder was then heated in an oven and transformed into red pigment. This finding supports earlier studies in which researchers determined that red PRS paintings contain a variety of oxidation and hydration states of iron, suggesting the prehistoric painters modified the mineralogy via heat to produce the desired pigments. The use of fire to transform yellow mineral pigment into red is well documented in the ethnographic liter-ature of Indigenous America.

In Mesoamerica, and likely the Lower Pecos as well, color meaning was not only determined by the inorganic or organic nature of raw materials used in paint, but by how the raw materials were processed. For example, Aztec deities associated with heat, such as fire and solar gods, were painted with red ocher. Inorganic materials, such as ocher, whose provenance is of the earth were not associated with heat, but with the cold, dark, telluric forces of the underworld. Through processing ocher, however, artists instilled the essence of fire into the pigment. They exposed yellow ocher to extreme heat in a fire to transform it into red ocher, thus, red ocher was considered a "burnt substance" and was associated with the sun and fire. It both emitted and received heat. The relationship of fire and solar gods with heat, therefore, was not only communicated through the color used to paint them (red), but how red pigment was produced. Form, color, materiality, and processing came together to vivify the Aztec pantheon and to express interrelationships between different layers of reality.

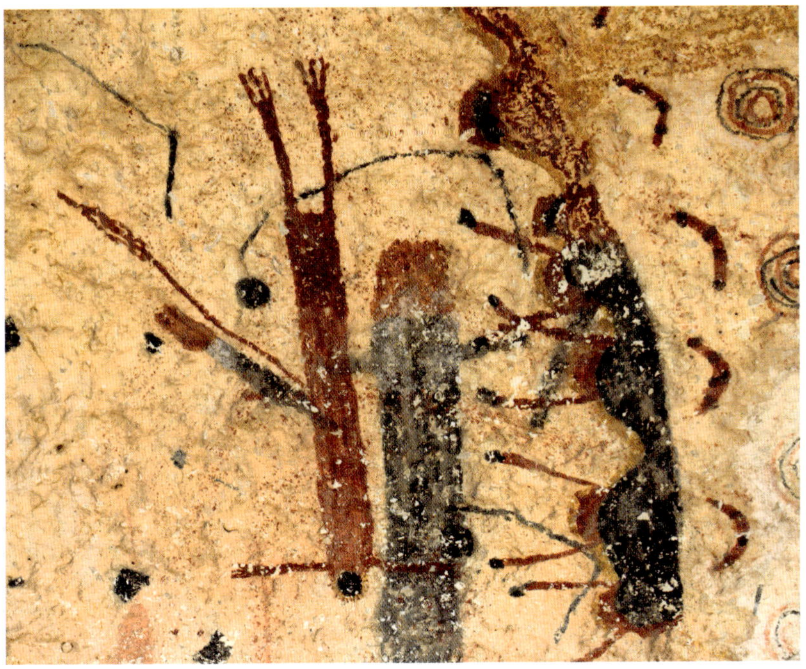

[FIG. 43]
An ancestor carrying torches to fuel the birth of the sun.

As discussed above, Lower Pecos artists used a similar process to obtain red pigment. Although red ocher occurs naturally in the region, artists expended additional time and resources to transform yellow siltstone into red pigment. The process infused the raw material with the essence of fire. In the White Shaman Mural, the black objects with red tips held by the black anthropomorphs are torches [FIG. 43]. The five figures represent the first ancestors who carried torches to light their path through the dark, watery underworld and to fuel the sun at the dawn of time. For the creators of the mural, the torches were not simply graphic representations of firelight; the red paint contained the very essence of fire. They were aflame.

Throughout the White Shaman Mural, the artist juxtaposed black and red paint as in the torches and the black bodies and red heads of the anthropomorphs. At the intersection of the two colors, they applied a thin layer of white. One of the most distinctive components of Aztec and other Indigenous cosmologies is the division of the cosmos into oppositional pairs such as red/black, male/female, hot/cold, fire/matter, and day/night. Creation is sparked by the union of these oppositional pairs. In the Aztec language, the powerful couplet metaphor "burning water" (*atl tlachinolli*) represented the struggle between matter/water (black) and fire/spirit (red). If matter won, spirit was destroyed. If spirit won, the body burst into flames, thus creating a new light that gave birth to the sun. All that exists on earth resulted from the union of these two opposing elements. The black and red torches in the White Shaman Mural signify the union of fire (red) and matter (black). So, too, do the black bodies and red heads of the figures. In the Huichol story of creation, the primordial ancestors not only carried the fire to fuel the sun but were themselves fiery sky bearers placed at the four corners and the center of the cosmos to sustain the newly born sun. Their black bodies, like the black portion of the torches they carry, are analogous to the cold, feminine essence of matter. Their red heads are analogous to the hot, masculine essence of fire and the sun. The juxtaposition of black and red, therefore, invokes the idea of creation. The white paint applied at the point of intersection between the two colors may indicate the location at which the oppositional forces of cold/hot, matter/fire, and feminine/masculine are joined to produce a third state— smoke, vapor, or clouds. It represents transformation from one state to another, the fiery sacrifice that fuels the sun. Again, from an Indigenous perspective, the torches and the anthropomorphs in the mural are not merely images, they are actively and perpetually providing the sacrifice required to fuel the sun's birth and creation. Color, raw materials, and the processing of the materials conveyed meaning and imbued images with life and purpose. So, too, did the order in which the artists applied layers of color to the limestone wall to create the narrative.

Painting Process

Using digital microscopy, researchers have identified the painting sequence for the White Shaman Mural. They analyzed 192 locations of intersecting paint layers to identify stratigraphic relationships among the 117 figures in the mural. The principle of superposition establishes that layers at an archaeological site are deposited in chronological order. The same is true for a rock-art mural: paint layers closest to the limestone canvas were painted prior to those overlying them. The span of time between painting sequences could be a matter of minutes or millennia, however; if paint layers of a polychromatic figure are simultaneously over and under paint layers of another figure, they are part of the same painting event. In the White Shaman Mural, figures are interwoven to form a single composition.

When the artists approached the blank limestone canvas, they applied black paint first [FIG. 44, top left]. Every black dot, line, and figure in the mural interacted directly with the wall. Black overlies black but never overlies any other color. This paint application order often appears counterintuitive. For example, numerous figures in the mural are infilled with black dots. In each case, the black dots were painted before other colors were applied, which created a canvas covered in a multitude of black dots. After the black paint dried, the artist applied red [FIG. 44, bottom left]. The red paint overlies black paint, but the black paint never overlies red. In the same fashion, yellow paint overlies red and black [FIG. 44, top right]. Finally, white overlies all other colors [FIG. 44, bottom right]. This order—black, red, yellow, white—wove the polychromatic images together into a complex tapestry, with elements of one figure simultaneously over and under elements of another. The small red antlered figure discussed above is sandwiched between the black and yellow of the crenellated arch from which it is emerging. Together, the crenellated arch and the anthropomorph are interwoven with a black and white line that extends the length of the mural. The black line is under the arch and under the anthropomorph, the white overlies both figures.

Layers of Meaning

Nothing about the White Shaman Mural is random. Its location on the landscape, its viewshed, the arrangement of figures, the selection of figure attributes, and the raw materials used to make the paint carried meaning. But it was the artists' selection and application of color that engendered life. Pigment transformed and enlivened the images. Each layer of paint represents a layer of human behavior—a layer of choice and meaning. The muralists began with black, the color of femininity, the watery underworld, and primordial time, a time of perpetual darkness broken only by the cool light of the stars. Soon after the black paint dried, the artists applied red, the color associated with masculinity, fire, and blood. It is the color of crepuscular light, the fiery red glow appearing on the horizon just before sunrise. The union of red and black, masculine and feminine, fire and matter, initiated creation and gave birth to the sun. The next color applied was yellow, the color associated with the rays of the morning sun as it warms the earth and overcomes the cold black of night and the red of predawn. Finally, the artists applied white, the color associated with the zenith and the light of midday. It is the light that renders all of creation shadowless. It is the color of sacrificial transformation and transcendence and the return to primordial time. Moving from darkness (black) to light (white), from chaos to transcendence, artists participated in divine creation, weaving cycles of time and meaning into the murals through their choice of materials, color, and paint application.

From a Western perspective, rock-art panels are viewed as a collection of lifeless iconographic signs and symbols. The rock art of the Lower Pecos, however, challenges that perception and proposes a reality in which the artists imbued images with life through color and the deliberate selection and processing of raw materials, placement on the landscape, and manner of execution. The muralists lived in a universe in which all things were alive and equally real. In this perception of reality,

[FIG. 44]
Next page spread: The artists who created the White Shaman Mural followed a strict painting sequence: (top left) black; (bottom left) red; (top right) yellow; and (bottom right) white.

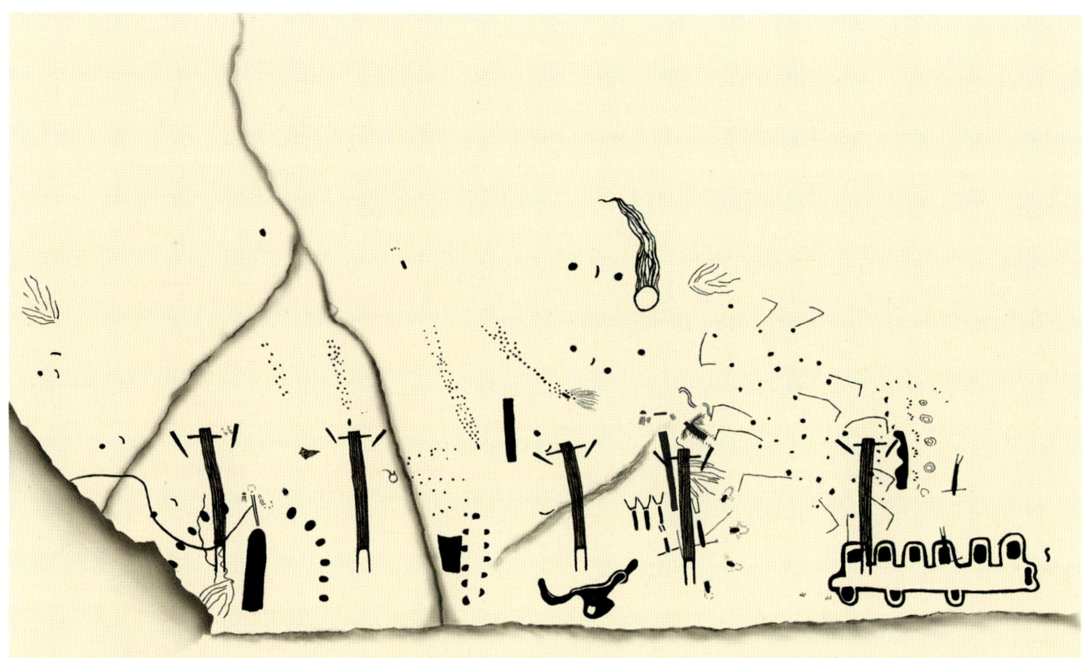

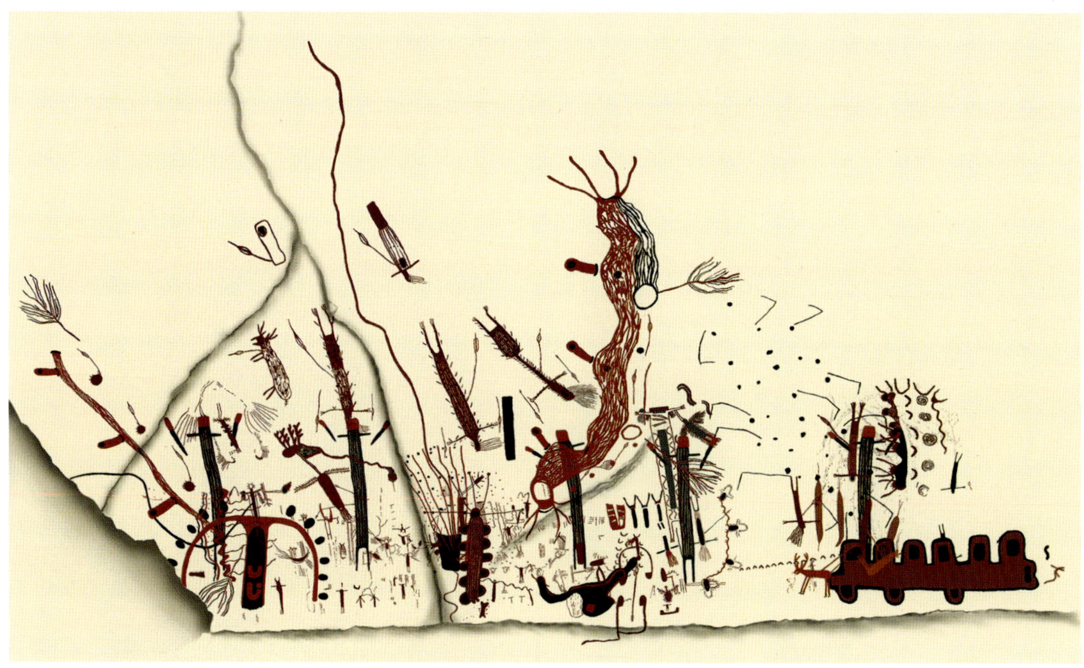

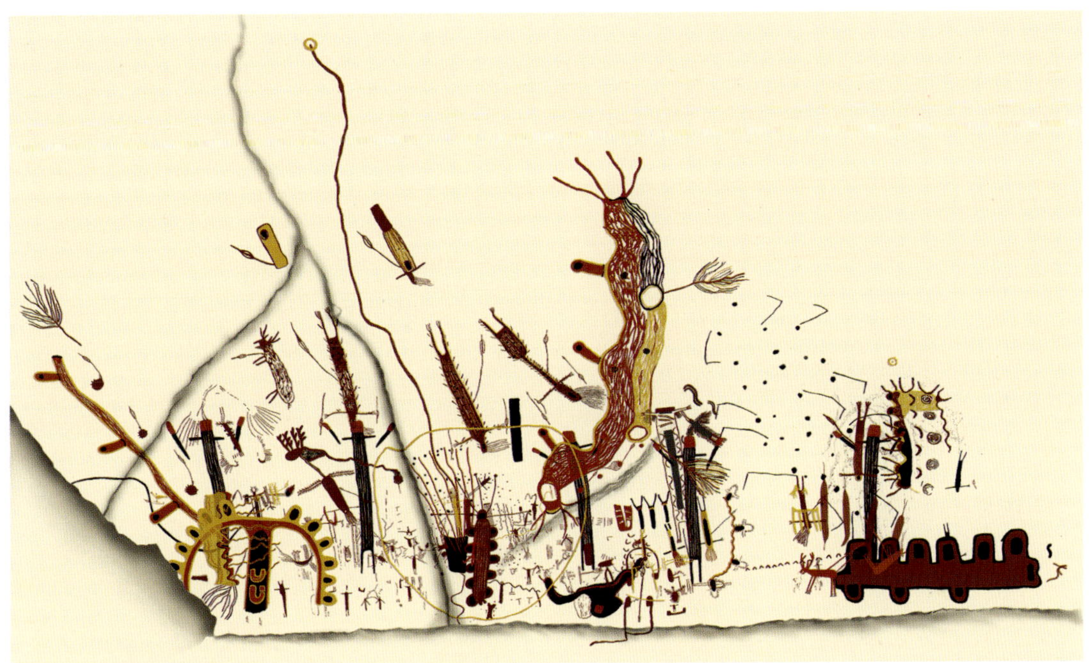

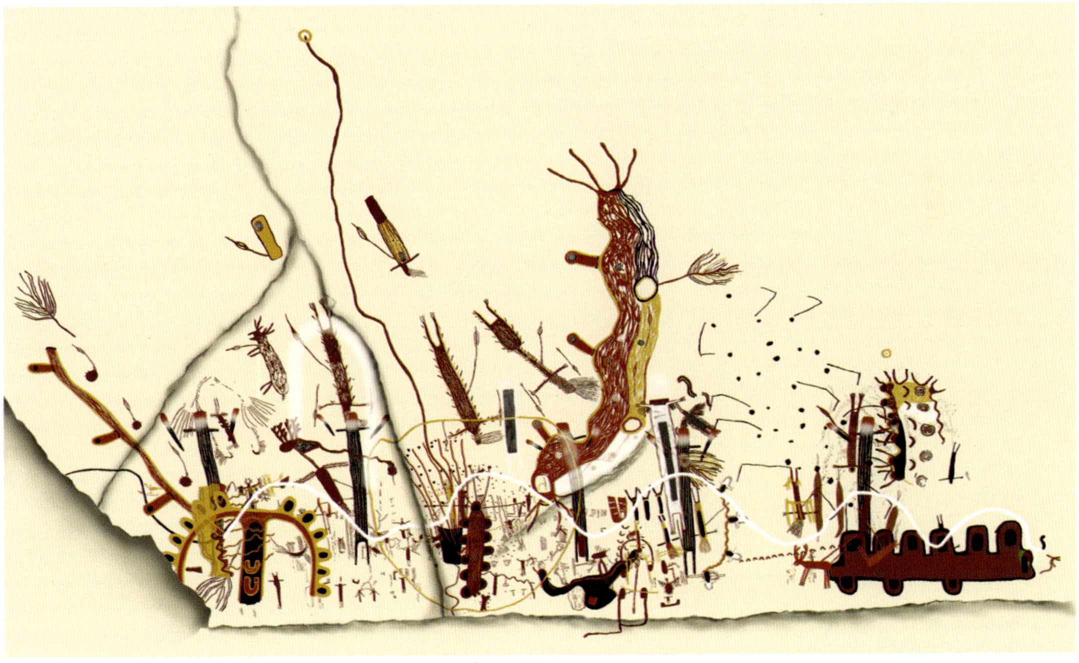

everything—including art—possessed the ability to act and react. The paintings were not merely decorative, instructional, or records of past events; they were, and continue to be, powerful, sentient beings that possess their own point of view and intentionality. From their place on the shelter wall, the incarnated images look upon and interact with the creation for which they are responsible.

Transmedial Simulations: Bronze Corrosions and Copper-Based Pigments in Chinese Art

Quincy Ngan

Introduction

Chinese painting and ancient bronzes are often displayed in different galleries, so it has been easy to overlook the intertwined relationship between pigments and bronze corrosion. Scholarship in the last fifty years has offered insight into this relationship by identifying the pigments and the corrosion products that appeared on ancient Chinese bronze vessels from the Shang and Zhou dynasties (ca. 1600–256 BCE). Copper-based pigments are closely related to copper corrosion products in terms of their chemical composition and appearance. Using this fact as a guide, this essay discusses "the mimetic power of pigments" (see Karin Leonhard's essay in this volume) in the context of Chinese art. It focuses on various copper-based pigments and explores how Chinese artists and craftsmen used them to paint, forge bronze corrosion, and enhance the aesthetics of bronze vessels and related objects. This essay demonstrates how copper-based pigments break down the boundaries established by the rigid taxonomy of mediums and reveal the deliberate choice of materials that artists made to enrich the visual effects and the depth of meaning in their creations. The transmediality of copper-based pigments—the way in which they establish connections among paintings, stone sculptures, and cast-bronze vessels—prompts scholars to synthesize an art-historical narrative with conservation science in the studies of pigments and dyes.

Transmediality—that is, the collapse of medial boundaries—has received serious treatments in both theoretical and art-historical discourses of Euro-American art. Such fruitful discussions can expand modern understanding of traditional Chinese pigments. Following this line of inquiry, this essay reveals that Chinese painters and craftsmen also used materials to reference other mediums, completing the functions and meanings of their creations along the way. This discussion demonstrates Chinese artists' "material intelligence"—that is, the skill with which they manipulated the unique characteristics of materials, including the "materiality of color," or the aesthetic, socioeconomic, and religious values of pigments and dyes in visual art. Such discussion is particularly important because the relationship of color to its manipulation is one of the least understood systems of communication in Chinese art.

This narrative uses the technical analyses of ancient Chinese bronze vessels and Chinese paintings carried out by the National Museum of Asian Art, Washington, D.C., as a point of departure. Since its publication in 1969, few studies have interwoven their findings into any form of art-historical narrative on pigments or theoretical framework about mediums beyond acknowledging that copper-based pigments appear on bronze vessels. The reports of the museum's scientific analyses of Chinese paintings were published in 2005 and 2021. While they corroborate their findings with historical painting manuals, how the choice of pigments become a strategy for constituting meaning remains an unexplored topic. In fact, pigments can create performative simulations—they convey the passage of time and evoke the visual and material characteristics of other materials and mediums along the way.

The first part of this essay explains how the love of color, or chromophilia, in the appreciation of bronze vessels led to the representations of bronze corrosion across mediums when chromophobia, or the disdain for color, is a prominent aspect in Chinese aesthetics. The second part focuses on azurite blue and malachite green, two of the most important and common copper-based pigments in the history of Chinese painting and in the practice of simulating bronze corrosions. The third part focuses on the transmediality and material intelligence embodied in using two artificial copper-based green pigments discussed in Barbara Berrie's essay in this volume: verdigris and atacamite.

Chromophilia and Chromophobia

Artist and writer David Batchelor (b. 1955) once said, "Chromophobia might not really have its opposite in chromophilia; chromophobia might be seen as chromophilia's weak form." His statement not only implies that color can bestow pleasure and anxiety upon us but also hints at the close relationship between the love of and disdain for color. The handscroll *Wu Dacheng's Collected Antiques* [FIG. 45] by the painter Ren Xun (1835–1893) aptly illustrates Batchelor's notion. The painting depicts the famed collector, antiquarian, and government official Wu Dacheng (1835–1902) surrounded by highly corroded ancient bronze vessels from his collection. This scroll is a composite of painting and rubbings that reveals both the love and the fear of color in the practice of admiring antiques. This threat of color becomes conspicuous when we consider pigments' power in simulating corrosions and bestowing a specious passage of time on newly cast bronze objects.

Composed of a colored painting and a colophon filled with ink rubbings, *Collected Antiques* illustrates the close relationship between chromophobia and chromophilia in Chinese antiquarianism. From the Northern Song dynasty (970–1127) onward, ancient bronze vessels with prominent blue-green corrosion were highly coveted among antiquarian collectors. These collectors studied the history, culture, and language of the past via its objects. In his own writings, Wu articulated his fondness for blue, green, and red corrosion. However, such obsession with colorful bronze vessels was discouraged among government officials, who were supposed to focus instead on national affairs. To counteract this restriction and to highlight the quality of his collection, Wu added, via a colophon, rubbings of the actual vessels depicted in the painting. The rubbings are made of ink, a material that epitomizes the chromophobic aesthetic in Chinese painting. From the ninth century onward, art critics and scholar-painters championed the ink and deemed colors a distraction. Therefore, ink became the predominant aesthetic. In this handscroll, the rubbings capture the ancient characters cast on the vessels. The study of the ancient words that often appear on these vessels—which inevitably probe into ancient history and society—has long been celebrated as both a pastime and a topic of scholarship among government officials. While it is common for a Chinese painting to have attachments like a colophon, the allure and the anxiety of color occasioned the equal importance of the colored painting and the ink rubbing in this handscroll. This equal importance of two different mediums is what the artist Seth Kim-Cohen called heteromedia: a "simultaneous, non-hierarchical, not-necessarily-coordinated, mixture of media ... [that] do their own thing, at the same time, with no inherent appeal to primacy or hierarchy."

While bronze corrosions could betray the indecorum of chromophilic government officials, corrosion products could evince the passage of time or convey an aura of supposed authenticity, a point attested to by scientific analyses, Chinese connoisseur handbooks, and Wu Dacheng's handscroll. Because the Shang and the Zhou dynasties were celebrated by many historical elites as the origin and model of Chinese civilization, bronze vessels and objects from this long epoch were particularly valuable. Bronze vessels and objects from Shang and Zhou were usually made of alloys of copper, tin, and lead. Each of these elements interacted over time with elements in the air and soil and created a variety of products in different colors. Traditional Chinese connoisseurs also regarded the presence of corrosion as the necessary attestation to the passage of time that established the authenticity and archaic temporality of the vessels and went to great lengths to discuss how corrosion occurred and how they differentiated between original and fake corrosion. In the historical discourse on *guse* (archaic color), traditional Chinese antiquarians

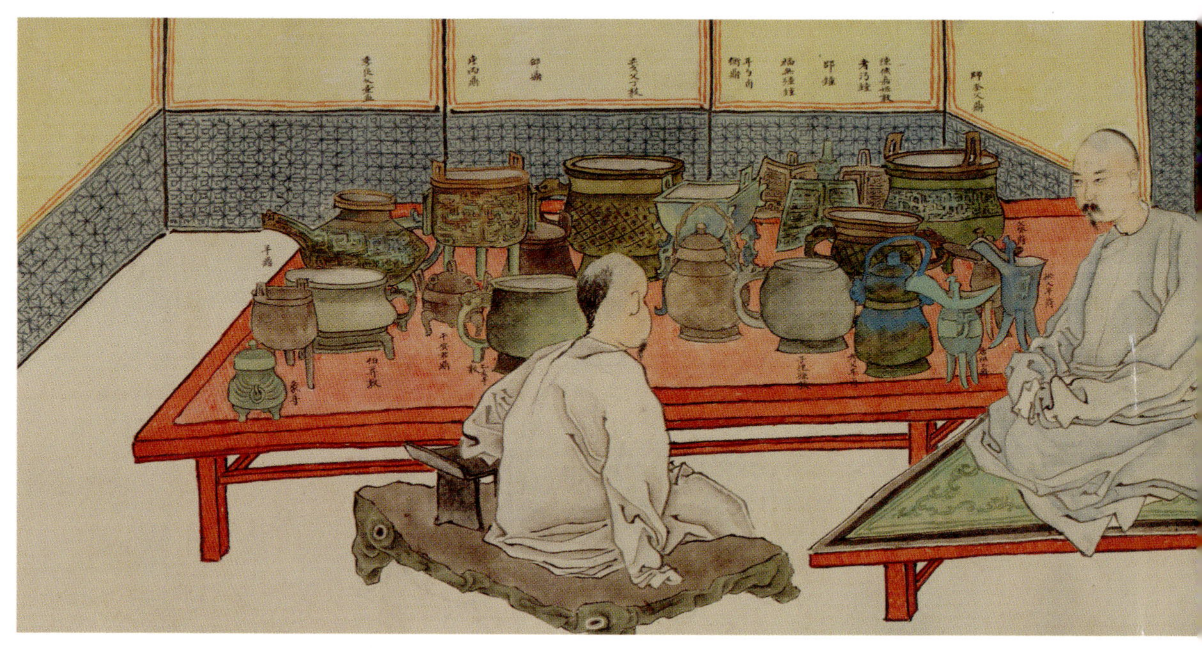

[FIG. 45]
Ren Xun, *Wu Dacheng's
Collected Antiques*, 1892.
Ink and color on silk.
41.5 × 1,452 cm (with
colophon, not pictured).
Shanghai Museum.

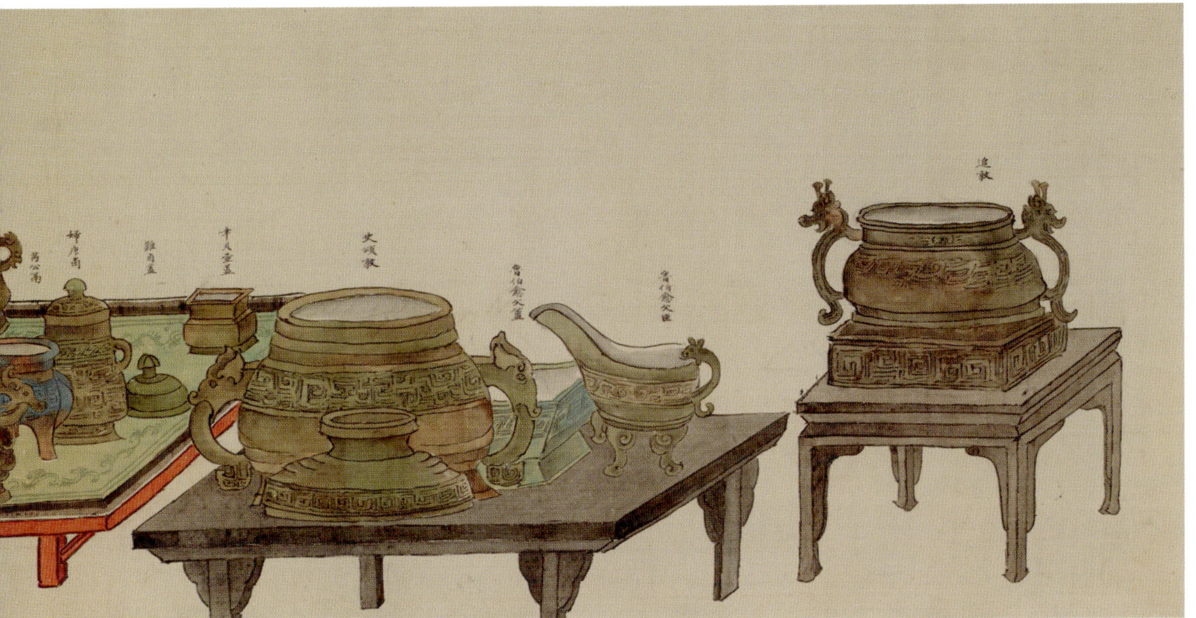

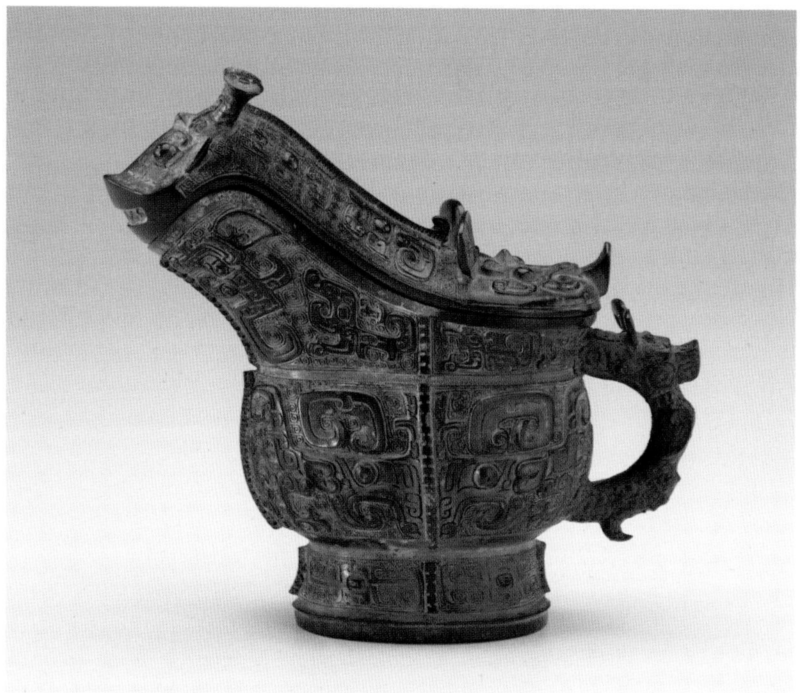

described corrosion with a variety of color terms that simulate an aura
of authenticity and archaic temporality in decorative arts. These archaic
colors include blue, green, lacquer black, silver, brown, yellow, and red,
most of which appear in *Collected Antiques*.

Simulating corrosion with pigments, a practice that is rooted in
chromophilia, resulted in simulacra that could both reinforce and
threaten the spell cast by authentic ancient bronze vessels. Scientific
analyses of the ancient bronze vessels in the Freer and the Sackler reveal
that a handful of them come with repair patches and parts covered with
a mixture of wax and azurite and malachite. These pigmented layers,
which are disguised as corrosion products, were meant to hide the
seam connecting the restoration and the original body and to simulate
a passage of time consistent with the rest of the object. For example, a
pitcher from the twelfth century BCE is adorned, especially on the restored
handle, with green nodules made of powdered malachite and an organic
binder [FIG. 46]. Some connoisseur handbooks state that the most coveted
bronze vessels featured excessive blue and green corrosions because
they indicated the period of utmost antiquity, the Xia, Shang, and Zhou
dynasties (2070 BCE–256 BCE). These handbooks add that those without
such corrosions were only from the Han dynasty (206 BCE–220 CE) and

therefore of lesser value. It thus comes as no surprise that some bronze objects from the Freer and the Sackler collections are adorned with pigmented mixtures that emulate the passage of time. Although these vessels genuinely date from earliest antiquity, the lack of corrosion on the bodies would have posted a threat to their authenticity in the mindset of traditional connoisseurs. Along the same vein, connoisseur handbooks warn novices of forgers who used this method to deceitfully enhance the aesthetics and values of newly cast objects.

For more than a millennium, ancient Chinese bronzes with colorful corrosion have been highly valued by elites due to their association with the history and culture of the distant past. Their eminent status has led to their omnipresence across mediums. Beyond being vessels-qua-vessels, they also appeared as motifs in paintings, and their forms were carved into jade and other semiprecious stones. This transmediality raises questions regarding how artists represented bronze corrosion in different artistic mediums.

Transmedial Simulations Using Azurite and Malachite

Revisiting Wu's handscroll and engaging with a stone curio of a bronze vessel carved from a mineral ore composed of azurite and malachite turns the discussion to how bronze corrosion is represented in painting and stone curios and the extent to which artists and craftsmen were aware of the transmedial bond established by their materials. Through examining these disparate-seeming artifacts informed by transmedial discourse, this section contemplates how azurite and malachite function within the color system of communication in Chinese art.

While Wu's *Collected Antiques* has not been tested for its colors, any blue or green pigments used for depicting the bronze corrosion could indicate the transmedial presence of pigments. Azurite and malachite had been used for millennia in China, so they are the most likely candidates when attempting to identify pigment origin. A case in point is the anonymous painting *Old Scholar Playing the Qin* (Freer, F1911.163a), which depicts an old scholar appreciating a wide array of cultural artifacts, ranging from bronze vessels to ceramics to scrolls. This painting has been tested for its colors. Azurite and malachite were used for the blue and green motifs. Scientific analyses reveal that azurite was the most common blue in scroll paintings before artificial pigments became popular in the wake of the First Opium War (1839–42). Thus, in the late nineteenth century, when Wu's scroll was made, several blue and green pigments were available: smalt, ultramarine, Prussian blue, and Paris green. All these artificial pigments, as scientific analyses reveal, were also used together with azurite and malachite. In addition, each of these pigments was used for forging bronze corrosion and enhancing the aesthetics of the bronze objects. Therefore, Ren's choice of any of these pigments could be said to illustrate the transmedial bond established by the similar compositions between copper-based pigments and some corrosion products.

While it is difficult to ascertain whether any given painter was aware of the transmedial bond that azurite and malachite can establish, a handful of Chinese paintings reveal that artists were conscious of the self-referencing power of materials. One such instance is *Portrait of a Military Officer and His Wife* [FIG. 47]. Executed on silk, it depicts a couple seated in a hall of their mansion beneath a tiled roof. While almost every inch of this painting was covered with pigment, at its center, which is also the center of the imaginary hall, an area of bare silk is left largely unpainted. On this almost bare surface the artist added some landscape elements in ink to simulate an ink landscape painting on silk hung in the pictorialized space. This painting-within-a painting is meant to indicate the scholarly taste of the deceased couple; the hanging of an ink landscape painting hanging behind the sitters also had deep imperial roots to convey a ruler's power. The artist drew on the self-referencing power of his materials or the physical equivalence between the bare silk ground and an ink painting on silk. He wove together multiple surfaces into a single pictorial space: first is the ground of the overall painting, or the surface of blank silk on which the pictorial elements are drawn, and second is the implied surface of the virtualized scroll hanging in the hall. These two surfaces literally coincide and give rise to a third illusional space in which various surface effects—ranging from "unpainted" to "ink painted" to "pigmented"—work in synergy. These surfaces help viewers to see the largely unpainted part of the silk ground as "a painting on silk"; the material literally conflates with what it represents, a phenomenon apparent in many other paintings like the Song dynasty (960–1279) series *Ten Kings of Hell* (Metropolitan Museum of Art, 30.76.292). In each of these heavily pigmented paintings on silk, there is a standing screen with an ink landscape painting devoid of color.

A Qing-dynasty curio [FIG. 48] serves as an example of how Chinese craftsmen intentionally used their materials to establish connections between carved stone curios and cast-bronze vessels. This curio is made entirely of a rock composed of azurite, malachite, and other naturally coexisting minerals and embodies the intricate relationship between the two minerals and bronze corrosion, but a few spots of blue-green pigments were noticeably added to the object to enhance its aesthetics, a practice also used for enhancing the appearance of newly cast bronze objects and miniature curios made of semiprecious stones. During the Qing dynasty, jade and other precious stones were carved into a variety of ancient bronze vessels in miniature. This practice spoke to the broader aesthetics in which one material was used to imitate, evoke, or simulate

[FIG. 47]
Unknown artist, *Portrait of a Military Officer and His Wife*. Qing dynasty, 18th–19th century. Hanging scroll; ink and color on silk, 75.5 × 107.5 cm. Royal Ontario Museum, Canada, The George Crofts Collection.

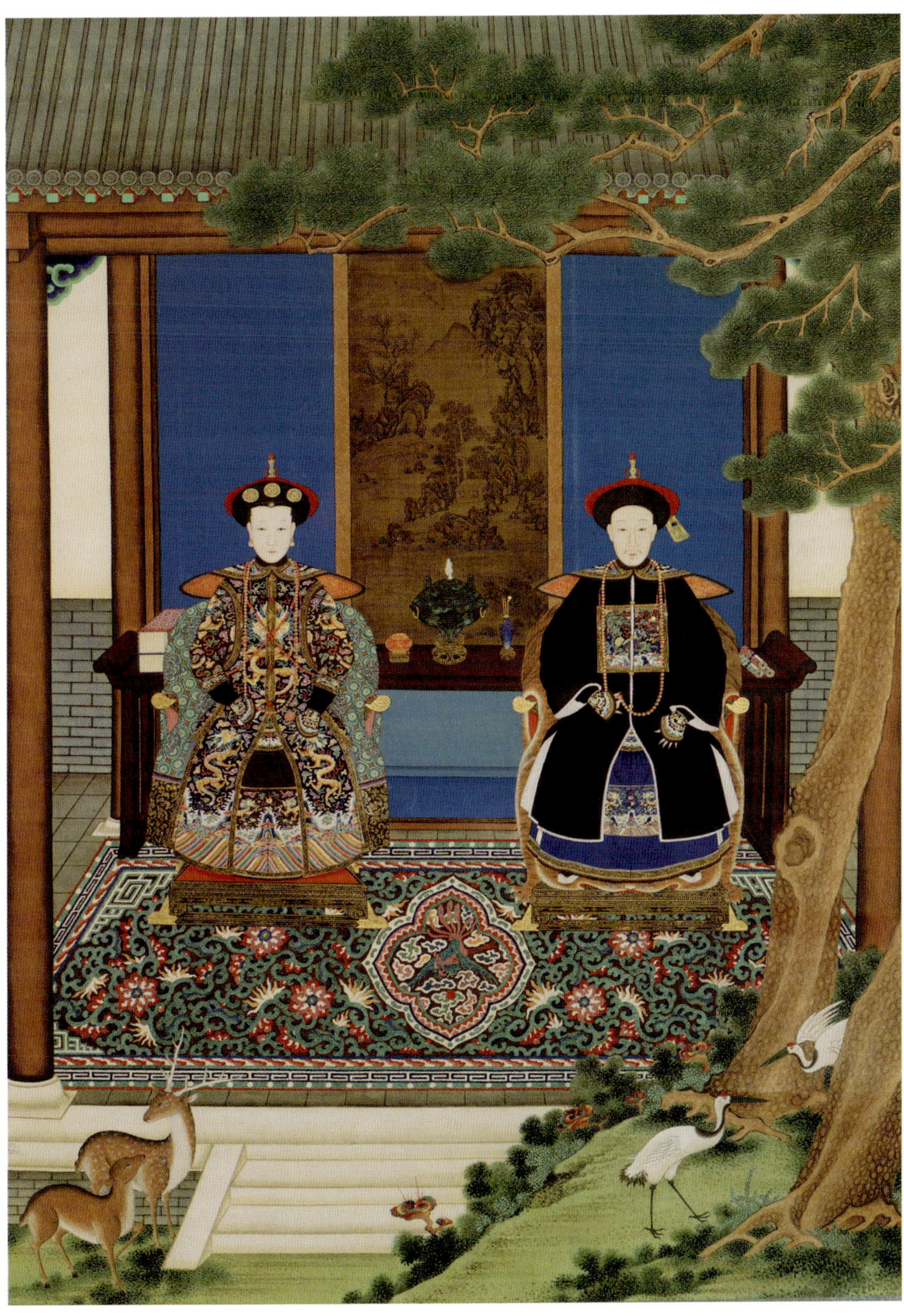

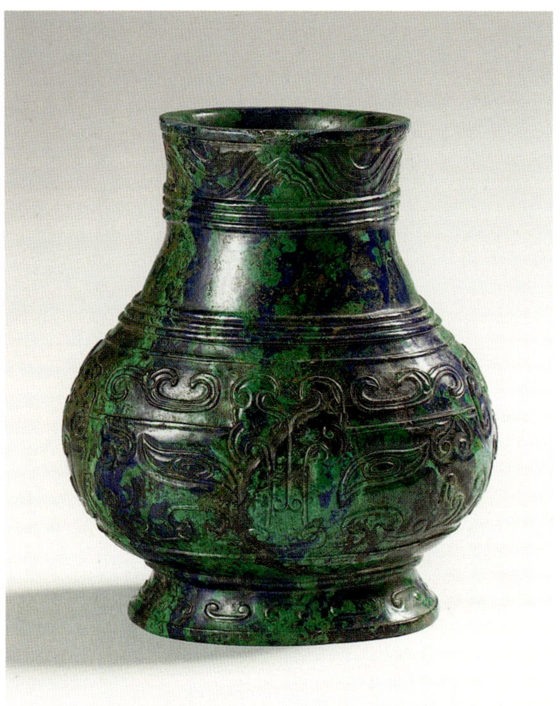

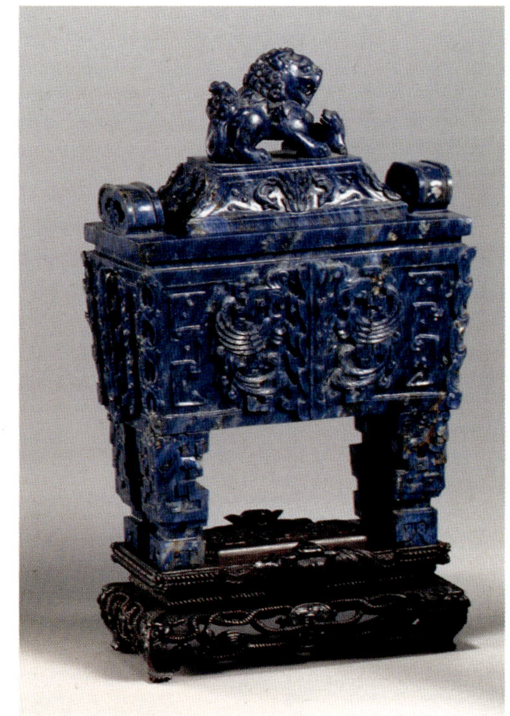

[FIG. 48]
Unknown artist, *Zun Vessel with Animal-Face Design*. Qing dynasty. Azurite, malachite, and other minerals, 12.4 × 8.2 × 10.7 cm. The National Palace Museum.

[FIG. 49]
Anonymous artist, *Incense Burner in the Form of a Square Ding*. Qing dynasty, 18th–19th century. Lapis lazuli, 19.69 × 14.29 × 7.62 cm. Norton Museum of Art, West Palm Beach, Florida, Gift of R. H. Norton (42.98a–b).

a different material. For example, a curio [FIG. 49] in the shape of a square *ding* vessel is carved entirely out of a lapis lazuli ore to apparently imitate a bronze vessel with excessive blue corrosions. Azurite and malachite occur on ancient bronze vessels as natural corrosions, and artists have been using the minerals to simulate corrosion products for centuries. Therefore, one can reasonably conclude that the craftsman of the Taipei curio intentionally drew on the material and visual similarities between the mineral ore and excessively corroded vessels. Unlike the example with lapis lazuli, which merely hints at the color of actual corrosion products, this Taipei curio is carved of azurite and malachite, themselves bronze corrosions, to represent bronze corrosions in a remarkable work of material intelligence. In other words, the material is conflated with what it represents. Apparently, the craftsman was conscious of the self-referencing power of azurite and malachite.

Two observations can be made from this liminality between mediums. First, the choice of material becomes a strategy for constituting meaning. Carvings utilizing azurite and malachite ore to represent excessively corroded bronze vessels rely on the ore's unique natural coloration. This relationship between the curio and the actual bronze is intermedial in the sense that one medium, stone, imitates a distinctly different one, cast bronze. This intermedial reference can also be gleaned from using copper-based pigments to simulate the hue of dyed textiles in Chinese painting, a point discussed below. Second, intramedial relationships exist when artificially aged vessels imitate naturally corroded ones, as when both objects issue from the same sculptural medium—in this case, bronze casting. This use of the two minerals to perform intramedial reference is akin to their functions in Chinese painting. A host of Song and Yuan literati-painters used azurite and malachite to convey a sense of archaism in their paintings in conjunction with modeling the styles of ancient works.

Transmediality and Material Intelligence in Using Artificial Pigments

Like azurite and malachite, copper trihydroxychlorides—which include atacamite, botallackite, clinoatacamite, and paratacamite—form a versatile, important group of green pigments because they appear on murals, scroll paintings, architectural decorations, and bronze vessels with both natural and forged corrosions. Copper trihydroxychlorides establish transmediality when these pigments were used to simulate the color of textiles in painting. In addition, verdigris, an uncommon pigment due to its instability, highlighted one monk's material intelligence and established an intermedial connection between mural painting and cast-bronze objects.

Chinese painters often used copper trihydroxychlorides and the mineral pigments cinnabar and azurite to mimic the color of textiles dyed with plant-based colorants, which underscores painters' pragmatic choices. Copper trihydroxychlorides establish an intermedial connection between painting and textile when painters used the pigments to simulate the color of green garments. In the anonymous *Portrait of Yang Hong* (Sackler, S1991.77), the attendant on the right wears a green robe generously covered with atacamite, the most common copper trihydroxy-chloride. Green color on a silk robe would have been accomplished by first applying a yellow dye (for example, from the bark of cork trees or the flowers of pagoda trees) and then indigo blue dye to degummed silk fabric. However, when such dyes are applied to the often not degummed silk ground of Chinese painting, the color appears dull. The silk ground also darkens over time, which would explain why the creator of *Portrait of Yang Hong* used atacamite instead. Atacamite can be artificially produced and could yield an equally brilliant green, which made it a more economical choice than malachite in traditional China. This desire to simulate the actual hues of dyed textiles can be gleaned from the use of azurite and cinnabar in the portrait as well. For example, scientific analysis reveals that the different shades of blue on the collar and sleeves of Yang Hong's robe and of the robe of the attendant at left were represented by different grades of azurite, which aptly simulate the colors of indigo-dyed silk garments. In dyeing, different shades of blue were achieved by using different vats and/or dying the fabric repeatedly. To simulate such tonal variations, Chinese painters could mix azurite with other pigments or, as in the portrait, use azurite of different particle sizes; for azurite and malachite, finer particles meant lighter hues. The collapse of layers of visual and material characteristics of pigments and textiles into a homogenized whole produced an intermedial reference when painters used materials to simulate a completely different medium.

Although verdigris was rarely used in Chinese painting because it erodes the surface of paper or silk, a textual record illustrates the material intelligence that this pigment conveyed. *The Record of Eminent Monks*, composed during the Southern Liang dynasty (502–57), contains an anecdote about the monk Fa'an (active early fifth century). Toward the middle of the Yixi period (405–19), Fa'an wanted to paint a mural in a temple in Xinyang county. Due to the scarcity of resources, he could not find verdigris. A person came to him in a dream and told him that two bronze bells were hidden in his bed. When Fa'an awoke, he dug up the bells, used them to make verdigris—possibly by applying vinegar—and finished the mural. Later, Fa'an gave one of the bells to his teacher, who melted it down to cast a bronze sculpture of a Buddhist deity. Fa'an's story was reiterated with slight variations in the Tang dynasty (618–907) Buddhist canonical anthology *Forest of Pearls from the Dharma Garden*. In this later account, Fa'an first preferred azurite for the mural, probably due to its relative stability. When he was unable to find the mineral, he sought verdigris but could not find it until he dreamt of the bells. Therefore, Fa'an originally intended to use verdigris to simulate the effect of azurite. These two records underscore Fa'an's material intelligence, perseverance, and religious devotion, notwithstanding the limited availability of resources, and convey how the understanding of materials, especially their chemical reactions and malleability, could facilitate creations.

Conclusion

The intramediality, intermediality, transmediality, and heteromediality performed by pigments, which are informed by the materiality of color, illustrate the mimetic power of pigments in Chinese art. Copper-based pigments, versatile materials, appear on objects ranging from paintings to bronze vessels, murals, and to curios. Through them, artists conveyed their socially and historically bound messages and desires, as seen in the chromophobia and chromophilia in Ren Xun's handscroll and the remarkable material conflation embodied in the Taipei curio. Pigments acted as vectors for communication among different mediums and between artists and their audiences. The conclusion that Chinese artists used the unique colorations and chemical compositions of copper-based pigments to create simulacra that transcend medial and material boundaries is reached by synthesizing conservation science and art-historical narratives. The material intelligence of Chinese artists, from the monk Fa'an to the curator of the Taipei curio, attests to the dictum that "there is no pure medium."

Acknowledgments

I am in debt to Jenny F. So and the editors of this volume for comments on this paper.

"All of It Green, Which Is a Pleasure to Look At": The Uses of Green Pigments in South American Artistic Practices

Gabriela Siracusano

When we first glance over the American continent, the recurrence of a certain color—green—becomes apparent. The signs of land that Columbus and his navigators would have noticed after long days and nights on the ocean were a green reed and a green fish. Among the initial perceptions of the American landscape, "come the day, they saw an island 15 leagues long, flat and without mountains, full of very green trees." On Saturday, October 13, 1492, a day after he had set foot on land, Columbus declared: "This island is very large and very flat and with very green trees and many waters and a lagoon in the middle very large, without any mountain, and all of it green, which is a pleasure to look at it."

America was imagined as a great orchard, humid and warm. In South America, in the territories of the Tawantinsuyu, which would later become the Viceroyalty of Peru, and in the jungle eastern regions, green would acquire these connotations and others. The exuberant American vegetation is shown in the first images by Europeans with deep, shrill, exotic shades of green, often in contrast to celestial blue skies, Indigenous inhabitants with their colorful outfits, and chromatic animals such as macaws and camelids.

Within the Inca visual culture, green was part of the set of dyed colors, not natural, and identified the Inca family and its environment. According to the descriptions of the clothes of the Incas made by Felipe Guamán Poma de Ayala in his *Nueva corónica*, we know that Maita Capac—fourth Sapa Inca of the kingdom of Cuzco—wore a shirt with a chess pattern made of *cumbi*, a fine fabric in white, green, and red. Capac Yupanqui—fifth Sapa Inca of the kingdom of Cuzco—wore a green and blue helmet and a shirt that combined dark blue with *tocapus* (geometrical motifs) in the middle and green at the bottom. The sixth Inca, Sapa Roca, wore a light green blanket. Guamán provides similar descriptions of the clothes of the *cuyas*, or queens, such as Mama Cora Ocllo, Cusi Cimbo Mama Micay, and Chuqui Llanto, who combined their *llicllas* (blankets),

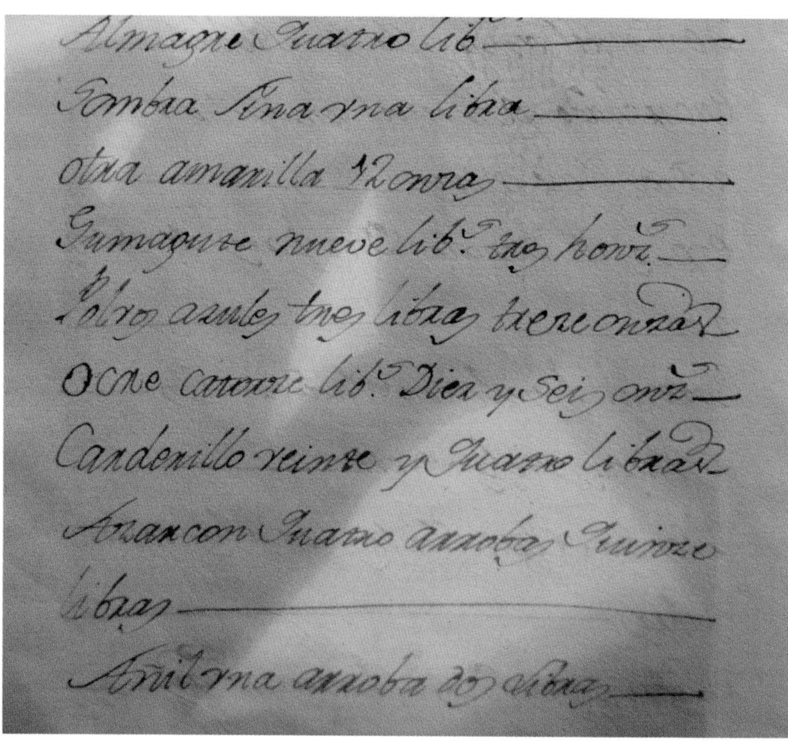

[FIG. 50]
List of pigments from
a Guarani Jesuit mission.
From *Testimonio de las
diligencias actuadas en
el pueblo de San Ignacio
Miní de indios Guaranís
sobre el extrañamiento
a la Compañía*, 1768–78.
Archivo General de la Nación
Argentina, Colonia, sección
gobierno, S.9-22-6-3.

chunbe (waist girdle), and *acxos* (skirts) with colors that would allow the
light and the dark greens to stand out. The precision in the colors and
the tones reinforced their distinctive character in a hierarchical society.
Guamán's description can be contrasted with the colors in the illustrations of painted Incas and Cuyas in the *General History of Piru* by Martín
de Murúa (1616). As recent studies have pointed out, green recurs in these
illustrations, primarily in the form of various dyes and pigments mostly
based on copper.

Other mentions of green during pre-Hispanic times appear in colonial
accounts linked to stones, bird feathers, and Andean ritual practices. Now,
as we know, the European entry into these lands came along with an
iconic artillery that would function for the purposes of political, economic,
and spiritual domination. There was a new visual system, with its protag-
onists and techniques.

Which pigments were used by painters to achieve the necessary green
tonalities for their visual stories? In principle, mixtures of blue and yellow
pigments were the predominant choice for producing green tones. Indigo,
azurite, or Prussian blue (since the eighteenth century), mixed with
orpiment or superimposed by glazes, were frequently used for green in

the painting of landscapes, the clothes of figures, and the iridescence of the wings of angels. The most common green pigments used for painting canvases in the workshops of Lima, Cuzco, and Potosí were copper-based pigments that either came already manufactured from Europe or from ores and mines in the Andes. Written colonial accounts mention pre-Hispanic pigments called *copaquiri* or *copaquira*—mostly referring to verdigris. According to these sources, in Andean cultures, many colors, and their corresponding material substances conveyed healing properties through looking, ingesting, touching, or even kissing and blowing powdered pigments to the rainbow in ritual ceremonies.

From an "archaeology of the making," we can confirm the presence of many copper-based pigments such as malachite; verdigris, or *cardenillo* (mostly used as a copper resinate); Verona green; and other green earths in a huge number of South American objects. Many of these pigments appear in the European painting manuals that circulated within artists' workshops in the territories of Perú, Bolivia, and the Jesuit province of Paracuaria under the Viceroyalty of Peru. How were they used and applied by the painters, most of them of Indigenous origin? Are we talking about the simple incorporation of these foreign practices and traditions, or can the material dimension of objects serve as testimony of an active Indigenous act of appropriation?

Let us focus on two groups of images: one from the area of the Jesuit missions of Paraguay; and the other from the highlands of Chile and Bolivia and around Lake Titicaca. The imagery produced in the Jesuit missions is well known for its representations of the ideological and visual programs of the order and for its testimony to the cultural inter-actions between the friars and the diverse Guarani ethnic groups that lived in the region. Although this was an unequal relationship, there are many signs that the Indigenous people found a way to express and maintain certain local traditions in the creation of meaningful simulacra and in the manipulation of foreign and local materials. For the latter, we know from the inventories compiled after the expulsion of the Jesuits from America in 1767 that storage areas were full of European and local pigments [FIG. 50]. Green shades for paintings and sculptures could be obtained by mixing indigo or Prussian blue with orpiment, by using different layers (or *velature*), or by applying malachite, verdigris, or green earth directly, usually over a gypsum layer. Written sources like Father Sánchez Labrador's manuscripts or the above mentioned Jesuit inven-tories frequently mention the presence of verdigris in the mission's workshops. Verdigris used as a copper resinate has been identified in Guarani Jesuit sculptures such as the busts of Saint Leon Pope and Saint Gregory Magnus (La Plata Museum, Argentina) that belonged to the Jesuit mission of Trinidad. The green pigment—often named *cardenillo*—was likely mixed with a local conifer resin. Another green pigment present in the copes of the pope and of God the Father [FIGS. 50, 51] in a wooden tabernacle and in the Virgin's cloak in a sculpture of the Immaculate Conception at the same mission is a green earth, or *verdacho*, a natural dark green mineral composed of glauconite or celadonite. Painting manuals such as the one by Palomino de Castros (1795–97) describe it as a "grayish green mineral paste suitable for all manner of painting, especially that from Verona." There is no evidence of this pigment in the Jesuit inventories or in other local sources, but it might have come from the European market.

Let us now move to the highlands of the Andean region. Nowadays, many different greenish and bluish shades color the hillsides and mountains. Together with the yellow and red tones, they are testimony of the variety of minerals that comprise the geology. Since pre-Hispanic times, there is evidence of several green minerals being used on objects and walls. For example, archaeological research developed in the north of Chile, within the Atacama Desert and the Tarapacá region, has shown the presence of copper oxides, copper sulfates, and copper chlorides in agglutinated pigments (pigments mixed with a binder such as animal fat) used in cave paintings, in leather objects like masks or helmets, and in the form of powders in funerary contexts. This discovery reinforces the idea of an ancestral technology for the use of these green copper minerals developed from antlerite, brochantite, chrysocolla, malachite, and atacamite, among others. Following the Spanish domination over the lands of the Incas, new green shades and mixtures would arrive, but the former ones remained in the memory and in the cultural practices of the local peoples.

The Indigenous painters active in workshops around Cuzco, Lake Titicaca, and Potosí followed manuals such as Vicente Carducho's *Diálogos de la pintura* (1633), Francisco Pacheco's *Arte de la pintura* (1641), and Antonio Palomino de Castro y Velasco's *El museo pictórico y escala óptica* (1715–24) in everything concerning the uses of pigments, dyes, binders, and varnishes in order to achieve experience in the novel techniques. The temperas and oils displayed on "new" supports such as canvas, wood, and walls required an understanding of that alchemy to paint the cloak of the Virgin, the blood of Christ, flowers and animals in biblical stories, and the iridescent colors of the rainbow. Malachite and verdigris were often found in the workshops and mentioned in contracts, inventories, and wills. As we know, the use of malachite—a basic carbonate of copper—in artistic practices is quite old. Pliny the Elder and Cennino Cennini mention it. Manuals refer to it as green *verditer*, *verde montaña*, *granillo*, *terra verde*, chrysocolla, or "green earth." In the Andes, Father Bernabé Cobo wrote that this "green stone that the Indians from the province of Lipes bring

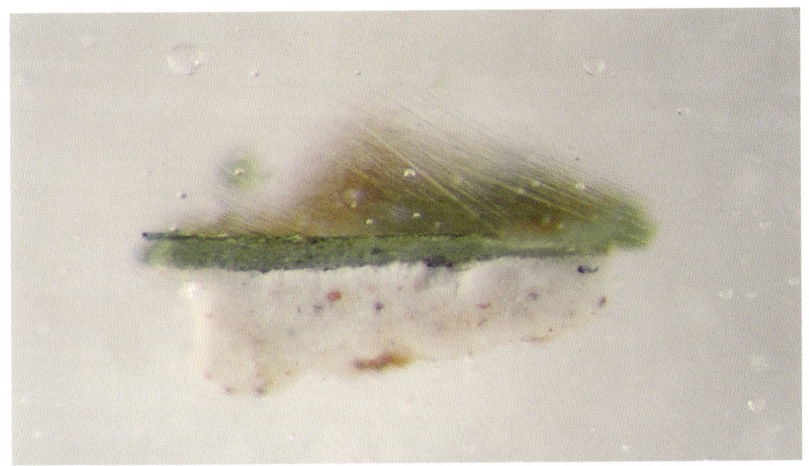

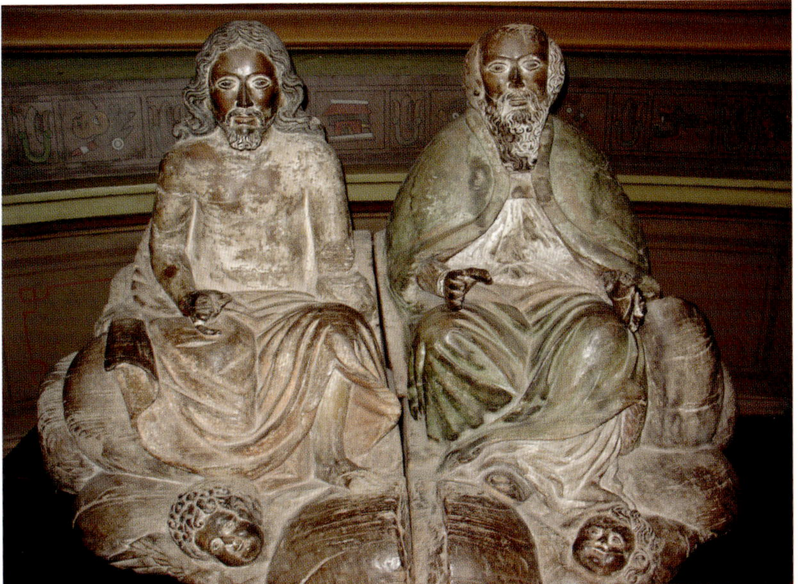

[FIG. 51]
(above) Green earth, or *verdacho*. Stratigraphic cut of the green section of the cope of God the Father. (below) *The Holy Trinity*, ca. 1750. Guarani Jesuit Mission of Trinidad. La Plata University Museum, Argentina.

from their ancient mines to Potosí for sale, and is called coravari by the Indians of Peru … is none other, it seems, than the gem Dioscorides named chrysolite. Besides being useful for painters for its lovely green hues, it is of avail for many other purposes" (1890, 272).

Those "other purposes" are related to malachite's pharmacological and healing properties. This pigment could be found in numerous ores in copper mines such as Cerro Sapo, near Cochabamba (Bolivia), and Caspana in the Antofagasta province (Chile), as written sources attest. Mixed with linseed oil, we identified it in three eighteenth-century paintings that belonged to the Toxo Marquis, at the north of Argentina: *Saint Augustine's Ecstasy* (Tafna, Jujuy), *Lord of Vilque* (Rinconada, Jujuy), and *El Carmen Virgin* (Yavi, Jujuy). The first two were painted in Alto Perú (Bolivia) and the last one was made in Cuzco. Another interesting case is its use as a copper resinate in the *Virgin of the Rosary of Pomata* (Casabindo, Jujuy) attributed to Mateo Pisarro, an indigenous painter who is supposed to having worked for the marquis Juan José Campero and Herrera by 1690. Pisarro applied it in subtle brushstrokes to paint the feathers in the crowns of the Virgin and Child and the leaves of the roses surrounding them.

As for verdigris, known in Spain as *cardenillo*, there is evidence of the use of this basic copper acetate called *copaquiri* in the Andes in pre-Hispanic times. It was applied in the Viceroyalty in a glaze to achieve intense greens, though it was usually not mentioned in manuals. According to the art theorist Francisco Pacheco, "Shun verdigris as you do shun the pestilence, for it is your greatest enemy." Nevertheless, it appears as one of the most common greens in the Andean region, often named in merchandise lists, contracts, and inventories. From recipes in the manuals and books of secrets that circulated throughout the Viceroyalty of Peru, we know that the Spanish tradition suggested it be mixed with a vegetable resin like copal. This copper resinate was used directly on the base layer for intense green hues or on a dried base of indigo for making *velature*. It is present in many late seventeenth- and eighteenth-century Cusquean paintings such as the series of Saint Catherine of Siena in Córdoba (Argentina). The painter Mateo Pisarro experimented with this pigment to obtain different hues by applying it as a *velatura* on azurite for the Virgin's garment in Yavi's *Coronation of the Virgin by the Holy Trinity*. Another traditional use of verdigris is found in two monumental series of the *Four Last Things* (Carabuco and that of Caquiaviri), both around La Paz and Lake Titicaca. Here, a transparent green copper pigment colored by copper salts of resinic acids was identified on samples from *The Purgatory* and *The Glory* painted by José Lopez de Los Ríos in 1684 in Carabuco. This copper resinate was also found in *The Glory of Caquiaviri*, in a mixture of resin, verdigris, and lead white [FIG. 52]. In both cases the bright green

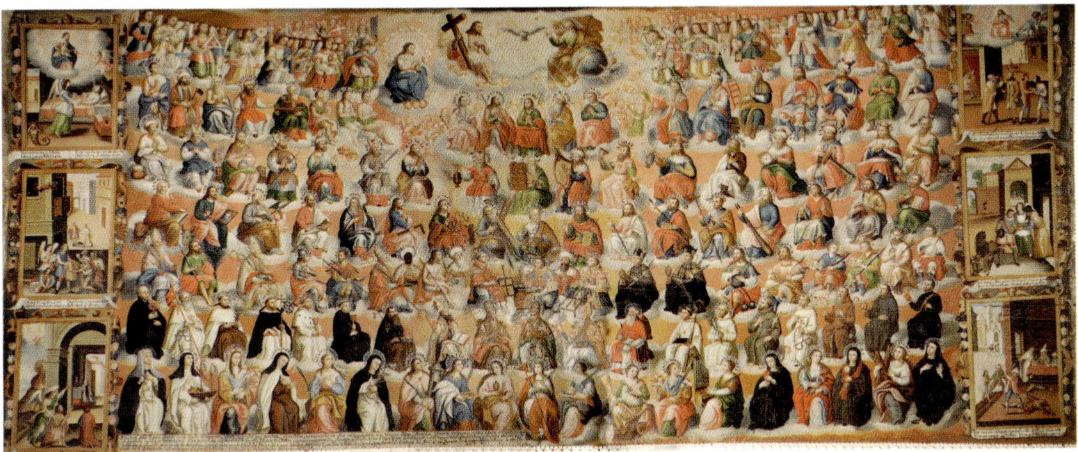

[FIG. 52]
Unknown artist, *The Four Last Things: The Glory*, 1739. Church of Caquiaviri, Bolivia.

hues, present in the tunics, clothing, and wings of saints and angels, speak to the Final Judgment, when the irruption of light in the "heavens would prepare the house of the righteous beloved of God" and "the moon will shine like the sun, and the sun seven times brighter than now" (*Tercero Catecismo*, 1585, fol. 740). The intense green tonalities would contribute to the spectacle sought by the priests who commissioned those paintings for evangelization purposes.

These symbolic connotations between pigments, chromatic perceptions, and the sacred enable lead to the final green pigments in this essay: antlerite, brochantite, and atacamite—copper-based pigments that do not appear in any of the Spanish manuals but were the main ingredients in the polychromy of sculptures and wall painting in the Andes.

Antlerite—a basic copper sulfate and green mineral—and brochantite are found in the northern region of the Chilean and Argentinian Andes. There is some evidence of their presence in European illuminated manuscripts and paintings on wood in the fourteenth century, though limited. In South America these green pigments were known and used by pre-Hispanic cultures, mainly as funerary offers. A leather headdress from an important man called the "Lord of Pica" from the Tarapacá region has shown the presence of antlerite, probably extracted from the mines of Collahuasi. The knowledge of the qualities and the possibilities of these pigments persisted during colonial times.

The geographic landscape that goes from Potosí (Bolivia) to the Pacific coast in Arica (Chile) provides some of the most beautiful views in the Andes and the highlands. It also witnessed the greatest circulation of goods and people in the entire region during the Peruvian Viceroyalty, especially those linked to the most coveted metal. Its extraction and use by the Spanish crown contributed not only to the world economy of the

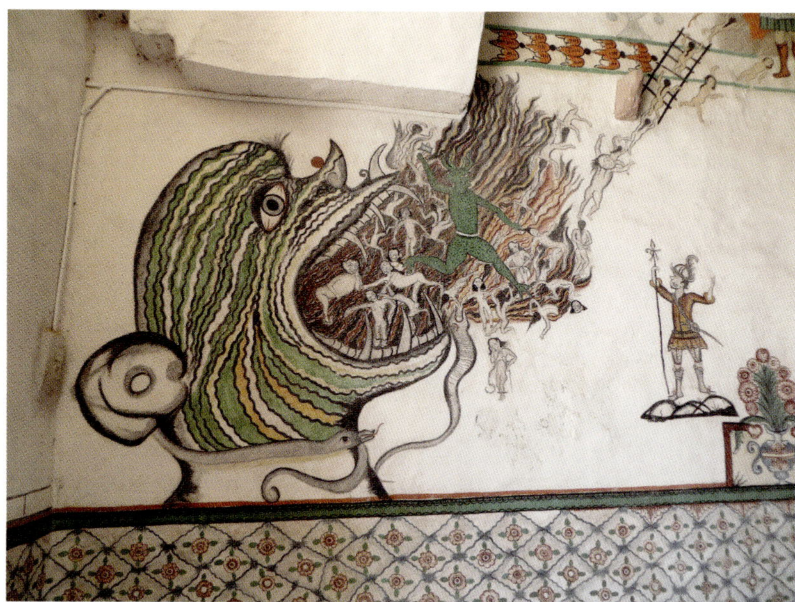

Hell, 18th century. Church of Our Lady of Copacabana in Andamarca, Bolivia. Detail showing presence of antlerite in Leviathan and the devil.

time but also to political upheaval and wars. I am referring to silver. This famous path is known as the Silver Route. All along this route are small chapels with adobe walls and thatched roofs, built between the seventeenth and the eighteenth centuries. They are in towns such as Pachama and Parinacota in Chile, and Andamarca, Curahuara de Carangas, Corque and Soracachi in Bolivia, among others. Their walls and most of the interior of their roofs are completely covered with paintings of subjects from the Old and the New Testaments: Last Judgment and Hell, Noah's Ark, the Massacre of the Innocents, the Life of Christ, the Virgin, and the saints, all of them surrounded by depictions of flowers, birds and other animals, and hanging textiles. Since 2010 different projects led by researchers from Chile, Bolivia, and Argentina have been studying the processes and purposes of the painting campaigns, the people involved in them, and their materials and techniques. In Saint Andrew of Pachama church, in the section where Saint Michael Fighting the Dragon is represented, we have identified a *secco* technique with calcium sulfate as the plaster, the use of a mixture of siccative linseed oil and egg as pigment binders, and a colorful palette that includes cochineal lake, smalt, indigo, hematite, vermilion, orpiment, carbon-based black, and, of course, green pigments such as the ones discussed in this essay. The presence of antlerite and brochantite, as natural mineral pigments and not a degradation of other colors such as malachite, has also been identified in another chapel on the Silver Route: Our Lady of Copacabana in Andamarca, a location on the west side of Lake Poopó, in Bolivia. This chapel contains one of the most interesting depictions of Hell, with the souls of the damned falling into Leviathan's open mouth aided by a scary green demon [FIG. 53]. The pigments used to color this devil were brochantite and antlerite, applied in a thin layer over a calcium sulfate ground layer. The recurrent use of these pigments from the pre-Hispanic tradition into the colonial period speaks of the survival of certain cultural traditions that had not disappeared even in the eighteenth century.

One final green pigment deserves our attention due to its significance and implications for the history of Andean sacralities and devotions. The late sixteenth-century Huarochiri manuscript is a Quechua text that is known for its collection of Andean myths, traditions, and rituals. The text discusses the *huaca*, a term that designates all the Inca sacralities and defines a sacred space: "While Macahuisa would speak, llacsa llacsa would blow from his mouth as if it were smoke going out [of her]." In a seventeenth-century *Vocabulario* (1608), the term *llacsa* relates to the action of disturbing or intimidating, but it is also linked to cast metal or bronze. In his *Historia del Peru,* Martín de Murúa mentions that the Inca gave his governors a necklace made of *llacsa* stones. *Llacsa* also appears in the list of offerings that Joseph of Arriaga—a Jesuit who participated in the extirpation campaigns of idolatry in Peru—describes as color powders used in ritual ceremonies in his book *La extirpación de la idolatría en el Peru* (1621). He states that *llacsa* "is green in the form of powder or stone like the cardenillo." It seems clear that Arriaga was associating this green pigment with the one he knew. Geological and metallurgical dictionaries dedicated to America, however, mention the term *lajsa* as an Aymara word referring not to *cardenillo* but to atacamite—a polymorph of the

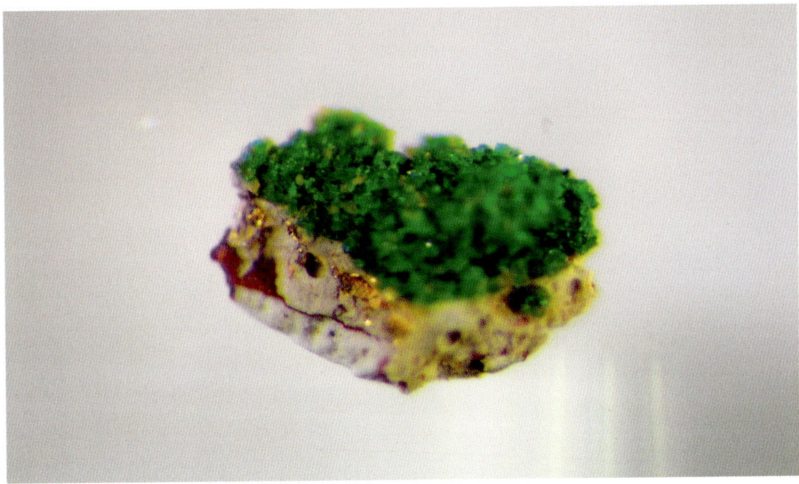

[FIG. 54]
Green sample with atacamite in *estofado* technique. Retable of Ancoraimes, 16th century. Bolivia.

basic copper (II) chloride minerals group. In South America it could be found in sacred spaces such as the temple of Pachacamac and on Inca funerary objects all around the north of Chile and Argentina, like the other copper green pigments we have mentioned. The Heuland brothers identified it as a native copper of the Lipes mines in Atacama after their royal mineralogical expedition in 1795 and named it atacamite. It subsequently appeared in European texts. Atacama used to be a region of the province of Potosí, about which Alvaro Alonso Barba—a connoisseur and an inhabitant of Lipes—said, "[T]here are many copper ores in all of these provinces. . . . Potosí is surrounded by hills where there are many of these mines. . . . There are very great veins in Atacama and some of them face the sea in large cliffs of this solid metal." So, it sounds quite reasonable that this green pigment was also useful for painters during the viceregal period, especially for local ones who lived in the region. Such is the case of Francisco Tito Yupanqui, who traveled around Potosí and is associated with two important religious objects for the Andean culture. By 1583 he would be the creator, main sculptor, and painter of the image of Our Lady of Copacabana, one of the most important devotions in the Andes. Chemical analysis of its polychromy revealed the presence of atacamite as a green pigment in the Virgin's veil, with a Spanish technique called *estofado* that combined the use of gold, Armenian bol, gypsum, and the green pigment. The same technique and green pigment were found in the retable of Ancoraimes, a small village near the southeast side of Lake Titicaca [FIG. 54]. The retable is known as one of the oldest in Bolivia, and art history has often associated it with the one Tito Yupanqui helped to paint, while learning to polychrome and gild the image of the Virgin. The coincidence of the same material and technique reaffirms that hypothesis. The survival of the use of this local green pigment, laden with symbolism in the Andean traditions, seems to have remained as a material memory reimagined in a new sacred space. Together with the antlerite and brochantite on walls or sculptures, they represent the silent witnesses of past cultural practices that, far from disappearing, would be readapted and given new significance by future patrons, painters, and spectators for the creation of new visual tales.

Pigmenting the Skin: When Spice Makes Race

Anne Lafont
Translated from French by Miriam Rosen

Pigmentum, a term from medieval Latin designating pigment, in the sense of the coloring used to paint (*pingere*), and *pimiento*, a term from colonial Spanish designating what has come to be known as *piment* in French (*chili* or *chili pepper* in English; the plant was discovered by Europeans in the Americas during the sixteenth century), are both associated with spices. As such, they constitute the two poles of this essay, situated in the interpretive space that French lexicology and etymology have created around the common noun *pi(g)ment*. The double origin, from Latin and Spanish, explains the semantic scope of the word *pigment* in French and English alike as well as its various metamorphoses in the visual arts. It is, therefore, from this perspective—encompassing material culture and natural history, the history of visual mediums and that of printing techniques—that I would like to reexamine the study of pigment in the convergent domains of eighteenth-century art and anatomy.

When Geneviève [FIG. 55] arrived in Paris from the colonial island of Santo Domingo in 1777, the scientific and artistic attention she attracted was duly noted by the naturalist Buffon and his colleague the illustrator Jacques de Sève in the supplement to volume five of *L'Histoire naturelle* (Paris, 1778). They set about to describe the unusual skin coloring (that is, the *pigmentation*) of this young woman, whose racial blackness did not correspond to the physical whiteness they observed. The question of *blafardise* (paleness, pallor), to borrow Buffon's term, which thus implied the unhealthy nature of Geneviève's skin color and that of albinos in general, or the question of the *Négres blancs* (white Negros), according to a more widespread vernacular expression, was already a subject of ongoing discussion.[1] The interest was first manifested in texts concerning the mathematician, philosopher, and essayist Maupertuis's *Dissertation physique à l'occasion du Nègre blanc* (Physical treatise on the white Negro, 1744) and the same author's *Vénus physique* (Physical Venus, 1745). Some thirty years later, the attention was more visual, as attested by de Sève's

1. The term *blafard* (from the Middle High German *bleichvar*, meaning "pale," applying to colors), appearing in French as *blaffert* (1342) and then *blaffard* (1549), had the same concrete meaning but took on the connotations of "sickly," "wan," "sad," or "washed-out"; see *Le grand Robert de la langue française* (Paris: Le Robert, 1992), vol. 2, p. 14). For Enlightenment naturalists like Buffon, the *blafards* were, by extension, "pigmentless."

plates, soon followed by the picturesque canvases of the 1780s, especially those showing the dwarf Siriaco, such as José Conrado Roza's *Mascarade nuptiale* (1788; Musée du Nouveau Monde, La Rochelle, France).

Is White a Pigment?

Scholars of the time sought to grasp the incongruous category represented by albinism in order to understand how the racial system for conceiving the world's different populations in terms of four skin colors (black, white, yellow, and red), as epitomized by the Swedish scientist Carl Linnaeus's *Systema naturae* (System of nature, 1735–58), could sometimes fail. And to determine the meaning of this exception.

At the time of the transatlantic slave trade, the "pale" white pigmentation of Geneviève's skin consequently appeared as the only divergence from the racial characterization of this young African woman from the West Indies. Neither her hair nor the shape of her lips or that of her nose differed from the racial features associated with blackness. It was thus necessary to investigate the origin of the skin color of Blacks and, as in this instance, its marked absence in some cases or its partial nature in others (that is, individuals affected by vitiligo, who were then commonly called Nègres-Pie (literally 'black and white Negros', known in English as Piebald Negros). Buffon and de Sève also devoted one plate in their *Natural History* to the Colombian Maria-Sabina [FIG. 56], who manifested what was equally known as *piebaldisme*, or "piebald skin" (Buffon, 1778, supplement to vol. 5, 566–67).

These rare examples came to be the cornerstones of the understanding of humanity's pigmentary system at a time when the exception proved the norm in a science of observation serving to demonstrate natural coherence and thus, in the scholar's eyes, divine coherence. In his vast undertaking, Buffon aspired to an all-encompassing enumeration that was clearly distinct from the systematic thought of Linnaeus but no less committed to understanding and explaining the natural irregularities—compared to the general if not the norm—that he had collected in his chapter on "monstrosities" in the supplement to volume 5 of *Natural History*.

Thus, after careful empirical reflection on Geneviève's body—after a manual exploration that led him to study the nature of her down, the abundant wrinkles on her hands, which are visible in the illustration, the firmness of her "breasts" and the size of her "nipples" as well as her "periodic flow" and the dimensions of her eyes—Buffon concluded that the specificity of these "pale" individuals did not actually make them a separate race because their physical structure stemmed from the "degeneration" or "degradation" of an original color, as observed in examples from different populations (American, African, and so forth).

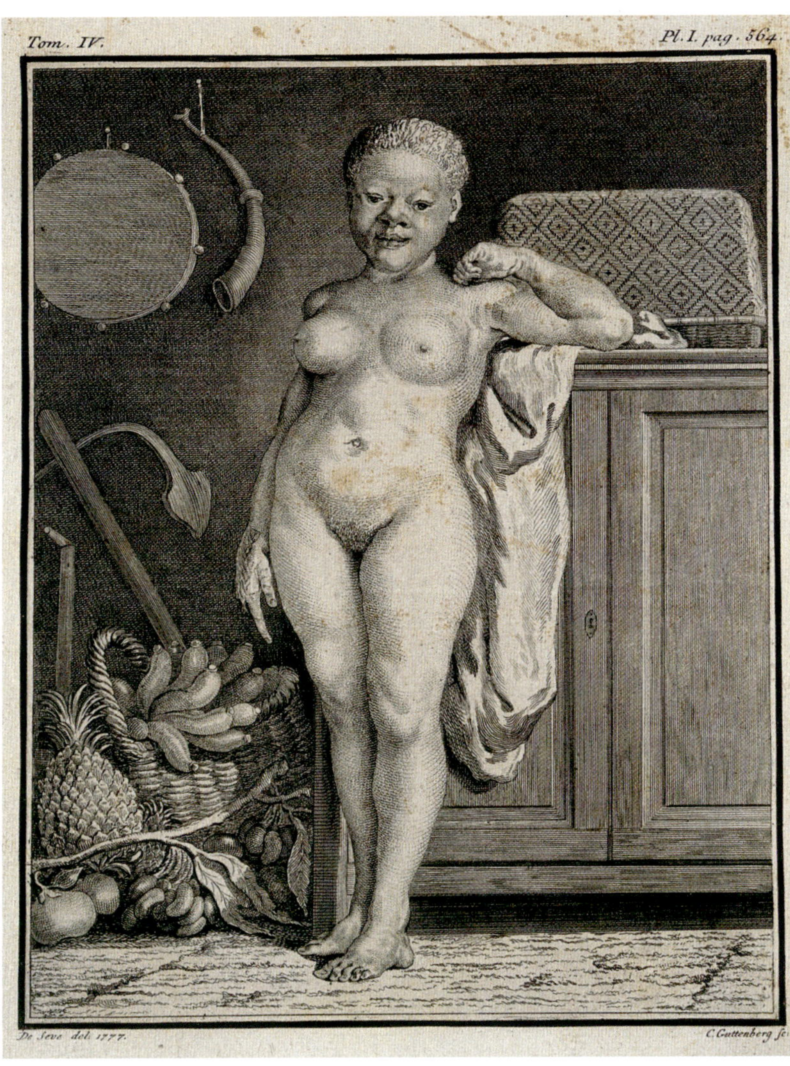

[FIG. 55]
C. Guttenberg after Jacques
de Sève, *Geneviève*, 1777.
Engraving, 22.9 × 17 cm.

This conclusion was consistent with the logic of monogenism, which saw the unity of the human species as the resolution of the biblical explanation of our origins (Adam and Eve) with natural history (a common core unique to all human beings was altered according to different climates, resulting in the observed diversity of the species [Maupertuis, 1745; Buffon, 1778]).

When Buffon's colleague de Sève represented Geneviève in 1777, his illustration transposed the scholar's entire demonstration while suggesting, for better or worse, the model's modesty (her downward gaze and the slight displacement of her left leg to block prying glances) and tenseness (her clenched right hand). We can easily imagine the brutality, at the very least moral, that Geneviève had endured. Indeed, such visual records often reveal the subject's point of view, even unintentionally. Buffon, conversely, made only one mention of Geneviève's emotion in his long article, where he wrote that he had occasionally detected on the young woman's face "a faint trace of crimson on her cheeks when she came close to the fire, or when she felt ashamed to be seen nude" (Buffon, 1778, p. 561).

De Sève's composition was destined for the eyes of the scholar-voyeur, who was interested not only in the question of skin color but also in the morphology of this "racially" black woman with white skin. Geneviève's breasts and pubis, visually associated with the mouth-watering pineapple and other exotic fruits in the basket at her feet and the musical instruments on the wall, including the horn, go beyond her subjection to the gluttony of Buffon and de Sève, along with that of the *Natural History* reader, who was supposed to derive both instruction and pleasure from it. The association of women's nude bodies, often the breasts, with fruits and sometimes flowers is a constant in literature and the visual arts, as demonstrated by art historian Linda Nochlin, who emphasized the gendered dimension by adding that this savory eroticism tied to the joys of the mouth had been imagined "for men's enjoyment, by men" (Nochlin, 1972, p. 9).

Through the otherwise concise medium of engraving, the illustration presenting Geneviève suggests the pallid whiteness of albinism and also raises questions about the use of the category of pigmentation as a marker of race. In other words, the figure of Geneviève, her exemplary nature, allows us to approach *pigment* from pictorial and dermatological points of view. These two semantic regimes, the material and the professional, are constituents of the concept of "pigment" in the eighteenth century, when the term encompassed its nature as a spice endowed with both culinary and medicinal virtues and its double effectiveness as a dyestuff and a phenomenon coloring the tissues of a living organism. One word, *pi(g)ment* (*pigment/chili* in English), opens at least three closely connected

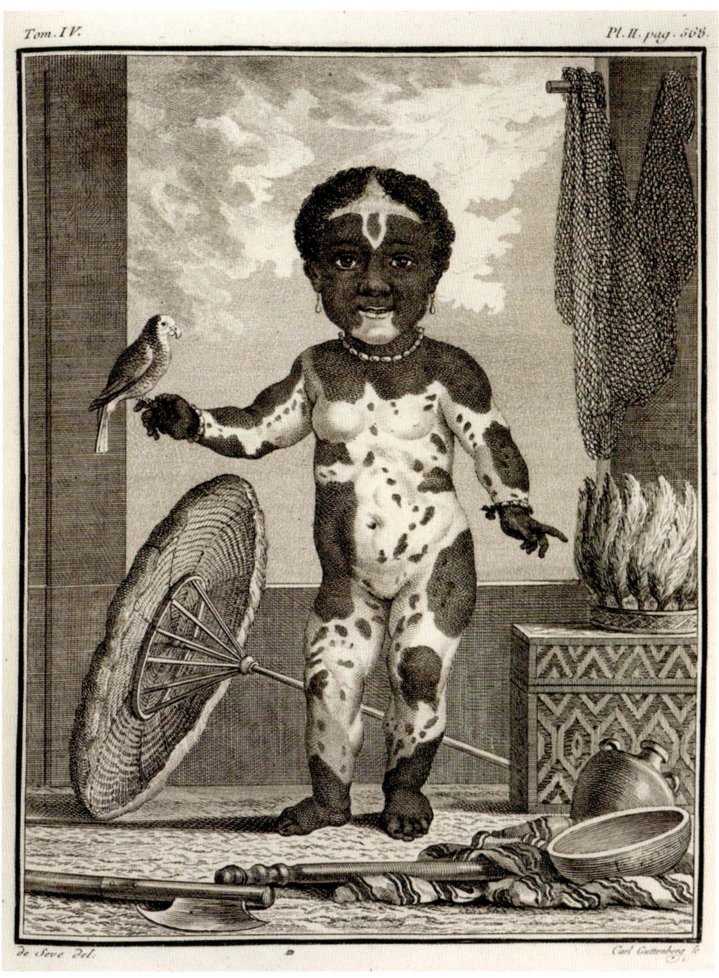

[FIG. 56]
Marie Sabina. Engraving after a drawing by Jacques de Sève in *Supplément à l'histoire naturelle de l'homme de Buffon* (Paris, 1778), vol. 5.

fields of meaning: the *piment/chili* as a cultivated fruit, pigment as a painter's material, and pigmentation as a dermatological phenomenon.

A Colonial Spice

In its original, natural state, the chili is the fruit of a plant growing in the humid tropical regions of Central and Latin America. This fruit, which can be red, green, or yellow, is oblong and has a smooth, shiny skin. Its size varies from one species to another, just as its colors and production sites have multiplied since its discovery by European colonizers—compare, for instance, India and the French Basque country. Spanish and British colonial settlers borrowed the name given to it by Indigenous Mesoamerican growers: *chili*. However, etymological studies do not agree that the word *chili* is named for the chili pepper, a lexical genealogy that would permit the association of the Latin American territory (the country known as Chile in Spanish and English, Chili in French) with the pepper.

It is interesting to note, however, that the phenomenon of skin pigmentation, which was identified at the end of the eighteenth century by the new medical branch engaged in treating skin diseases—dermatology— was based precisely on symbolic shortcuts of this type—namely, semantic migrations corresponding to various naturalizations of social codes. In medieval Europe, the need to distinguish Jews from the Christian community, to identify them within the urban social space, took concrete form in, among others, their relegation to one area of the city, the ghetto, and the obligation to wear at all times a small piece of yellow cloth sewn onto their clothing, the badge (Latin: *rota;* French: *rouelle* or *roue;* English: "wheel") that was the antecedent of the yellow star imposed by the Nazis in the 1930s. While yellow was not exclusive in the history of this badge and its Muslim and European variants, it was nonetheless the dominant color used to distinguish the Jewish community from the thirteenth century on because of its association with betrayal and, by extension, the Jewish people's supposed betrayal of Jesus. It was thus easy to go from the ancient Greek and Roman theory of the four humors, used for the moral qualification of human beings based on the supposed color of their bile, to an interpretation of the world no longer based on the color of the organism's internal fluids but on the color of the skin. And this framework had the additional advantage of being accessible on the body's surface, whereas it had previously been necessary to invent concealed differences, inside the body, to create distinctions between Christian, Jewish, and Muslim Europeans.

That said, the demand for a distinctive mark in the form of a yellow cloth conspicuously sewn on the clothing amounted to an admission of failure on the part of ecclesiastical authorities because the badge compensated for the absence of natural evidence. Paradoxically, the yellow identifier had to be performed culturally because it could not be detected naturally. If the treachery of the Jews were proven by the yellowish color of their skin—according to the humoral theory of human anatomy—it would not have been necessary to wear an ostentatious sign of that innate, visible immoral quality.

This example demonstrates the extent to which the projection of a custom imposed on a human community has a performative, essentializing function that depends on the process of naturalizing a totally invented distinction. The same was true in the eighteenth century, when the testimonies of European explorers like Jacques Lafitau led to the acceptance of the idea that the repeated use of annatto dye (or *roucou*) by the Indigenous peoples of Brazil wound up transforming this makeup (*tattoo* was, in fact, the ad hoc term used because makeup, especially white powder, was reserved for the cosmetics of European aristocrats) into a dominant natural aspect of their complexion. This particularity was therefore understood as an inherent, hereditary element.

During the Enlightenment, the same conceptualization of skin color corresponded to scientific belief in the effects of climate (today, we would say environment) on the nature of individuals to the point where the color perceived—in this case, red—was thought to result from the incorporation of a natural additive which, by analogy with the development of a photograph, would reveal the individual's essence—in other words, his or her "red" race. European travelers, impressed by their encounters with Indigenous populations, transformed a social and cultural practice involving the care and decoration of the skin into the principal marker of otherness. For purposes of classification, *mask* and *skin* were merged into a determinant biological element of identity, which they extended to all the Indigenous populations of the Americas. The colonizers thus made that marker into the touchstone of the demarcation between *Them*, the redskins, and *Us*, the whites. Race was now based primarily on the generalized construct of skin color and provided de facto confirmation of the inflexible essentialization of what was in reality a combination of sanitary and ritual traditions.

Race was thus at the heart of the social order and a paradigm for organizing the world into intelligible entities—a system serving the distribution of the tasks of each human community—and as such, it needed to be based on a simple, comprehensible division of the world's diversity. In the context of this superficial, approximate classification, skin color proved to be particularly effective. Throughout the eighteenth century, the conceptualization of an identifiable pigmentation and its ongoing process of transformation into a stable scientific factor made race a fundamental, trustworthy tool of the emerging discipline of anthropology.

The dynamics of the natural history of populations, whether based on the exception, as shown by the engraved portrait of Geneviève, the albino, or on a global scale, adapting racial categorization to a new anatomical given at world level—colonization—in a way prepared the terrain for the semantic weight of the notion of pigment, at first anatomically and then medically.

The exploration of the world in its physical, cultural, social, and topographical diversity required scholars of the time—the naturalists of the Enlightenment—to acquire the necessary means for making this diversity understandable. And perhaps it also required them to use the metaphorical imagery of the New World's resources to express the paradigm change at work regarding the knowledge of humanity in the era of the so-called great discoveries—the time of the African slave trade, when more than eleven million human beings were displaced from one continent to another. This forced migration gave rise to the symptomatic expression "ebony wood," which marked the objectification of the Africans as a necessary process for their enslavement. It also illustrated the merger of nature and culture—in other words, the absence of distinction between the individuals and the natural resources of a single territory to better exploit both. It contributed as well to euphemizing the extreme brutality of the trade in human beings. It is possible that the poetic dimension of "ebony wood" also served to conceal an activity that was not only disgraceful but also illegitimate in the eyes of eighteenth-century Abolitionists and soon illegal, given that the slave trade was prohibited in France as of 1815, when the term seemingly began to spread.

In the modern colonial empires, the massive demographic transformations caused by the displacement of the Africans who would be sold as slaves for plantations and the decimation of the Indigenous populations with the colonial conquest of the Americas necessarily had a considerable impact on all human activities, including the visual arts.

The intersection of art and race can therefore be perceived through the prism of pigment, for the act of color—whether manual or chemical—is produced in the process of coloring organic tissues, namely the skin of human beings. From this perspective, the invention of color engraving in the mid-eighteenth century is emblematic of the dynamics, both scholarly and imaginative, governing the exploration of coloring techniques, in the context of engraving and printing in general, as well as the visual use of this process in the identification of an anatomical phenomenon that was omnipresent in the imperial world: pigmentation. It might thus be argued that art provided medical science with a descriptive, or even analytical, model, as documented by the very word *pigmentation*. The production of the pigment (the material made by a combination of naturally colored spices and fixatives), like the art of painting more broadly (the art of

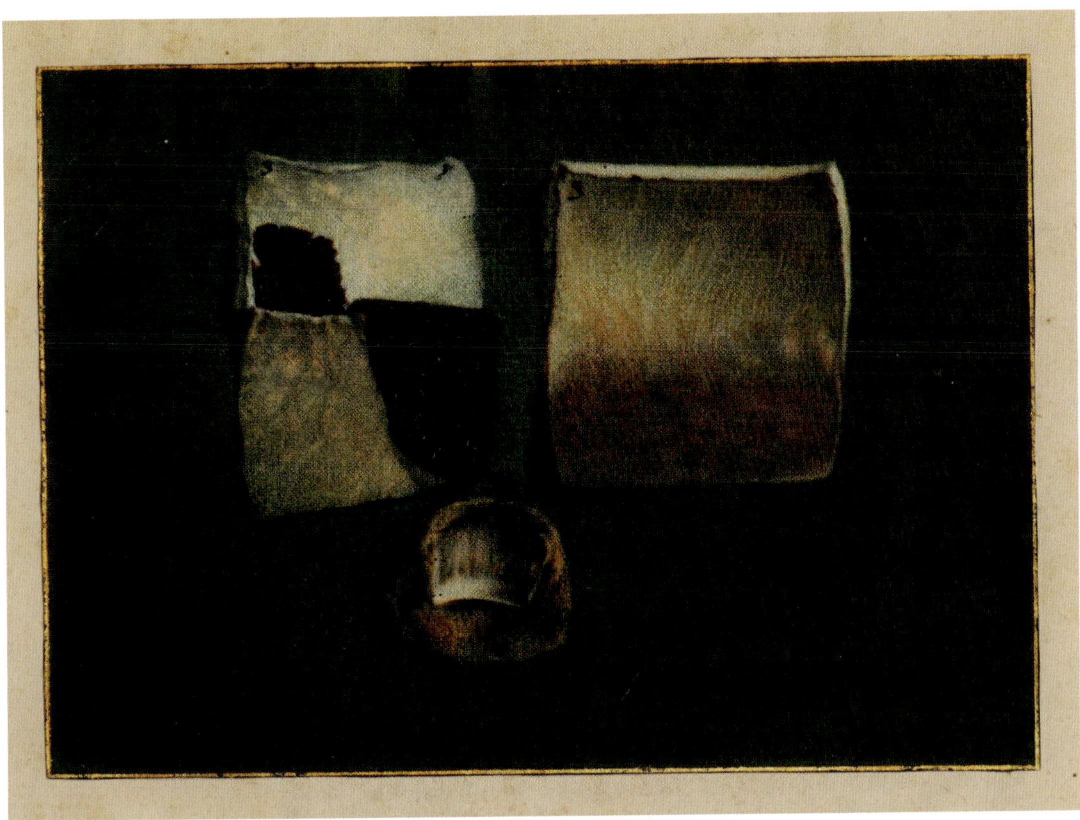

[FIG. 57]
.Ian l'Admiral, illustration
in Bernhard Siegfried
Albinus, *Dissertatio secunda
de sede et caussa coloris
Aethiopum et caeterorum
hominum* (Leiden, 1737).

applying this synthetic material on a canvas), could then be associated with the natural phenomenon of pigmentation in the emerging science of dermatology, pioneered in France by the doctor Jean-Louis Alibert (1768–1837), author of *Description des maladies de la peau* (Description of skin diseases, Paris, 1806), which includes more than fifty hand-colored illustrations.

The Colored Body

The material investigations of a remarkable artist and inventor, Jacques-Fabien Gautier d'Agoty (1711–1785), whose work was related to the experiments in printing taking place in various European cities, marked a crucial step in the history of the intersection of the visual arts and the naturalists' knowledge about pigments. In concrete terms, they allow us to relate these two theoretical and practical systems within a lexical perspective that, from the end of the eighteenth century, included the pigment of painting and that of the skin.

Gautier d'Agoty was born in Marseilles, where he developed a particular sensitivity to the opulent colors of the Oriental textiles he saw in the port, which was then open to Asian and North African trade. In the 1730s he went to Paris, where he studied with Jacob Christoph Le Blon (1667–1741), the inventor of a pioneering technique for three-color printing. This process, which consisted of overlaying mezzotint plates that were successively inked with blue, yellow, and red colorants, capitalized on the mezzotint's subtle rendering of the passage from shadow to light. Le Blon presented his method in an illustrated English and French publication *Coloritto; or, The Harmony of Colouring in Painting* (1725), and two of his students, Gautier d'Agoty and Jan l'Admiral (1699–1773), were to draw on these discoveries to further the knowledge of the human body (Fend, 2017).

L'Admiral thus illustrated the anatomist Bernhard Siegfried Albinus's treaty on the origin of the color of Blacks, *Dissertatio secunda de sede et caussa coloris Aethiopum et caeterorum hominum* (1736), with a plate showing samples of the skin of a Black woman, her thumb, breast, and heel presented as specimens [FIG. 57]. Gautier d'Agoty, meanwhile, set up a family workshop with his four sons where they produced numerous color prints in the second half of the century. In particular, he created fantasy-like anatomical plates in which the nervous system, muscles, and veins belonging to the unseen world of the human organism beneath the skin were not only revealed but rendered in all their chromatic richness. The black-and-white world of the print could now offer a more detailed characterization of its subjects within the regime of representation, but it also underwent a kind of spectacularization. *L'Ange de l'anatomie* [FIG. 58], an incunabulum of color printing, is the best-known plate from Gautier

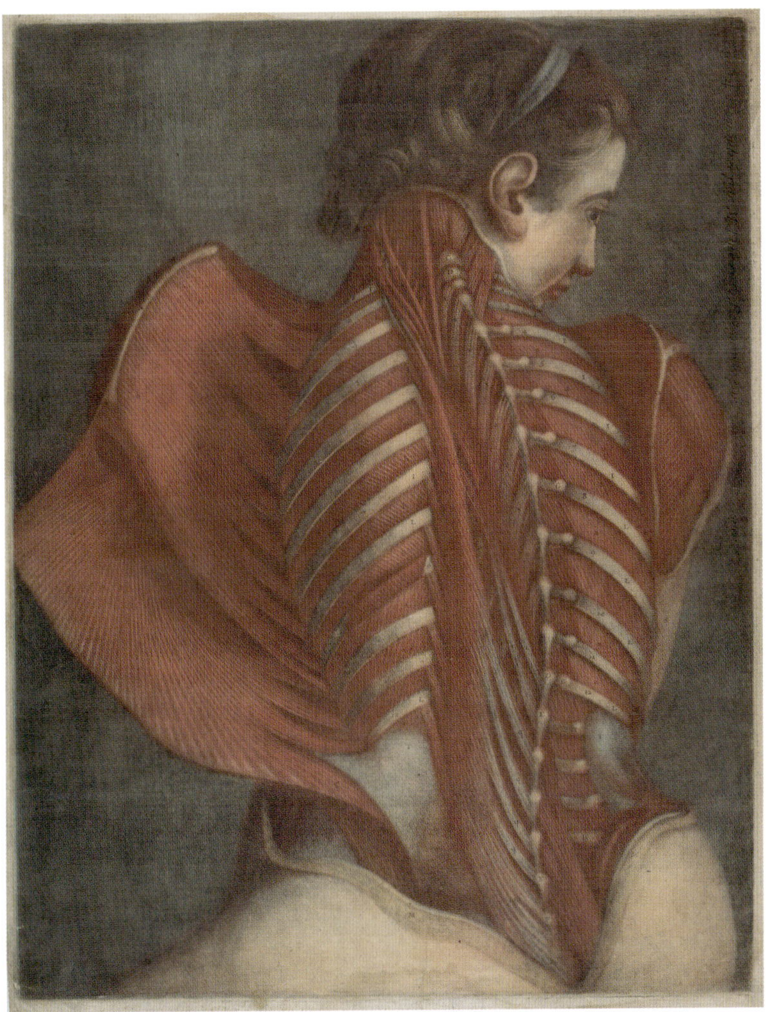

[FIG. 58]
Jacques-Fabien Gautier
d'Agoty, *L'Ange de l'anatomie*
(*The Anatomical Angel*) or
*Dissection of a Woman's
Back*, 1746. Color mezzo-
tint, 61.2 × 46 cm. National
Gallery of Art, Washington,
D.C., Gift of Ruth Cole
Kainen (2012.92.47).

d'Agoty's anatomical atlas (1746), paradoxically aimed at disclosing the glistening diversity of the organs under the skin, or perhaps *under the race,* as read through the surface color of the epidermis.

While Gautier d'Agoty drew on Le Blon's technical discovery to investigate the depths of the human body, he was also using the colorist process racially, as seen in his contemporary print depicting Madame du Barry, mistress of Louis XVI, served by a Black page in red livery [FIG. 59]. The page is presumably the famous Zamor (1762–1820), a native of Bengal (now in Bangladesh), who was Madame du Barry's servant for more than twenty years. He is shown offering the king's favorite a cup of what we can assume to be a warm beverage brewed from a colonial spice like coffee or chocolate. Dressed in a white negligee, she turns her back to the mirror; behind her, the presence of bedding suggests that she has just awakened and that the young Black servant thus participated in the intimacy of her morning toilette. In d'Agoty's print, he not only serves her but looks at her with admiration, as we often see in portraits of white aristocrats and their young Black pages throughout the eighteenth century.

The perfection of the color engraving technique, which was directly related to the exploration of human diversity and the improved knowledge of the inner workings of the body, also paralleled the development of the medium of pastel. This dry pigment is composed of a colored powder (either mineral or vegetable) and a filler (such as chalk or plaster), held together with a binder (often gum arabic from Senegal). The mixture produces a particular type of paste that is at once greasy and light. It is sufficiently compact to take the form of a stick that serves as a crayon for color drawing.

Although it had already been used in the visual arts, pastel was especially popular in the eighteenth century. The most famous pastel artists of the time included Rosalba Carriera, followed by Maurice Quentin de la Tour, Jean-Marc Nattier, and Jean-Baptiste Perronneau, and owing to the medium's association with a specific genre, they were the most celebrated portraitists of Enlightenment circles. Because of its consistency, pastel renders the surface to which it is applied opaque, like oil paint, but lends itself to effects that are at once diaphanous and velvety, and these are particularly suited to the representation of the skin. Its reputation as the medium of the portrait, and, more precisely, as that of the portrayal of skin because of its intermediate position between drawing and painting, sheds an interesting light on Perronneau's choice of pastel to represent the albino Maponde, a West African, in a portrait commissioned by the Count de Caylus for the Countess de Tessin [FIG. 60]. The countess, who was the wife of Sweden's ambassador to Paris from 1739 to 1742, seemingly decided to obtain a portrait of the young African, who, a few decades before Geneviève, had become a focus of attention in the French

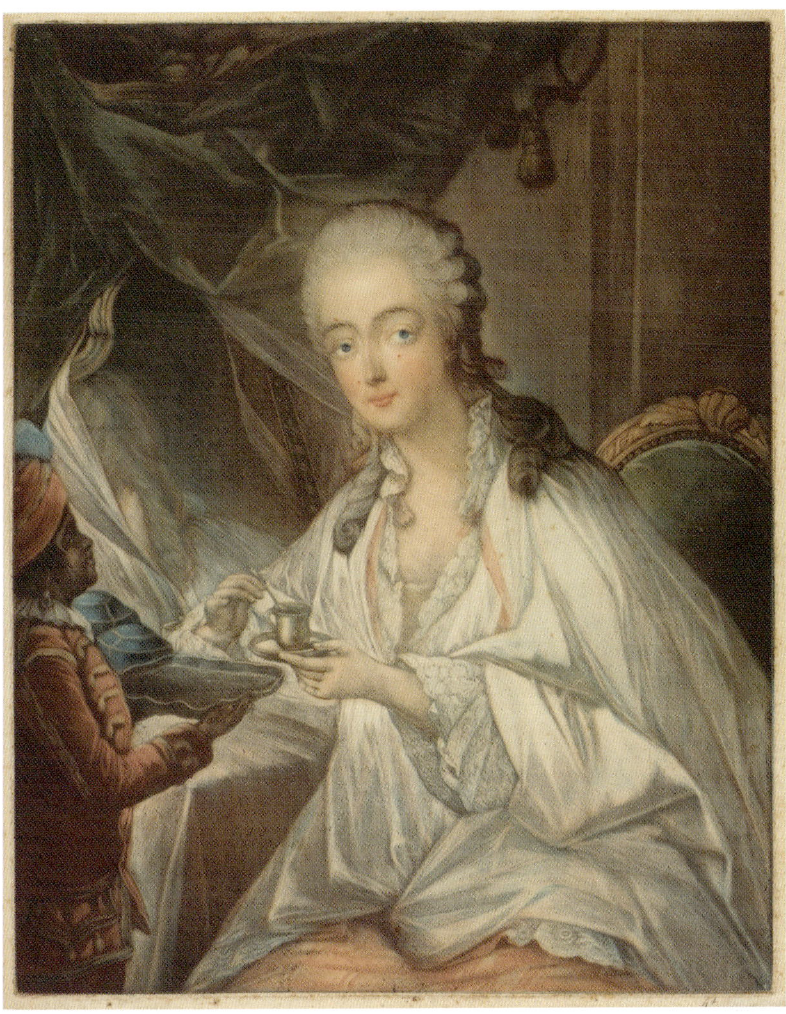

[FIG. 59]
Jacques-Fabien Gautier
d'Agoty after François-
Hubert Drouais, *Madame
du Barry*, 1771. Color mezzo-
tint. National Gallery of Art,
Washington, D.C., Widener
Collection (1942.9.2273).

capital because of the singularity of his skin. Indeed, Maupertuis was to mention him in *Vénus physique* (1745), his book on "white Negros" and the origin of the color of Blacks, as proof of genetic theory or, more precisely, as a borderline case regarding assumptions about human procreation.

Perronneau, who had not yet exhibited at the official Salon organized by the Académie des Beaux-Arts, was still overshadowed by the pastel artist Quentin de la Tour. But now he found himself commissioned to execute the portrait of Maponde, who, as we learn from the inscription on the reverse of the work, was "born to a Negro and a Negresse in Cabende, from the Moyo nation, and was traded [sold as a slave] in the forenamed Cabende, coast of Angola, on 15 January 1743" and "painted by J.-B. Peroneau en 1745" ("né d'un nègre et d'une négresse à Cabende, de nation Moyo, et a esté traitté au dit Cabende, coste d'Angolle, le 15 janvier 1743" and "peint par J.-B. Peroneau en 1745"). The Countess de Tessin's interest in this pigmentary curiosity and the resulting racial enigma that was stirring up the Parisian intellectual elite could thus be satisfied by acquiring a picture of Maponde. We do not know who decided on the artist, but Perronneau turned out to be an appropriate choice insofar as his preferred medium, pastel, gave him a formidable tool for rendering the specific nature of the model's skin color. The result is an extremely gentle portrait, both formally and with regard to Maponde's gaze, which is directed at his portraitist and therefore, indirectly, at his viewers. The red frock coat refutes any scientific or exotic context, for Maupertuis could hardly be imagined examining the strange skin of a young man wearing such a costume. The subtle plays of the white, yellow, pink, blue, and green pastels—at once dense and muted—convey the color of Maponde's face and hair but also animate them.

The year 1745 thus marked the entry of pigment into the question of skin. At the same time, yet owing to different materials, it took hold of the body of the *Anatomical Angel* and that of Maponde and blurred the notion of color as a fixed marker of race. The white person proved to be made of an intertwining of blood vessels and organs of all colors beneath the skin. But another white was also a possibility, a kind of avatar of the matrix common to the origin of all humanity. This was the case for the rare form of Africanness that Buffon mistakenly qualified as *blafard*, while on the contrary, Perronneau's portrait, thanks to the pastel's dry but pasty consistency, highlights the pinkish white tint of the young albino's cheeks and forehead with vermilion. Even if he does not manifest any emotion, Maponde is full of life.

As a result, this portrait also turned out to be a precocious refutation of pro-slavery rhetoric, a counterexample that was neglected by the discourse favorable to maintaining slavery in the young American republic. Indeed, future president Thomas Jefferson, in his *Notes on the*

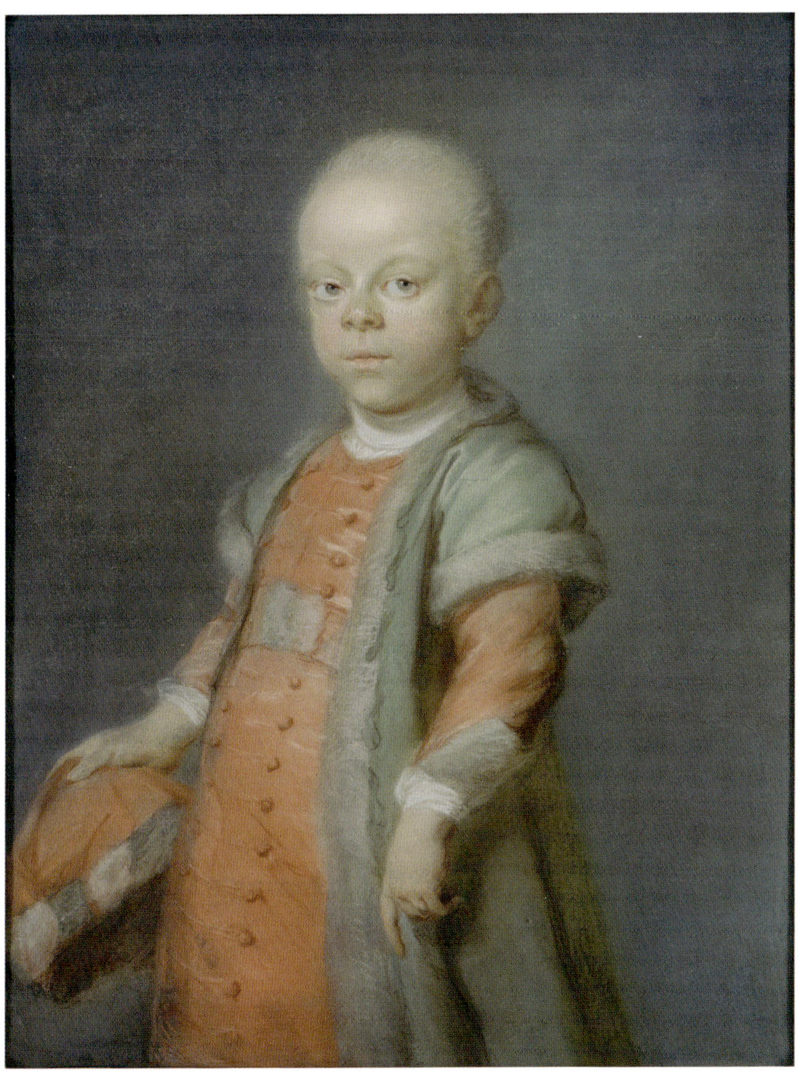

[FIG. 60]
Jean-Baptiste Perronneau,
Maponde, 1745. Pastel
on paper, 75 × 56 cm.
Nationalmuseum Stockholm
(NMB 1674).

148

State of Virginia (1781, revised 1782, 1783), justified the non-inclusion of Blacks in the new state on the pretext that black pigmentation rendered the skin so opaque that the emotions of those endowed with it, the Blacks, were invisible, inaccessible to the others, those who kept company with them in the supposed transparency of their whiteness. Jefferson's skin-based argument maintained that political community and political equality could not adapt to a distortion involving the way each party read the other's soul in other words, that there could not be transparent citizens on the one hand and, on the other, citizens whose emotions were covered with an "immovable veil of black" (p. 145).

Politics

Pi(g)ment, as spice and coloring that animated the inside and outside of the human body, became the blind spot of the age of "Enlightenment" and an obstacle to the participation of those who bore its dark trace in the political community. Black skin coloring, because of the privation of the civil rights that it required as a matter of course, consequently summed up the impossibility for Blacks to emancipate themselves, given their "essence," their pigmentation, which doomed them to political marginality.

Pigmented skin thus became the threshold of otherness. As the Dutch draftsman, anatomist, and physician Petrus Camper (1722–1789)—the famous inventor of the theory of facial angle for measuring the stage of advancement of individuals on the scale of humanity—recalls in the first paragraph of his Introduction to *Treatise on the Natural Difference of Features in Persons of Different Countries and Periods of Life* (1791):

> Painting, and whatever is relative to the Art, have been my favourite amusements since my earliest years: and as the characteristic differences in men and animals appeared to me the most interesting objects in nature, I was disposed to pay more than ordinary attention to these.—To draw, and to model in clay, were the recreations of my childish hours. As I grew older, I was particularly struck with the figure and colour of the Moor [*Mooren*]; and with the difference in features and complexion between the East Indian blacks [*Swarten*] and the natives of Africa.[2]

In this way, the scholar's childish vocation was inscribed in the practice of observation as demonstrated by his interest in a system of visual notation (drawing and visual arts) while his memory, so vividly impressed, retained the souvenir of Black morphology and skin color. These first sentences of Camper's work on natural differences laid out a program in which the visual arts contribute to racial investigation, while pigment, an artistic material, and pigmentation, a dermatological phenomenon, constitute the

2. Like most of the eighteenth-century studies cited here, Petrus Camper's writings were rapidly published in various translations. What is particularly interesting in this passage, however, is the marked difference between the English and the French translations of the original Dutch terms *Mooren* and *Swarten*: while the English translator uses the equivalent words "Moors" and "Blacks," the French translator opts in the first instance for *Noirs* ("Blacks") and, in the second, for *Nègres*, from the Latin *niger*, via the Portuguese *negro*, with the pejorative sense of "Negros" in English.

two sides of the same coin, the two pillars of the scientific inquiry on the diversity of the human species.

The history of pigment thus highlights the connection between the pre-modern European coloring material and the colonial spice suitable for staining. It also relates the less familiar story of eighteenth-century experimentation with drawing and color aimed at obtaining a vibrant representation of human skin. These artistic experiments prepared the scholar's eye to recognize the complex physiological phenomenon of skin coloring. Indeed, Alibert's invention of dermatology at the end of the century occurred at the intersection of the history of painting, colonial history, and the history of graphic and coloring techniques, for these knowledge systems had converged to place *pigment* and *piment/chili* at the heart of a new body of expertise that was itself at the articulation of the medicine of the skin and physical and cultural anthropology.

Further Reading and Bibliography

Pigment Worlds: An Introduction

Bahn, Paul G. *Prehistoric Rock Art: Polemics and Progress.* Cambridge: Cambridge University Press, 2010.

Bolland, Charlotte, and Tarnya Cooper, eds. *The Real Tudors: Kings and Queens Rediscovered.* Exh. cat. National Portrait Gallery, London, 2014.

Chapman, Clare, and Ossian Ward. *Anish Kapoor.* Exh. cat. Gallerie dell'Accademia di Venezia and Palazzo Manfrin Venier. Venice: Marsillio Editori, 2022.

Finlay, Victoria, and Narayan Khandekar. *An Atlas of Rare & Familiar Colour: The Harvard Art Museums' Forbes Pigment Collection.* Los Angeles: Atelier Éditions, 2017.

Forbes, Edward W. "The Technical Study and Physical Care of Paintings," *Art Bulletin* 2, no. 3 (1920): 160–70.

Ganio, Monica, et al. "From Lapis Lazuli to Ultramarine Blue: Investigating Cennino Cennini's Recipe Using Sulfur K-edge XANES." *Pure and Applied Chemistry* 90, no. 3 (2018): 463–75.

Hersey, Mark D. *My Work Is That of Conservation: An Environmental Biography of George Washington Carver.* Athens: University of Georgia Press, 2011.

Kirsh, Andrea, and Rustin S. Levenson. *Seeing through Paintings: Physical Examination in Art Historical Studies.* New Haven: Yale University Press, 2000.

Phipps, Elena. "Cochineal Red: The Art History of a Color." *Metropolitan Museum of Art Bulletin* 67, no. 3 (2010): 5–48.

Sanders, Eulanda A., and Chanmi Hwang. "George Washington Carver: Textile Artist." *Textile Society of America Symposium Proceedings* (2014), n.p.

Smith, Pamela H. "Knowledge in Motion: Following Itineraries of Matter in the Early Modern World." In *Cultures in Motion,* edited by Daniel T. Rodgers, Bhavani Raman, and Helmut Reimitz. Princeton: Princeton University Press, 2013, 109–33.

Stenger, Jens, et al. "The Making of Mark Rothko's Harvard Murals." *Studies in Conservation* 61, no. 6 (2016): 331–47; and "Conservation of a Room: A Treatment Proposal for Mark Rothko's Harvard Murals." Ibid., 348–61.

Svoboda, Marie, and Caroline Cartwright. *Mummy Portraits of Roman Egypt: Emerging Research from the Appear Project.* Los Angeles: J. Paul Getty Museum, 2020.

Pigment Histories in European Painting

Anderson, Christy, Anne Dunlop, and Pamela H. Smith, eds. *The Matter of Art: Materials, Practices, Cultural Logics, c. 1250–1750.* Manchester: Manchester University Press, 2015.

Anguissola, Anna, and Andreas Grüner, eds. *The Nature of Art: Pliny the Elder on Materials.* Turnhout, Belgium: Brepols, 2020.

Bell, Janis C. "Color and Theory in Seicento Art: Zaccolini's 'Prospettiva del Colore' and the Heritage of Leonardo." Ph.D. diss. Brown University, 1983.

Beta, Simone, and Maria Michela Sassi, eds. *I colori nel mondo antico: Esperienze linguistiche e quadri simbolici. Atti della giornata di studio.* Fiesole: Cadmo, 2003.

Biggam, Carole P., and Kirsten Wolf, eds. *A Cultural History of Color.* 6 vols. London: Bloomsbury Publishing, 2021.

Boehm, Gottfried, and Matteo Burioni, eds. *Der Grund: Das Feld des Sichtbaren.* Munich and Paderborn: Wilhelm Fink Verlag, 2012.

Bohde, Daniela. *Haut, Fleisch und Farbe: Körperlichkeit und Materialität in den Gemälden Tizians.* Emsdetten, Germany: Edition Imorde, 2002.

Bolland, Charlotte, and Tarnya Cooper, eds. *The Real Tudors: Kings and Queens Rediscovered.* Exh. cat. London: National Portrait Gallery, 2014.

Boskamp, Ulrike. *Primärfarben und Farbharmonie: Farbe in der französischen Naturwissenschaft, Kunstliteratur und Malerei des 18. Jahrhunderts.* Weimar: VDG, 2009.

Brachert, Thomas. *Lexikon historischer Maltechniken: Quellen—Handwerk—Technologie—Alchemie.* Munich: Callwey, 2001.

Bruno, Vincent J. *Form and Colour in Greek Painting.* London: Thames & Hudson, 1997.

Brusatin, Manlio. *Lezioni sui colori.* Venice: Cafoscarina, 1995.

Bucklow, Spike. *The Alchemy of Paint: Art, Science and Secrets from the Middle Ages.* London: Marion Boyars, 2009.

Bushart, Magdalena, and Friedrich Steinle, eds. *Colour Histories: Science, Art, and Technology in the 17th and 18th Centuries.* Berlin and Boston: De Gruyter, 2015.

Clarke, Mark. *Mediaeval Painters' Materials and Techniques: The Montpellier Liber diversarum arcium.* London: Archetype Publications, 2011.

DeLancey, Julia A. "Dragonsblood and Ultramarine: The Apothecary and Artists' Pigments in Renaissance Florence." In *The Art Market in Italy, 15th–17th Centuries,* edited by Marcello Fantoni, Louisa C. Matthew, and Sara F. Matthews Grieco. Modena: F. C. Panini, 2003, 141–50.

Eastaugh, Nicholas, Valentine Walsh, and Tracey Chaplin. *Pigment Compendium: A Dictionary of Optical Microscopy of Historical Pigments.* Burlington: Elsevier, 2008.

Eastlake, Charles Lock. *Methods and Materials of Painting.* 1st ed., 1847. New York: Dover, 2001.

Elkins, James. *What Painting Is: How to Think about Oil Painting, Using the Language of Alchemy.* New York: Routledge, 1999.

Eyb-Green, Sigrid, and Joyce Townsend, eds. *The Artist's Process: Technology and Interpretation.* Proceedings of the Fourth Symposium of the Art Technological Source Research Working Group. London: Archetype Publications, 2012.

Feeser, Andrea, ed. *The Materiality of Color: The Production, Circulation, and Application of Dyes and Pigments, 1400–1800.* Farnham: Ashgate, U.K., 2012.

Fehrenbach, Frank. "Calor nativus—Color vitale: Prolegomena zu einer Ästhetik des 'Lebendigen Bildes' in der frühen Neuzeit." In *Visuelle Topoi: Erfindungen und tradiertes Wissen in den Künsten der italienischen Renaissance,* edited by Ulrich Pfisterer and Max Seidel. Munich: Deutscher Kunstverlag, 2003, 151–70.

Gage, John. *Colour and Culture: Practice and Meaning from Antiquity to Abstraction.* Boston: Little Brown, 1993.

Gage, John. "Colour in History: Relative and Absolute." *Art History* 1 (1978), 106.

Göttler, Christine. "Yellow, Vermillion, and Gold: Colour in Karel van Mander's Schilder-Boeck." In *Materialized Identities in Early Modern Culture, 1450–1750,* edited by Susanna Burghartz et al. Amsterdam: Amsterdam University Press, 233–80.

Hall, Marcia B. *Color and Meaning: Practice and Theory in Renaissance Painting.* Cambridge: Cambridge University Press, 1992.

Hall, Marica B. *The Power of Color: Five Centuries of European Painting.* New Haven and London: Yale University Press, 2019.

Harley, Rosamond D. *Artists' Pigments c. 1600–1835.* London: Butterworths, 1982.

Hermens, Erma, Annemiek Ouwerkert, and Nicola Costaras, eds. *Looking through Paintings: The Study of Painting Techniques and Materials in Support of Art Historical Research.* Leids Kunsthistorisch Jaarboek 11. London: Archetype Publications, 1998.

Kemp, Martin. *The Science of Art: Optical Themes in Western Art from Brunelleschi to Seurat.* New Haven and London: Yale University Press, 1990.

Kern, Ulrike. "The Origins of Broken Colours." *Journal of the Warburg and Courtauld Institutes* 79 (2016): 183–211.

Kirby, Jo, Susie Nash, and Joanna Cannon, eds. *Trade in Artists' Materials: Markets and Commerce in Europe to 1700.* London: Archetype Publications, 2010.

Krieger, Verena. "Die Farbe als 'Seele' der Malerei: Transformationen eines Topos vom 16. Jahrhundert zur Moderne." *Marburger Jahrbuch für Kunstwissenschaft* 33 (2006): 91–112.

Lehmann, Ann-Sophie. "How Materials Make Meaning." *Nederlands kunsthistorisch jaarboek* 62 (2012): 6–27.

Leonhard, Karin. *The Eloquence of Color: Rhetoric and Painting in the French Classical Age.* Berkeley: University of California Press, 1993.

Leonhard, Karin. "Painted Poison: Venomous Beasts, Herbs, Gems, and Baroque Colour Theory." In *Art and Science in the Early Modern Netherlands/Kunst en wetenschap in de vroegmoderne Nederlanden.* Nederlands Kunsthistorisch Jaarboek 61 (2011), 116–47.

Leonhard, Karin. "Pictura's Fertile Field: Otto Marseus van Schriek and the Genre of Sottobosco Painting." *Simiolus* 34, no. 2 (2009–10): 95–118.

Leonhard, Karin. "'The Various Natures of Middling Colours We May Learne of Painters.' Sir Kenelm Digby Looks at Rubens and Van Dyck." In *Knowledge and Discernment in the Early Modern Arts,* edited by Christine Göttler and Sven Dupré. London and New York: Routledge, Taylor & Francis, 2017.

Leonhard, Karin. "White Earth, or How to Cultivate Color in the Field of Painting—Still Life and Baroque Color Theory." In *Vision and Its Instruments,* edited by Alina Payne. University Park: Pennsylvania State University Press, 2015.

Lichtenstein, Jacqueline. "Making Up Representation: The Risks of Femininity." *Representations* 20 (1987): 77–87.

Lindberg, David C. *Auge und Licht im Mittelalter: Die Entdeckung der Optik von Alkindi bis Kepler.* Frankfurt am Main: Suhrkamp, 1987.

Muntwyler, Stefan, ed. *Das Farbenbuch: 367 Pigmente und Farbstoffe, 17 Pigmentanalysen von Gemälden, 19 Farbgeschichten.* Elsau, Switzerland: alataverlag, 2022.

Pietsch, Annik. "Farbentheorie und Malpraxis um 1800: Die handwerkliche Produktion des künstlerischen Kolorits nach den 'Gesetzen der Ästhetik und Physik.'" In *Verfeinertes Sehen: Optik und Farbe im 18. und frühen 19. Jahrhundert,* edited by Werner Busch. Munich: R. Oldenbourg, 2008.

Railing, Patricia, ed. *18th Century Colour Palettes: From Treatises of Robert Dossie, "The Handmaid to the Arts," 1758, Jean Félix Watin, "The Art of the Painter, Gilder and Varnisher," 1773, Placide Auguste le Pileur d'Apligny, "Treatise on Material Colours," 1776, Pierre-Barthélemy-Alexandre de Constant de Massoul, "A Treatise on the Art of Painting and the Composition of Colours," 1797.* Forest Row, East Sussex: Artists Bookworks, 2018.

Railing, Patricia, ed. *17th Century Colour Palettes: A Compendium on Pigments and Studio Practice Given in Ten 17th Century Treatises.* Forest Row, East Sussex: Artists Bookworks, 2017.

Railing, Patricia, ed. *16th century Colour Palettes: Pigments Given in Treatises by Leonardo da Vinci, Raffaello Borghini, Giovanni Paulo Lomazzo, Paintings by Titian.* Forest Row, East Sussex: Artists Bookworks, 2017.

St. Clair, Kassia. *The Secret Lives of Colour.* London: John Murray, 2016.

Shapiro, Alan E. "Artists' Colors and Newton's Colors." *Isis* 85, no. 4 (1994): 600–630.

Sheldon, Libby. "Palette, Practice and Purpose: Pigments and Their Employment by Native and Anglo-Netherlandish Artists in Tudor and Jacobean Painting." In *Painting in Britain,* edited by Tarnya Cooper et al. Oxford: Oxford University Press, 2015, 128–37.

Siracusano, Gabriela. *Pigments and Power in the Andes: From the Material to the Symbolic in Andean Cultural Practices, 1500–1800.* London: Archetype Publications, 2005.

Smith, Pamela H., "Vermilion, Mercury, Blood, and Lizards: Matter and Meaning in Metalworking." In *Materials and Expertise in Early Modern Europe: Between Market and Laboratory,* edited by Ursula Klein and Emma Spary. Chicago: University of Chicago Press, 2010, 29–49.

Stumpel, Jeroen. "On Grounds and Backgrounds: Some Remarks about Composition in Renaissance Painting." *Simiolus* 18 (1988): 219–43.

Taylor, Paul. "Coloring Nakedness in Netherlandish art and Theory." In *The Nude and the Norm in the Early Modern Low Countries,* edited by Karolien De Clippel et al. Turnhout: Brepols, 2011, 65–79.

154

Taylor, Paul. "From Mechanism to Technique: Diderot, Chardin, and the Practice of Painting." In *Knowledge and Discernment in the Early Modern Arts*, edited by Christine Göttler and Sven Dupré. London and New York: Routledge, Taylor & Francis, 2017.

Wallert, Arie, ed. *Still Life: Techniques and Style: An Examination of Paintings from the Rijksmuseum.* Exh. cat. Zwolle: Waanders, 2000.

Pigment Science
Making/Treatises

Broecke, Lara. *Cennino Cennini's Il libro dell'arte: A New English Language Translation and Commentary with Italian Transcription.* London: Archetype Publications, 2015.

Greenfield, Amy Butler. *A Perfect Red: Empire, Espionage, and the Quest for the Color of Desire.* New York: HarperCollins, 2009.

Helwig, Kate. "A Note on Burnt Yellow Earth Pigments: Documentary Sources and Scientific Analysis." *Studies in Conservation* 42, no. 3 (January 1, 1997): 181–88. https://doi.org/10.1179/sic.1997.42.3.181

Henshilwood, Christopher S., et al. "A 100,000-Year-Old Ocher-Processing Workshop at Blombos Cave, South Africa." *Science* 334, no. 6053 (2011): 219–22. https://www.science.org/doi/10.1126/science.1211535

Hilliard, N., et al. *A Treatise Concerning the Arte of Limning.* Manchester: Mid Northumberland Arts Group, Carcanet Press, 1992.

Norgate, Edward. *Miniatura; or, The Art of Limning.* New Haven: Yale University Press, 1997.

Pigment Science
General

Ball, Philip. *Bright Earth: Art and the Invention of Color.* Chicago: University of Chicago Press, 2003.

Berke, Heinz. "The Invention of Blue and Purple Pigments in Ancient Times." *Chemical Society Reviews* 36, no. 1 (2007): 15–30. https://doi.org/10.1039/B606268G

Bomford, David, et al. *Art in the Making: Impressionism.* London: National Gallery, 1990.

Braun, Kevin L., and Kristin Jansen Labby, eds. *Contextualizing Chemistry in Art and Archaeology: Inspiration for Instructors.* American Chemical Society, 2021. https://pubs.acs.org/doi/book/10.1021/bk-2021-1386

Butler, Anthony R., Christopher Glidewell, Joseph Needham, and Sharee Pritchard. "Mosaic Gold in Europe and China." *Chemistry in Britain* 19, no. 2 (1983): 132–35.

Clarke, Mark. "Anglo-Saxon Manuscript Pigments." *Studies in Conservation* 49, no. 4 (2004): 231–44. https://doi.org/10.2307/25487700

Feller, Robert L., et al., eds. *Artists' Pigments: A Handbook of Their History and Characteristics.* 4 vols. Washington, D.C.: National Gallery of Art, 1986–2007.

Finlay, Victoria. *Color: A Natural History of the Palette.* New York: Random House, 2004.

Kirsh, Andrea, and Rustin S. Levenson. *Seeing Through Paintings: Physical Examination in Art Historical Studies.* New Haven and London: Yale University Press, 2000.

Siddall, Ruth. "Mineral Pigments in Archaeology: Their Analysis and the Range of Available Materials." *Minerals* 8, no. 5 (2018): 201. https://www.mdpi.com/2075-163X/8/5/201

U.S. Food and Drug Administration. Color Additives History, 2017. https://www.fda.gov/industry/color-additives/color-additives-history

Pigment Science
Change

Berrie, Barbara H., and Yoonjoo Strumfels. "Change Is Permanent: Thoughts on the Fading of Cochineal-Based Watercolor Pigments." *Heritage Science* 5, no. 1 (July 26, 2017): 30. https://doi.org/10.1186/s40494-017-0143-4. https://doi.org/10.1186/s40494-017-0143-4

Casadio, Francesca, et al., eds. *Metal Soaps in Art: Conservation and Research.* Cham, Switzerland: Springer, 2019.

Coccato, Alessia, Luc Moens, and Peter Vandenabeele. "On the Stability of Mediaeval Inorganic Pigments: A Literature Review of the Effect of Climate, Material Selection, Biological Activity, Analysis and Conservation Treatments." *Heritage Science* 5, no. 1 (March 29,

2017): 12. https://doi.org/10.1186
/s40494-017-0125-6

Eikema Hommes, Margriet van.
"Painters' Methods to Prevent
Colour Changes Described in
Sixteenth to Early Eighteenth
Century Sources on Oil Painting
Techniques." *Leids Kunsthistorisch
Jaarboek* (1998): 91–131.

Gaetani, Maria Carolina, Ulderico
Santamaria, and Claudio Seccaroni.
"The Use of Egyptian Blue and
Lapis Lazuli in the Middle Ages:
The Wall Paintings of the San Saba
Church in Rome." *Studies in Con-
servation* 49, no. 1 (2004): 13–22.
https://doi.org/10.2307/1506927;
http://www.jstor.org/stable
/1506927

Monico, Letizia, et al. "Evidence for
Degradation of the Chrome Yellows
in Van Gogh's *Sunflowers*: A Study
Using Noninvasive In Situ Methods
and Synchrotron-Radiation-Based
X-Ray Techniques." *Angewandte
Chemie International Edition* 54
(2015). https://doi.org/10.1002
/anie.201505840

Saunders, David, and Jo Kirby.
"Light-Induced Colour Changes
in Red and Yellow Lake Pigments."
*National Gallery Technical Bulle-
tin* 15 (1994): 79–97. http://www
.nationalgallery.org.uk/technical
-bulletin/saunders_kirby1994

Subcommittee D01.57 on Artist
Paints and Related Materials.
ASTM International. https://www
.astm.org/get-involved/technical
-committees/committee-d01
/subcommittee-d01/jurisdiction
-d0157

Pigment Science
Analysis Methods

Aceto, Maurizio, et al. "Characterisa-
tion of Colourants on Illuminated
Manuscripts by Portable Fibre
Optic UV-Visible-NIR Reflectance
Spectrophotometry." *Analytical
Methods* 6, no. 5 (2014): 1488–5000.
https://doi.org/10.1039/c3ay41904e

Campanella, Beatrice, et al. "The
Shining Brightness of Daylight
Fluorescent Pigments: Raman and
SERS Study of a Modern Class
of Painting Materials." *Microchemical Journal* 152 (January 2020):
104292. https://www.science
direct.com/science/article/abs/pii
/S0026265X19320508?via%3Dihub

Derbyshire, Alan, and Robert
Withnall. "Non-Destructive
Pigment Analysis Using Raman
Microscopy." *Conservation Journal*
30 (January 1999). http://www
.vam.ac.uk/content/journals
/conservation-journal/issue-30
/non-destructive-pigment-analysis
-using-raman-microscopy/

Derbyshire, Alan, and Robert
Withnall. "Pigment Analysis
of Portrait Miniatures Using
Raman Microscopy." *Journal
of Raman Spectroscopy* 30,
no. 3 (1999): 185–88. https:
//doi.org/10.1002/(SICI)1097
-4555(199903)30:3<185::AID
-JRS357>3.0.CO;2-U

Eastaugh, Nicholas, et al. *Pigment
Compendium: A Dictionary and
Optical Microscopy of Historical
Pigments*. Oxford: Butterworth-
Heinemann, 2008.

Fiorillo, Flavia, et al. "Non-Invasive
Technical Investigation of English
Portrait Miniatures Attributed
to Nicholas Hilliard and Isaac
Oliver." *Heritage* 4, no. 3 (2021):
1165–81. https://www.mdpi.com
/2571-9408/4/3/64

Fuster López, Laura, Maartje Stols-
Witlox, and Marcello Picollo. (2020).
UV-Vis Luminescence Imaging
Techniques/ Técnicas de imagen
de luminiscencia UV-Vis. Valencia:
Universitat Politècnica de València,
2020. http://hdl.handle.net/10251
/138517 https://www.lalibreria
.upv.es/portalEd/UpvGEStore
/products/p_1100-2-1

Infrared & Raman Users Group.
http://irug.org/

Liang, Haida. "Advances in Multispectral and Hyperspectral Imaging
for Archaeology and Art Conservation." *Applied Physics A* 106, no. 2
(2012): 309–23.

Mazzeo, Rocco, ed. *Analytical Chemistry for Cultural Heritage*. Cham,
Switzerland: Springer, 2017. https://
doi.org/10.1007/978-3-319-52804-5

Moffitt, Kirsten. "Orpiment in Colonial Williamsburg: Challenges with
the Identification of Yellow Arsenic
Sulphides in Historic Housepaints."
Microscopy and Microanalysis 27,
no. S1 (2021): 3012–13. https://doi.
org/10.1017/S1431927621010461

Shugar, Aaron N., and Jennifer L.
Mass. *Handheld XRF for Art and
Archaeology*. Leuven: Leuven:
University Press, 2012.

Pigment Science
Trade and Commerce

Historic Black Pigments without Color Index Names. http://www.artiscreation.com/black.html#historic_pigments

Kirby, Jo, Susie Nash, and Joanna Cannon. *Trade in Artists' Materials: Markets and Commerce in Europe to 1700.* London: Archetype Publications, 2010.

Observatory of Economic Complexity (OEC), Prepared Pigments, https://oec.world/en/profile/hs92/prepared-pigments

Reutersvärd, Oscar. "The 'Violetto-mania' of the Impressionists." *Journal of Aesthetics and Art Criticism* 9, no. 2 (1950): 106–10.

Romani, Martina, et al. "Analytical Chemistry Approach in Cultural Heritage: The Case of Vincenzo Pasqualoni's Wall Paintings in S. Nicola in Carcere (Rome)." *Microchemical Journal* 156 (May 1, 2020): 104920. https://doi.org/10.1016/j.microc.2020.104920.

Vellekoop, Marije, et al. *Van Gogh's Studio Practice.* Belgium: Mercatorfonds, 2013.

Pigments in Baroque and Rococo European Painters' Palettes

Berrie, Barbara H. "Mining for Color: New Blues, Yellows, and Translucent Paint." *Early Science and Medicine* 20, nos. 4–6 (2015): 308–34.

Clarricoates, Rhiannon, Helen Dowding, and Alexandra Gent, eds. *Colour Change in Paintings.* London: Archetype Publications, 2016.

Eikema Hommes, Margriet van. *Changing Pictures: Discoloration in 15th–17th Century Oil Paintings.* London: Archetype Publications, 2004.

Taylor, Paul. *Condition: The Ageing of Art.* London: Paul Holberton Publishing, 2015.

Van de Wetering, Ernst. *Rembrandt: The Painter at Work.* Amsterdam: Amsterdam University Press, 1997.

Color Engenders Life: Pigment and Process in Prehistoric Rock Art

Applegate, Richard B. "The Black, the Red, and the White: Duality and Unity in the Luiseño Cosmos." *Journal of California and Great Basin Anthropology* 1 (1979): 71–88.

Boyd, Carolyn E. "Images in the Making: Process and Vivification in Pecos River Style Rock Art." In *Ontologies of Rock Art: Images, Relational Approaches and Indigenous Knowledge*, edited by Oscar Moro Abadía and Martin Porr. New York: Routledge, (2021): 245–63.

Boyd, Carolyn E., and Kim Cox. *The White Shaman Mural: An Enduring Creation Narrative in the Rock Art of the Lower Pecos.* Austin: University of Texas Press, 2016.

Bu, Kaixuan, James Cizdziel, and Jon Russ. "The Source of Iron-Oxide Pigments Used in Pecos River Style Rock Paints." *Archaeometry* 55, no. 6 (2013): 1088–1100.

Cajete, Gregory. *Look to the Mountain: An Ecology of Indigenous Education.* Durango, Colorado: Kivaki Press, 1994.

Campbell, Paul D. *Earth Pigments and Paint of the California Indians.* San Diego: Sunbelt Publications, 2007.

Dupey García, Élodie. "Making and Using Colors in the Manufacture of Nahua Codices: Aesthetic Standards, Symbolic Purposes." In *Painting the Skin: Pigments on Bodies and Codices in Pre-Columbian Mesoamerica*, edited by Élodie Dupey Garciá and María Luisa Vásquez de Ágredos Pascual. Tucson: University of Arizona Press, 2018, 186–205.

Dupey García, Élodie. "The Materiality of Color in the Body Ornamentation of Aztec Gods." *RES: Anthropology and Aesthetics* 65/66 (2015): 72–88.

Gutzeit, Emma, and Mary Virginia Carson. "Preliminary Report on Field Expedition Sent to West Texas by Witte Museum," 1931. Unpublished field report and watercolor paintings on file at the Witte Museum, San Antonio.

Hyman, Marion, Solveig Turpin, and Michael Zolensky. "Pigment Analysis at Panther Cave." *Rock Art Research* 13 (1996): 93–103.

Kirkland, Forrest, and W. W. Newcomb. *The Rock Art of Texas Indians.* Austin: University of Texas Press, 1967.

Koenig, Charles W., et al. "Portable X-Ray Fluorescence Spectroscopy of Pictographs: A Case Study from the Lower Pecos Canyonlands of Texas." *Archaeometry* 56 (2014): 168–86.

MacLean, Hope. "Sacred Colors and Shamanic Vision among the Huichol Indians of Mexico." *Journal of Anthropological Research* 57, no. 3 (2001): 305–23.

Maffie, James. *Aztec Philosophy: Understanding a World in Motion.* Boulder: University Press of Colorado, 2014.

Magaloni Kerpel, Diana. *The Colors of the New World: Artists, Materials, and the Creation of the Florentine Codex.* Los Angeles: Getty Research Institute, 2014.

Séjourné, Laurette. *Burning Water: Thought and Religion in Ancient Mexico.* 1st ed., 1957. London: Thames and Hudson, 1978.

Shafer, Harry, ed. *Painters in Prehistory: Archaeology and Art of the Lower Pecos Canyonlands.* San Antonio: Trinity University Press, 2013.

Transmedial Simulations: Bronze Corrosions and Copper-based Pigments in Chinese Art

Aru, Mariafrancesca, et al. "Mineral Impurities in Azurite Pigments: Artistic or Natural Selection?" *Journal of Raman Spectroscopy* 45 (2014): 1013–18.

Bagley, Robert, W. *Shang Ritual Bronzes in the Arthur M. Sackler Collections.* Washington, D.C.: Arthur M. Sackler Foundation and Arthur M. Sackler Museum, 1987.

Bai, Qianshen. "Antiquarianism in a Time of Crisis: On the Collecting Practices of Late-Qing Government Officials, 1861–1911." In *World Antiquarianism: Comparative Perspectives*, edited by Alain Schnapp, et al. Los Angeles: Getty Research Institute, 2014, 394.

Chase, W. T. "Chinese Bronzes: Casting, Finishing, Patination, and Corrosion." In *Ancient & Historic Metals: Conservation and Scientific Research*, edited by David A. Scott. Oxford University Press, 1995, 85–117.

Dan, Shūgō. "Tonkō bakkōkutsu hekiga no ganryō" (Colorants used in the murals at Dunhuang Mogao caves). *Bukkyō Geijutsu* 175 (1987): 90–100.

Feeser, Andrea, Maureen Daly Goggin, and Beth Fowkes Tobin, eds. *The Materiality of Color: The Production, Circulation, and Application of Dyes and Pigments, 1400–1800.* London: Routledge, 2012.

Fiedler, Inge, and Bayard Michael. "Emerald Green and Scheele's Green." In *Artists' Pigments: A Handbook of Their History and Characteristics*, edited by Elisabeth W. FitzHugh. Washington, D.C.: National Gallery of Art, 1997, vol. 3, 219–56.

Fleming, L. E. "Paintings on Silk and Paper from Dunhuang at the British Museum: Conservation Methods." In *Conservation of Ancient Sites on the Silk Road*, edited by Neville Agnew. Los Angeles: Getty Conservation Institute, 1997, 105–11.

Foong, Ping. *The Efficacious Landscape: On the Authorities of Painting at the Northern Song Court.* Cambridge: Harvard University Asia Center, 2015.

Gettens, Rutherford J. *The Freer Chinese Bronzes, Volume 2: Technical Studies.* Washington, D.C.: Smithsonian Institution, 1969.

Gettens, Rutherford J. "Patina: Noble and Vile." In *Art and Technology: A Symposium on Classical Bronzes.* Cambridge: MIT Press, 1970, 57–72.

Gettens, Rutherford J. "Pigments in a Wall Painting from Central China." *Technical Studies in the Field of Fine Arts* 7 (1938): 104–5.

Gettens, Rutherford J., and Elisabeth W. FitzHugh. "Malachite and Green Verditer." *Studies in Conservation* 19, no. 1 (1973): 2–23.

Giaccai, Jennifer, and John Winter. "Chinese Painting Colors: History and Reality." In *Scientific Research on the Pictorial Arts of Asia: Proceedings of the Second Ford Symposium at the Freer Gallery of Art*, edited by Paul Jett et al. London: Archetype Publications, 2005, 99–108.

Han, Jing. "The Historical and Chemical Investigation of Dyes in High Status Chinese Costume and Textiles of the Ming and Qing Dynasties (1368–1911)." Ph.D. diss. University of Glasgow, 2016.

Hay, Jonathan. *Sensuous Surface: The Decorative Object in Early Modern China.* Honolulu: University of Hawaii Press, 2010.

Hofmann, Christa, et al. "Studies on the Conservation of Verdigris on Paper." *Restaur* 36, no. 2 (2015): 147–82.

Kim-Cohen, Seth. "Worldmaking, Worldmarking, Wordmaking: The Heteromediality of Francis Alys." A talk delivered at the European Summer School in Cultural Studies, Heidelberg, Germany, August 2007.

Malenka, Sally, and Beth A. Price. "A Chinese Wall Painting and a Palace Hall Ceiling: Materials, Technique, and Conservation." In *Conservation of Ancient Sites on the Silk Road*, edited by Neville Agnew. Los Angeles: Getty Conservation Institute, 1997, 127–38 .

McCarthy, Blythe, and Jennifer Giaccai, eds., *Scientific Studies of Pigments in Chinese Paintings.* London: Archetype Publications, 2021.

Ngan, Quincy. "The Significance of Azurite Blue in Two Ming Dynasty Birthday Portraits." *Metropolitan Museum Journal* 53 (2018): 46–62.

Rajewsky, Irina O. "Intermediality, Intertextuality, and Remediation: A Literary Perspective on Intermediality." *Intermediality: History and Theory of the Arts, Literature and Technologies* 6 (2005): 43–64.

Ruitenbeek, Klaas, ed. *Faces of China: Portrait Painting of the Ming and Qing Dynasties (1368–1912).* Petersberg, Germany: Michael Imhof Verlag, 2017.

Scott, David A. *Copper and Bronze in Art: Corrosion, Colorants, Conservation.* Los Angeles: Getty Conservation Institute, 2002.

Shekede, Lisa, and Bomin Su. "Wall Paintings at the Mogao Grotto Site, Dunhuang, China: Color Use from Northern Wei to Tang." In *Color in Ancient and Medieval East Asia*, edited by Mary M. Dusenbury. Lawrence: Spencer Museum of Art, University of Kansas, 2015, 45–57.

Shen, Ai Guo, et al. "Pigment Identification of Colored Drawings from Wuying Hall of the Imperial Palace by Micro-Raman Spectroscopy and Energy Dispersive X-ray Spectroscopy." *Journal of Raman Spectroscopy* 37 (2006): 230–34.

Wang, Jinyu, and Wang Jingcong. "*Dunhuang shiku tonglü yanliao de yingyong yu laiyuan*" (The application and source of *tonglü* in the Dunhuang grotto). *Dunhuang yanjiu* (Dunhuang Research) 74, no. 4 (2002): 23–28.

Winter, John. *East Asian Paintings: Materials, Structures and Deterioration Mechanisms.* London: Archetype Publications, 2008.

Xia, Yin, et al. "Smalt: An Underrecognized Pigment Commonly Used in Historical Period China." *Journal of Archaeological Science* 101 (2019): 89–98.

Yang, Meili. "*Wan Ming Qing chu fanggu qi de zuose—yi tongqi, yuqi wei zhu de yanjiu*" (The artificial coloration of objects imitating ancient vessels—a study focusing on objects in bronze and jade). *Gugong xueshu jikan* (National Palace Museum Quarterly) 30, no. 3 (2005): 17–45.

Yong, Lei. "Copper Trihydroxychlorides as Pigments in China." *Studies in Conservation* 57, no. 2, 106–11.

Yu Fei'an. *Chinese Painting Color: Studies of their Preparation and Application in Traditional and Modern Times.* Translated by Jerome Silbergeld and Amy McNair. Seattle and London: University of Washington Press, 1988.

"All of It Green, Which Is a Pleasure to Look At": The Uses of Green Pigments in South American Artistic Practice

Arriaga, Pablo Joseph de. *La extirpación de la idolatría en el Perú.* 1st ed., 1621. Cuzco: Centro de Estudios Regionales Andinos "Bartolomé de las Casas," 1999.

Ávila, Francisco de. *Ritos y tradiciones de Huarochiri del siglo XVII (Dioses y Hombres de Huarochiri)*, edited by Gerald Taylor. 1st ed., 1598. Lima: Instituto de Estudios Peruanos/Instituto Frances de Estudios Andinos: 1987.

Carducho, Vicente. *Dialogos de la pintura: Su defensa, origen, esencia, definición, modos y diferencias.* Madrid: Turner, 1979.

Cobo, Bernabé. *Historia del Nuevo Mundo.* 4 vols. 1st ed., 1653. Seville: Sociedad de Bibliófilos Andaluces, 1890.

Colón, Cristobal. *Diario de a bordo,* edited by Luis Arranz. Madrid: EDAF, 2006.

Colón, Fernando. *Historia del Almirante Cristóbal Colón.* Volume 1. Madrid: Tomás Minuesa, 1892. Of how the admiral took land and possession of it in the name of the Catholic Monarchs, ch. 22. Alicante: Biblioteca Virtual Miguel

de Cervantes; and Madrid: Biblioteca Nacional, 2006. http://www
.cervantesvirtual.com/nd/ark:
/59851/bmcqn629

Cummins, Thomas B. F., and Barbara Anderson, eds. *The Getty Murua: Essays on the Making of Martin de Murua's Historia General del Piru, J. Paul Getty Museum Ms. Ludwig XIII 16.* Los Angeles: Getty Research Institute, 2008.

Doctrina Christiana y catecismo para instrucción de los indios, y de las de mas personas, que han de ser enseñadas en nuestra Sancta Fe. Con un confessionario y otas cosas necessarias para los que adoctrinan, que se contienen en la pagina siguiente. Lima: Antonio Ricardo, printer, 1584.

Fazio, Alejandra T., et al. "Fungal Deterioration of a Jesuit South American Polychrome Wood Sculpture." *International Biodeterioration & Biodegradation* 64 (2010): 694–701.

Gómez, Blanca A., et al. "Integrated Analytical Techniques for the Characterization of Painting Materials in Two South American Polychrome Sculptures." *e-Preservation science* 7 (2010): 1–7.

Guamán Poma de Ayala, Felipe. *El primer nueva corónica y buen gobierno.* Peru, ca. 1615. Danish Royal Library, Copenhagen, GKS 2232 4°; https://poma.kb.dk /permalink/2006/poma/info/en /frontpage.htm

Guzmán, Fernando, et al. "Programa iconográfico y material en las pinturas murales de la iglesia de San Andrés de Pachama, Chile." *Colonial Latin American Review* 25, no. 2 (2016): 245–64.

Murúa, Martin de. *Historia general del Peru, origen y descendencia de los Incas . . .* 1st ed., 1590. 2 vols. Madrid: Instituto Gonzalo Fernandez de Oviedo, 1962.

Pacheco, Francisco. *Arte de la pintura, su antigüedad y grandezas.* 1st ed., 1649. Madrid: Cátedra, 1990.

Palomino de Castro y Velasco, Antonio. 3 vols. *El museo pictórico y escala óptica.* Madrid, Ediciones Aguilar, 1988.

Rúa, Carlos, et al. "Identification of Pigments in Wall Paintings of the Colonial Period from Bolivian Churches in the Ruta de La Plata." *Conservation Science Cultural Heritage* 17 (2017): 117–35.

Seldes, Alicia, et al. "Green, Yellow, and Red Pigments in South American Painting, 1610–1780." *Journal of the American Institute for Conservation* 41, no. 3 (2002): 225–42.

Sepúlveda, Marcela, Valentina Figueroa, and José Cárcamo. "Pigmentos y pinturas de mineral de cobre en la región de Tarapacá, norte de Chile: Nuevos datos para una tecnología pigmentaria prehispánica." *Estudios Atacameños* 48 (2014): 23–37. http://www.jstor .org/stable/26395105

Siracusano, Gabriela. "Mary's Green Brilliance: The Case of the Virgin of Copacabana." *Journal of Interdisciplinary History* 45, no. 3 (2014): 389–406.

Siracusano, Gabriela, ed. *La paleta del espanto.* Buenos Aires: Unsam-Edita, 2010.

Siracusano, Gabriela. *Pigments and Power in the Andes: From the Material to the Symbolic in Andean Cultural Practices, 1500–1800.* London: Archetype Publications, 2011.

Siracusano, Gabriela, and Agustina Rodriguez Romero, eds. *Materia americana: The Body of Spanish American Images (16th to mid-19th Centuries).* Saenz Peña: Universidad Nacional de Tres de Febrero, 2020.

Tomasini, Eugenia P., et al. "Atacamite as a Natural Pigment in a South American Colonial Polychrome Sculpture from the Late XVI Century." *Journal of Raman Spectroscopy* 44 (2013): 637–42.

Tomasini, Eugenia P., et al. "Characterization of Pigments and Binders in a Mural Painting from the Andean Church of San Andrés de Pachama (Northernmost of Chile)." *Heritage Science* 6 (2018): 61.

Tomasini, Eugenia P., et al. "A Multianalytical Investigation of the Materials and Painting Technique of a Wall Painting from the Church of Copacabana de Andamarca (Bolivia). *Microchemical Journal* 128 (2016): 172–80.

Pigmenting the Skin: When Spice Makes Race

Albinus, Bernhard Siegfried. *Dissertatio secunda de sede et caussa coloris Aethiopum et caeterorum hominum.* Leyden, 1736. https: //wellcomecollection.org/works /jkfwrk3a

Buffon, Georges Louis Leclerc. *Supplément à l'histoire naturelle de l'homme de Buffon* (Paris: A l'Imprimerie royale, 1778), vol. 5.

Buffon, Georges Louis Leclerc. *Buffon's Natural History: Containing a Theory of the Earth, a General History of Man, of the Brute Creation, and of Vegetables, Minerals, &c.* Translated from the French by James Smith Barr. London: J.S. Barr, 1792. https://www.gutenberg.org/ebooks/author/42924

Camper, Petrus. *Two Books Containing a Treatise on the Natural Difference of Features in Persons of Different Countries and Periods of Life; and on Beauty*, translated by Thomas Cogan. London: C. Dilly, 1794; new ed., J. Hearne, 1821. https://archive.org/details/b21305122/page/n31/mode/2up?q=Painting%2C+and+whatever+

Cordez, Philippe. "Peau noire, bois d'ébène. Les meubles-esclaves d'Andrea Brustolon pour Pietro Venier (Venise, 1706)." In Vittoria Borsò and Andrea von Hülsen-Esch, eds., *Materialle Mediationen im Französisch-deutschen Dialog.* Berlin: de Gruyter, 2018, 109–34. https://archiv.ub.uni-heidelberg.de/artdok/7182/

Curran, Andrew. *The Anatomy of Blackness: Science and Slavery in an Age of Enlightenment.* Baltimore: Johns Hopkins University Press, 2011.

Doron, Claude-Olivier. *L'homme altéré: Races et dégénérescence.* Paris: Champ Vallon, 2016.

Fend, Mechthild. *Fleshing Out Surfaces: Skin in French Art and Medicine, 1650–1850.* Manchester: Manchester University Press, 2017.

Gautier d'Agoty, Jacques-Fabien, and Joseph-Guichard Duverney. *Myologie complète en couleur et grandeur naturelle, composée de l'essai d'anatomie en tableaux imprimés.* Paris: Gautier, 1746.

Jefferson, Thomas. *Notes on the State of Virginia.* 1st ed., Paris, 1781; 2nd ed., London: John Stockdale, 1787.

Katzew, Ilona. "White or Black? Albinism and Spotted Blacks in the Eighteenth-Century Atlantic World." In Pamela A. Patton, ed., *Envisioning Others: Race, Color, and the Visual in Iberia and Latin America.* Leiden and Boston: Brill, 2015, 142–86.

Lafont, Anne. *L'art et la race: L'Africain (tout) contre l'oeil des lumières.* Paris: Presses du réel, 2019.

Le Blon, Jacob Christoph. *Coloritto; or, The Harmony of Colouring in Painting.* London, 1725. Facsimile ed., introduction by Faber Birren. New York: Van Nostrand Reinhold, 1980.

Leclerc, Georges-Louis, comte de Buffon. *Histoire naturelle.* 36 vols. Paris: L'Imprimerie Royale, 1749–1804. https://gallica.bnf.fr/ark:/12148/bpt6k97490d.image

Linnaeus, Carl (Carl von Linné). *Systema naturae.* Leiden and Stockholm, 1735–58. *A general system of nature through the three grand kingdoms of animals, vegetables, and minerals; systematically divided into their several classes, orders, genera, species, and varieties with their habitations, manners, economy, structure, and peculiarities*, translated by William Turton. London: Lackington, Allen, and Co., 1802. https://archive.org/details/generalsystemof07linn

Lowengard, Sarah. *The Creation of Color in Eighteenth Century Europe.* New York: Columbia University Press, 2006. http://www.gutenberg-e.org/lowengard/

Moreau de Maupertuis, Pierre Louis. *Dissertation physique à l'occasion d'un Nègre blanc.* Leiden, 1744.

Moreau de Maupertuis, Pierre Louis. *Vénus physique.* Paris, 1745.

Nochlin, Linda. "Eroticism and Female Imagery in 19th-Century Art." In Thomas Hess and Linda Nochlin, eds., *Woman as Sex Object: Studies in Erotic Art, 1730–1970.* New York: Newsweek Books, 1972, 9–15.

Rosenthal, Angela. "Visceral Culture: Blushing and the Legibility of Whiteness in 18th Century British Portraiture." *Art History* 27, no. 4 (2004): 563–92.

Schaub, Jean-Frédéric, and Silvia Sebastiani. *Race et histoire dans les sociétés occidentales (XVe–XVIIIe siècles).* Paris: Albin Michel, 2021.

Contributors

Barbara H. Berrie is senior conservation scientist and head of the scientific research department at the National Gallery of Art, Washington, DC. She works broadly in the field of art conservation in collaboration with chemists, conservators, and art historians. She works extensively on the identification of pigments and what pigments reveal about artists and art-making.

David Bomford is the retired director of conservation at the Museum of Fine Arts, Houston. His numerous curatorial and publication projects include the following exhibits and associated catalogues for the National Gallery, London: *Art in the Making: Degas* (2004), *Art in the Making: Underdrawings in Renaissance Paintings* (2002), *Art in the Making: Impressionism* (1990), *Art in the Making: Italian Painting before 1400* (1989), and *Art in the Making: Rembrandt* (1988). Bomford was Slade Professor at Oxford in 1996–1997, and currently a trustee of the Victoria and Albert Museum, London.

Carolyn E. Boyd is an archaeologist and artist and holds the Shumla Endowed Research Professorship in the Department of Anthropology at Texas State University, San Marcos. She is the author of *Rock Art of the Lower Pecos* (Texas A&M University Press, 2003) and *The White Shaman Mural: An Enduring Creation Narrative in the Rock Art of the Lower Pecos* (University of Texas Press, 2016), which received the Society for American Archaeology Scholarly Book Award in 2017. Her work on the ancient pictographic murals of Texas and northern Mexico has been supported by National Geographic, the National Endowment for the Humanities, and the National Science Foundation.

Caroline Fowler is Starr Director of the Research and Academic Program at the Clark Art Institute. Her previous books include *Drawing and the Senses: An Early Modern History* (2017), and *The Art of Paper: From the Holy Land to the Americas* (2020).

Anne Lafont is an art historian and professor at the School for Advanced Studies in Social Sciences (EHESS) in Paris. Her research focuses on art, images, and material culture of the Black Atlantic, as well as on historiographical issues relating to the notion of African art. Her work on the different ways of visualizing pigmentation at the time of the invention of dermatology and on the auxiliary sciences of racism and their graphic notation resulted in *L'art et la race. L'Africain (tout) contre l'œil des Lumières* (to be published in English by the Getty in 2024). Lafont was a member of the scientific committee for the exhibition *Le modèle noir de Géricault à Matisse* (2019, Musée d'Orsay). In 2021 and 2022, she taught at Williams College as Clark Professor and was awarded Outstanding Mid-Career Scholar by the Bard Graduate Center in New York City. Her latest book, co-edited with François-Xavier Fauvelle, is *L'Afrique et le monde. Histoires renouées de la préhistoire au XXIe siècle* (Paris, La découverte, 2022).

Karin Leonhard is Professor for Art History at Konstanz University, with a focus on Dutch art history and theory. Her research interests include the history and theory of space and perspective, light and color in the early modern period, the methodology of art history, and especially the dialogue between art history and conservation science. She is the author of *Das gemalte Zimmer. Zur Interieurmalerei Jan Vermeers* (2003) and *The Fertile Ground of Painting: Seventeenth-Century Still Lifes and Nature Pieces* (2021).

Quincy Ngan is an assistant professor in the history of art and a research fellow at the MacMillan Center at Yale University. His research focuses on the materiality of pigments and dyes in early modern China, as well as on the significances of skin in contemporary Chinese art and visual culture. His recent publications explore the communicative power of colors and how the socioeconomic values of azurite and indigo factored into art-making in Ming China. His articles appear in *Metropolitan Museum Journal*, *Archives of Asian art*, and *Yishu: Journal of Contemporary Chinese Art*. He is currently writing a book titled *The Matter of Color in Early Modern China*.

Gabriela Siracusano is a principal scientific researcher at CONICET (National Research Council, Argentina), director of the Centro MATERIA at the Universidad Nacional de Tres de Febrero (UNTREF) in Argentina, and professor at UBA and UNTREF.

She was a Guggenheim Fellow (2006–2007) and Getty Scholar (2016). She has also served as visiting professor and researcher at Cambridge University, Universidad Nacional Autónoma de México, Getty Research Institute, UT Austin, l'École des Hautes Études en Sciences Sociales, and Kunsthistorisches Institute in Florenz, among others. Recently, she was awarded the Gratia Artis Prize (2022) by the National Academy of Fine Arts in Argentina. She is the author of many books and articles, including *El Poder de los Colores* (Fondo de Cultura Económica, 2005; ALAA award, 2006), *Pigments and Power in the Andes* (Archetype, 2011), *La Paleta del Espanto* (Unsamedita, 2011), and with Agustina R. Romero, *Materia Americana* (Eduntref, 2020, ALAA and Eleanor Tuft Honorable Mentions 2021).

Ittai Weinryb is an associate professor at the Bard Graduate Center. He is the author of *The Bronze Object in the Middle Ages* (2016), *Hildesheimer Avantgarde: Kunst und Kolonialismus in mittelalterlichen Deutschland* (2023), and the curator of *Agents of Faith: Votive Objects in Time and Place* (2018).

Index

Photography and Copyright Credits

© Anish Kapoor. All Rights Reserved, DACS 2023. Photo: Dave Morgan: 2

Antwerp X-ray Imaging and Spectroscopy Research Group, University of Antwerp, Belgium: 35

Jon Arnold Images Ltd / Alamy Stock Photo: 1

Art Institute of Chicago, Gift of Emily Crane Chadbourne: 4

Barbara Berrie and the National Gallery of Art, Washington: 21, 23, 25, 27, 29

Carolyn Boyd: 30, 44a–d

Bibliothèque Nationale de France: 14

Bridgeman Images: 10, 13

Centro MATERIA-UNTREF: 51, 54

Colonial Williamsburg Foundation: 26

John K. Delaney, Kathryn Dooley, and the National Gallery of Art, Washington, D.C.: 31

Daniel Giannone: 52

Courtesy of the Ny Carlsberg Glyptotek, Copenhagen. Imaging: Jens Stenger: 36

Private collection, courtesy of Haboldt & Co.: 15

Galerie De Jonckheere, Paris: 11

Golden Artist Colors, Inc.: 20

Digital Image © CNAC/MNAM, Dist. RMN-GrandPalais / Art Resource, NY. Photo: Georges Meguerditchian: 9

© President and Fellows of Harvard College. Photo: Caitlin Cunningham Photography: 6

Chester Leeds: 40

ISAAC Research Centre, Nottingham Trent University: 33

Minneapolis Museum of Art, Mary Griggs Burke Collection, Gift of the Mary and Jackson Burke Foundation: 17

© 2024 Museum of Fine Arts, Boston: 22

National Gallery of Art, Washington: 24, 28, 39, 58, 59

© National Gallery, London / Art Resource, NY: 8a, 36, 38

Photo © National Gallery, London: 37

© National Portrait Gallery, London: 16

National Library, St. Petersburg, Russia / Bridgeman Images: 13

Musée National de Stockholm: 60

National Palace Museum: 48

Newberry Library, Chicago, Edward E. Ayer Collection: 3

Norton Museum of Art, West Palm Beach, Florida: 49

© Kate Rothko Prizel & Christopher Rothko/Artists Rights Society (ARS), New York. Photo: President and Fellows of Harvard College: 5

Royal Ontario Museum, Canada: 47

Arthur M. Sackler Gallery, National Museum of Asian Art, Smithsonian Institution, Washington, D.C.: 46

Science Photo Library: 56

Shanghai Museum: 45

Shumla Archaeological Research and Education Center: 40, 41, 42, 43

Gabriela Siracusano: 50, 51a, 53

Staatliches Museum Schwerin: 12

Photo © Tate, London / Art Resource, NY: 18

Tuskegee University Archives: 7

UEBA ESOU Co. Ltd.: 19

V&A Images, London / Art Resource, NY: 32

Wellcome Collection: 55, 57

Björn Wylezich / Alamy Stock Photo: 8b